Now is the Winter
Thinking about Hockey

BOOKS BY JAMIE DOPP
On the Other Hand
Prospects Unknown: A Mystery With a Difference
The Birdhouse, Or

BOOKS BY RICHARD HARRISON
Fathers Never Leave You
Recovering the Naked Man
Hero of the Play
Big Breath of a Wish
Hero of the Play: 10th Anniversary Edition
Worthy of his Fall

Now is the Winter
Thinking about Hockey

Edited by
Jamie Dopp and Richard Harrison

Wolsak and Wynn

© Jamie Dopp and Richard Harrison, 2009

No part of this publication may be reproduced, stored in a retrieval system or transmitted, in any form or by any means, without the prior written consent of the publisher or a licence from The Canadian Copyright Licensing Agency (Access Copyright). For an Access Copyright licence, visit www.accesscopyright.ca or call toll free to 1-800-893-5777.

Richard Harrison photograph: Jennifer Weihmann
Jamie Dopp photograph: Stephen Dopp
Cover Image: Erin Riley
Book design: Julie McNeill, McNeill Design Arts
Printing: Ball Media, Brantford, Canada

The publisher gratefully acknowledges the support of the Canada Council for the Arts, the Ontario Arts Council and the Book Publishing Industry Development Program (BPIDP) for their financial assistance.

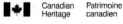

Wolsak and Wynn Publishers Ltd.
#102 69 Hughson Street North
Hamilton, ON
Canada L8R 1G5

Library and Archives Canada Cataloguing in Publication

Now is the winter: thinking about hockey / edited by Jamie Dopp and Richard Harrison.

Includes bibliographical references and index.
ISBN 978-1-894987-34-9

1. Hockey. 2. Hockey–History. 3. Hockey–Social aspects. I. Dopp, Jamie, 1957– II. Harrison, Richard, 1957–

GV847.N68 2009   796.962   C2009-904115-4

Printed in Canada on 100% post-consumer recycled content

Contents

JAMIE DOPP AND RICHARD HARRISON
Introduction
7

STEPHEN HARDY AND ANDREW HOLMAN
Periodizing Hockey History
One Approach
19

MICHAEL P. BUMA
"Save Our Team, Save Our Game"
Identity Politics in Two Canadian Hockey Novels
37

ANDREW HOLMAN
Frank Merriwell On Skates
*Heroes, Villains, Canadians and Other Others
in American Juvenile Sporting Fiction, 1890–1940*
53

RICHARD HARRISON
Stanley Cup/Superman
69

DAVID MCNEIL
The Story of Hockey Photography in the Early 1950s
81

JOHN SOARES
Boycotts, Brotherhood and More
*International Hockey from Moscow to
Colorado Springs via Squaw Valley (1957–1962)*
97

SAM MCKEGNEY
THE ABORIGINAL ART OF WAKE-SWIMMING
or The Media Mythologization of Jonathan Cheechoo   113

ANNE HARTMAN
"HERE FOR A LITTLE PICKUP?"
Notes on Women's Shinny Hockey in Toronto Public Parks   123

E. W. (ED) MASON
MEDIA FRAMING OF THE OTHER
Ice Hockey in the New Zealand Media   145

BRIAN KENNEDY
"WHAT EVER HAPPENED TO THE ORGAN AND THE PORTRAIT OF HER MAJESTY?"
NHL Spectating as Imaginary Carnival   155

CRAIG G. HYATT, WILLIAM M. FOSTER AND MARK R. JULIEN
"BUT WHAT ABOUT MY FEELINGS?"
Examining Edmonton Oilers Fan Reaction to Chris Pronger's Trade Demand from a Gift-Giving Perspective   171

KELLY HEWSON
"YOU SAID YOU DIDN'T GIVE A FUCK ABOUT HOCKEY"
Popular Culture, the Fastest Game on Earth and the Imagined Canadian Nation   187

Contributors   205

Index   211

Jamie Dopp and Richard Harrison

Introduction

At the *Canada's Game?* hockey conference in 2005, the organizer, Andrew Holman, arranged a shinny game for participants on the rink at Plymouth College, Massachusetts. So a group of academics, rec-league players, alumni of the NHL and the Western Hockey League, sports writers, historians, poets, novelists and a CBC TV film crew – men and women, from teenager to retiree – all tied on skates. We donned *Canada's Game?* jerseys (in home and away colours) and prepared to play wearing helmets and gloves borrowed from the college team, which also, thankfully, provided the goaltenders for each side. We selected our sticks from the rack and took to the ice for a "gentleman's game": no raising the puck, no checking. It didn't take long for first contact to be made. Shortly thereafter, the puck began to rise from the ice and connect with shins, or worse. Then the battles-in-the-corner began, and the game was on. And after the announced "last goal" settled it in the finest tradition of shinny, and we sat, exhausted, happy and slightly bruised in the dressing room, someone asked, "What happened out there?" The answer came back: "Hockey happened." And we laughed.

Though the essays in this collection grew out of papers given at the *Canada and the League of Hockey Nations Conference* organized by Jamie Dopp in Victoria, BC, in 2007, they retain the spirit – and some of the players – from that earlier game of shinny. The writers in this collection have all experienced the beauty, the exuberance and the occasional violence of the game of hockey, most of them directly, at one time or another, on the ice. And, like the players in Plymouth, the writers here have all responded to the game whether played or watched not just with feelings or physical effort but with questions.

What does it mean to say "hockey happened?" As satisfying as it is to give the word "hockey" the mythic power to be its own answer, hockey continues to intrigue, anger, draw and repel us precisely because it is a complicated thing – and it becomes more complicated the more we think and talk about it together. Hockey was created, as the story goes, by Canadian society before there was a Canada; in this way, hockey has been said to mark of the beginning of Canadian time. Thus, in turn, it has been the game through which Canada is often said to define much of itself. Adopted by other nations, hockey has become a point of contact across political lines. And also a mark of division. It has been a flashpoint for both national pride and anxiety about the national self.

Neither the evolution of the game nor of its scholarship has been easy. By the mid-twentieth century – about a hundred and fifty years after early versions of hockey were reported in Canadian settler communities – a broad swath of the Canadian populace identified themselves with the game. Canadians, at this time, were also indisputably the best in the world at it. Then "the Russians" won their first World Championship in 1954, after having committed to the game less than a decade earlier. Canada took the title back the following year. And then we sparred, the Soviet Union and Canada – Canada ruling the 1950s and early '60s, the Soviets doing the same from 1963 until 1971. But the configuration of Olympic and World Championship teams meant that the two countries avoided the confrontation of best vs. best until the 1972 Summit Series when the crown broke, and each of us came away with a piece. In the preface to *Hockey Showdown*, his reconstructed diary of the series, Team Canada coach Harry Sinden wrote, "Hockey has been the Canadian Game. We fostered it, loved it, nurtured it, thought it would be ours forever. This series showed us that there are many nations now who want to share this great game with us at its top level." In this he was acknowledging history. Then he added, "We should feel proud of this, not threatened," acknowledging, and trying to calm, the feelings of those who'd seen history get made. But many Canadians were threatened by the emergence of other great hockey nations. Many felt that losing hockey supremacy meant losing something of ourselves. Hockey was not a Canadian invention like the telephone or the Canadarm which only makes us prouder of Canada when employed by others around the world. When it was used exceptionally well by hands not our own, it felt like hockey made us less.

Perhaps it is that very possessive emotionality which accounts for the long delay in treating hockey and its literature as subjects of serious critical inquiry. Investigating hockey critically is to think of it not as expressing some real connection between nature and culture, but to see it as carrying a story, often expressed in mythic terms, that people desire to be true about themselves and their place in the world. The dominant hockey narrative in Canada has connected the game to what Richard Gruneau and David Whitson describe as a "happy naturalism, a direct expression of our [Canadian] ability to survive, indeed to thrive, in an inhospitable land of ice and snow, long winters, vast open spaces" (1). Canada's great narrative of its own "northern" character, with its emphasis on the personal virtues of hardiness, self-reliance, and self-sacrifice, and on the social values of small-town life and loyalty to the collective good, all leavened with a touch of ironic humour, has been told so often in the language of hockey that the two stories – of game and nation – can seem like one.

The two stories, of course, are separate. Though most of the writers in this book have come to hockey first as players and lovers of the game, and so have felt (and even continue to feel) the attractions of hockey's myths, the act of treating hockey as a subject for critical inquiry means shutting the eye that sees hockey as a mythic creation, shaping a society because of an essential nature that acts on the culture from the outside, and considering hockey, instead, as a social creation governed by and affecting the structures, emotions, ambitions and desires of society itself.

The touchstone book for understanding hockey in this way is Gruneau and Whitson's *Hockey Night in Canada*, published in 1993. In the 1990s the appreciation of popular culture by Canadian academics was still decidedly mixed. Although many scholars had accepted the arguments about the significance of popular culture made by various Western thinkers, the distinction between "high culture" and "low" still operated quite strongly, distinguishing between what was fit for critical investigation and what was not. As Gruneau and Whitson wrote less than twenty years ago, Canadians "with highbrow sensibilities" might have watched and enjoyed a hockey game, but the game itself was still "subjected to considerable intellectual snobbery" (12). Certainly this was the case in the departments of English Literature. There was (as there still is) a massive body of hockey writing in Canada; however, most of it was hockey journalism chronicling the exploits of colourful players, teams, or eras, and rarely, if ever, studied in the academy. Hockey-related biographies kept fans happy, but weren't curriculum material – the lone exception lying, perhaps, in Ken Dryden's groundbreaking and meditative 1983 memoir, *The Game*. And though there were also many hockey histories, events in hockey rarely figured in textbooks on Canadian history as a whole, with the exceptions of the Richard Riot in 1955 because of its connection with the Quiet Revolution, and the 1972 Summit Series because of its links to the Cold War. Both of these were cases in which the ever-present mix of hockey and politics exploded into public view. But up until the early 1990s literary- or cultural studies-based considerations of the meaning of hockey and its writing were few and far between despite the prominence of the game in Canadian life.

How things have changed might be glimpsed by reflecting on both the public and the academic receptions of Paul Quarrington's hockey novel *King Leary*, which was first published in 1987, six years before Gruneau and Whitson's book. Although *King Leary* won the 1988 Stephen Leacock Award for Humour and was shortlisted for Ontario's Trillium Book Award, it received little critical attention (comedy about hockey? the low speaking of the low), and the book went out of print. There was no published full-length study of the novel until the proceedings of 2001's *Putting It On Ice* conference in which Don Morrow hailed the book as among the first and few to give "literary voice to the meaning of a game to a culture so lacking in its own self-revelatory literature" (117). The novel was re-published only after its selection as one of the contenders in the 2008 edition of CBC Radio One's *Canada Reads* literary competition, and it was named the winner by the show's panellists over some of Canada's most critically praised novels – which means it belongs among them now, if it didn't always. As we write this, *King Leary*, perhaps a particularly Canadian tragedy comically told, can be heard on CBC Radio's *Between the Covers*, and several studies of the book are forthcoming.

Along with the increased attention to what is now commonly referred to as "Hockey Literature's" early works, since 1987 there has been a steady creation of literary writing either entirely or partially about the game. With Quarrington's *King Leary* (and his own later *Logan in Overtime*) and Roy MacGregor's 1983 novel *The Last Season* serving as the foundation for serious adult fiction about hockey, there came, among others, Bill Gaston's *The Good Body*, Mark Anthony Jarman's *Salvage King, Ya!*, Wayne Johnston's *The Divine Ryans*, and Richard B. Wright's *The Age of Longing*. In the title of Pete McCormack's *Understanding Ken*, we see another stage in the development of hockey literature: a book announcing itself in relation to hockey through the name of the author of an earlier book on the game and safely assuming that the reference is understood. (In a lovely twist on that understanding, the Ken that McCormack's protagonist seeks to understand is, of course, the author of the famously analytical *The Game*, but it is Ken's earlier, astounding decision to divorce himself from not just the Canadiens but hockey itself that the hero is left to comprehend on his own.) In Lynn Coady's *Saints of Big Harbour* and Cara Hedley's *Twenty Miles*, hockey and its literature, formerly dominated by male voices, is re-imagined by women in whose rich fiction hockey is less their characters' refuge than it is a place where they confront those forces that shape their personal lives. *The Hockey Player Sonnets* by John B. Lee and *Hero of the Play* by Richard Harrison, both from the 1990s, became two of Canada's best-selling books of poetry, and both were reprinted in tenth anniversary editions. Such successes in hockey poetry, like the post-1987 achievements in hockey fiction, did not come out of nowhere. There are precedents in Al Purdy's giant of a poem "Hockey Players," first published in 1965 and which famously and forever defined the game as a "combination of ballet and murder, " and in Stephen Scriver's 1980s explorations in the vernacular of the game, *All Star Poet!* and *More! All Star Poet*, its revised republication. Recently the ranks of hockey poets in Canada added two whose writing is focussed on the role of goaltender: Matt Robinson, who played the most unforgiving position in sport, with *no cage contains a stare that well*, and Randall Maggs, who studied goaltending's mysteries through a dramatic reconstruction of one of its most enigmatic greats. His *Night Work: The Sawchuk Poems* received front-page attention on the *Globe and Mail's* "Books" section, and is already in its second printing.

And there are several anthologies – *The Rocket, the Flower, the Hammer, and Me; Thru the Smoky End Boards; Going Top Shelf;* and *Ice: New Writing on Hockey* among them – devoted entirely to hockey poetry and short fiction. There have also been films like *The Divine Ryans, Perfectly Normal,* and the biopic *The Rocket.* As well, the realm of hockey non-fiction has expanded, and hockey has become an object of literary, sociological, even philosophical reflection: consider Bruce Dowbiggin's *The Meaning of Puck*, Dave Bidini's *Tropic of Hockey*, Bill Gaston's *Midnight Hockey*, Brian Kennedy's *Growing Up Hockey*, Stephen Brunt's *Searching for Bobby Orr*, Roy MacGregor's *Canadians* and Lorna Jackson's *Cold-Cocked*.

On the critical side, the number of articles, books and films on hockey's literary, social, historical and cultural place has also increased, including important social histories like John Chi-Kit Wong's *Lords of the Rinks*. Michael McKinley's pivotal book *Putting a Roof on Winter*, shows us that the transformation of hockey from an outdoor to an indoor sport was fundamental in the development of the modern game. Cecil Harris's *Breaking the Ice*, based on the experiences of the few black players to make it to the NHL, reopens the still-sensitive conversation about hockey and race. The recent, massive CBC documentary *Hockey: A People's History* and its accompanying book, also by McKinley, explores hockey not as mythic lore passed down from generation to generation of a select few "hockey people," but as a historical process both moved by and affecting the larger forces of the culture. In this approach, who and what we are can still be seen in the intimate relationship between hockey and its birth nation, but rather than a mythic identification in terms of lore and values, the "we" that can be seen through hockey is the "we" of economics, morality, demographics, politics, daily life, war and peace.

Even more significantly, perhaps, in terms of the tension between ways of looking at the game, are books which explicitly detach themselves from hockey's myth, like David Cruise and Alison Griffiths' *Net Worth: Exploding the Myths of Pro Hockey* and Laura Robinson's *Crossing the Line: Violence and Sexual Assault in Canada's National Sport*, both of which analyze hockey as a mass ritual with mechanisms, power structures and abuses protected by its almost sacred place in the culture. If hockey is us, argue such books, we can change it, and change ourselves for the better in doing so.

The last ten years have also seen the appearance of conferences and books of essays devoted completely to hockey: Colin Howell's *Putting It On Ice* and *Women's Hockey* conferences at the Gorsebrook Research Institute of St. Mary's University, Halifax, and the proceedings from these; Whitson and Gruneau's *Artificial Ice*, a multi-authored follow-up to the issues raised in and by their *Hockey Night in Canada*; and Andrew Holman's conference with a title both question and challenge: *Canada's Game?* And if a conference is a group of people devoted to the idea that their subject is worth their best intellectual efforts, we must include Brendan Shanahan's player-summoned gathering during the NHL's 2004/2005 lockout season to reconsider the rules of a professional game that had wrestled itself stale both on and off the ice. Conferences and writings such as these produce both a community of thinkers and a critical mass of discussion through which long-term and short-term ideas about the game and its place in both Canadian and world culture can come to life. Such perspectives give us greater insight into hockey as both the subtle and brutal cultural creation it is. And they can give us the means to argue effectively for change in the game, either to follow the society in which the game is played or, on occasion, to take the lead.

A few more words, then, about the *Canada and the League of Hockey Nations* conference, and this book made from the papers discussed there. *Now is the Winter* is not a proceedings. It does not represent the wide range of topics that we debated with passion and humour. The conference touched on more than the cultural, political and artistic meanings of hockey that form the main themes of this book. Papers on the wisdom of allowing bodychecking among younger players, on the challenges faced by families supporting their hockey-playing sons and daughters, on the economics of the professional game, on the ever-present topic of the relationship between violence and play, and on the governance of the NHL were all presented. The documentary *Valery's Ankle* was screened, and one of the most infamous episodes in the Summit Series was vigorously debated as, probably, it always will be. Authors gave readings from their poems, biographies, memoirs and fiction about hockey, and there was the generous and insightful after-dinner address by Harley Hotchkiss, part-owner of the Calgary Flames and then chairman of the NHL Board of Governors. Any number of these could form the cornerstone for a different anthology – or film or literary festival.

In different and exciting ways, the papers within this collection offer answers to the question that still fascinates so many of us: "What happens when hockey happens?" In hockey, Stephen Hardy and Andrew Holman see an innovative and powerful way to map international history, perceiving in the game's spread and contraction a pattern to map any number of activities caught up in "globalization," a process not without its battles. John Soares takes us into some of the Cold War's most intimate zones of contact and conflict, and finds, perhaps surprisingly to some, that the violent game of hockey has created bonds between players of opposing nations that in many ways transcend politics. Brian Kennedy combines cultural theory with direct research to explore the elements involved in the presentation of professional hockey games, thus offering a sophisticated analysis of how these games create their spectacular effects. Kelly Hewson, an outsider converted to the love of the game, sees hockey in a kind of stasis at the moment, one of its faces looking to a mythic past it cannot leave behind, the other to a future it has yet to enter, though it yearns to do so. Richard Harrison proposes that hockey's myth can still foster an international love of the winter that the game retreated from long ago. David McNeil's personal and meticulous analysis of the photographs of his father playing goal for Montreal in the '50s discusses how hockey photography gives us a record not just of how we saw the game, but of how we decided, through selecting some photographic technologies over others, how to see. And the way

Canadians see ourselves though hockey is the subject of Michael P. Buma's commentary on the act of self-salvation that Canadians often read into the struggle to retain teams in Canadian cities. Interestingly, while our on-ice performance is a show of Canadian power and competence, hockey's off-ice and business sides often leave Canadians feeling helpless and angry: witness Craig Hyatt, William M. Foster and Mark R. Julien's reconstruction of Chris Pronger's emotional departure from Edmonton as a failed relationship between fans who honoured the hero who brought glory to their city but whose actions told them that their city was not good enough.

Lastly, the consistent and perhaps inevitable division in hockey between those inside its world and those left out – the way that hockey continues to speak the language of self and other – is examined and challenged by four papers in this book. Sam McKegney points out that hockey still carries North American cultural assumptions of the past about the relationships between the European and Aboriginal peoples and with nature. Ed Mason uncovers a similar process at work in New Zealand, showing that hockey's processes still operate far from the game's usual domains. Anne Hartman's essay from the rinks of Toronto, where women's shinny must still contest its marginal space on public ice, looks forward to her doctoral work on how the politics of equity and inequality are still in play in game and nation alike. And Andrew Holman's analysis of sport fiction for youth shows how even the smallest of cultural and political differences in a common activity can become powerful divisions between "us" and "them." But an important lesson of all of the essays is that such borders are not fixed. The essays speak in their own ways of the hope, tentative but real, that differences between self and other can truly become no more important than home and away hockey sweaters: costumes that make the game possible but that we take off again when the game that brought us together has done its work and it's time to talk about the play.

Now is the Winter

Works Cited

Beardsley, Doug, ed. *The Rocket, The Flower, The Hammer and Me: An All-Star Collection of Canadian Hockey Fiction*. Winlaw, BC: Polestar, 1988.

Bidini, Dave. *Tropic of Hockey: My Search for the Game in Unlikely Places*. Toronto: McClelland & Stewart, 2000.

Brooks, Kevin, and Sean Brooks, eds. *Thru the Smoky End Boards: Canadian Poetry about Sports and Games*. Vancouver: Polestar, 1996.

Brunt, Stephen. *Searching for Bobby Orr*. Toronto: Random House, 2006.

Coady, Lynn. *Saints of Big Harbour*. Toronto: Random House, 2002.

Cruise, David, and Alison Griffiths. *Net Worth: Exploding the Myths of Pro Hockey*. Toronto: Penguin, 1991.

Dowbiggin, Bruce. *The Meaning of Puck: How Hockey Explains Modern Canada*. Toronto: Key Porter, 2008.

Dryden, Ken. *The Game: A Thoughtful and Provocative Look at Life in Hockey*. Toronto: HarperCollins, 1989. First published 1983 by McClelland & Stewart.

Gaston, Bill. *Midnight Hockey: All About Beer, the Boys, and the Real Canadian Game*. Toronto: Random House, 2006.

Gaston, Bill. *The Good Body*. Dunvegan, ON: Cormorant, 2000.

Gruneau, Richard, and David Whitson. *Hockey Night in Canada: Sports, Identities and Cultural Politics*. Toronto: Garamond, 1993.

Harris, Cecil. *Breaking the Ice: The Black Experience in Professional Hockey*. Toronto: Insomniac Press, 2003.

Harrison, Richard. *Hero of the Play: 10th Anniversary Edition*. Toronto: Wolsak and Wynn, 2004.

Hedley, Cara. *Twenty Miles*. Toronto: Coach House, 2007.

Hockey: A People's History. CBC Television, Fall 2006. www.cbc.ca/hockeyhistory.

Howell, Colin D., ed. *Putting it on Ice. Vol. 1, Hockey and Cultural Identities*. Halifax: Gorsebrook Research Institute, 2002.

Jackson, Lorna. *Cold-Cocked: On Hockey*. Emeryville, ON: Biblioasis, 2007.

Jacobs, Dale, ed. *Ice: New Writing on Hockey*. Edmonton: Spotted Cow Press, 1999.

Jarman, Marc Anthony. *Salvage King, Ya!: A Herky-Jerky Picaresque*. Vancouver: Anvil Press, 1998.

Johnston, Wayne. *The Divine Ryans*. Toronto: Random House, 1998. First published 1990 by McClelland & Stewart.

Kennedy, Brian. *Growing Up Hockey: The Life and Times of Everyone Who Ever Loved the Game*. Edmonton: Folklore, 2007.

Kennedy, Michael P. J., ed. *Going Top Shelf: An Anthology of Canadian Hockey Poetry*. Victoria: Heritage House, 2005.

Lee, John B. *The Hockey Player Sonnets*. Waterloo, ON: Penumbra, 1991.

MacGregor, Roy. *The Last Season*. Toronto: Penguin, 2005. First published 1983 by Macmillan.

MacGregor, Roy. *Canadians: A Portrait of a Country and Its People*. Toronto: Penguin, 2007.

Maggs, Randall. *Night Work: The Sawchuk Poems*. London, ON: Brick Books, 2008.

McCormak, Pete. *Understanding Ken*. Vancouver: Douglas & McIntyre, 1998.

McKinley, Michael. *Putting a Roof on Winter: Hockey's Rise from Sport to Spectacle*. Vancouver: Douglas & McIntyre, 2000.

McKinley, Michael. *Hockey: A People's History*. Toronto: McClelland & Stewart, 2006.

Morrow, Don. "Quarrington's Hockey Shtick: A Literary Analysis." In *Putting it on Ice*. Vol. 1, *Hockey and Cultural Identities*, edited by Colin D. Howell, 111–118. Halifax: Gorsebrook Research Institute, 2002.

Perfectly Normal. Directed by Yves Simoneau. Four Seasons Entertainment, 1991.

Purdy, Al. "Hockey Players." In *The Cariboo Horses*, 60–62. Toronto: McClelland & Stewart, 1965.

Robinson, Laura, *Crossing the Line: Violence and Sexual Assault in Canada's National Sport*. Toronto: McClelland & Stewart, 1998.

Robinson, Matt. *no cage contains a stare that well*. Toronto: ECW Press, 2005.

Said, Edward W. *Culture and Imperialism*. New York: Random House, 1993.

Scriver, Stephen. *All Star Poet!* Saskatoon: Coteau, 1981.

Scriver, Stephen. *More! All Star Poet: New and Selected Poems*. Saskatoon: Coteau, 1989.

Sinden, Harry. *Hockey Showdown: The Canada-Russia Hockey Series*. Toronto: Random House, 1972.

The Divine Ryans. Directed by Stephen Reynolds. Marystown, NL: Enterprise Newfoundland, 1999.

The Rocket. Directed by Charles Binamé. Montreal: Alliance Films, 2005.

Valery's Ankle. Directed Brett Kashmere. 15 Years in Productions, 2006.

Wright, Richard B. *The Age of Longing*. Toronto: HarperCollins, 1995.

Quarrington, Paul. *King Leary*. Toronto: Random House, 1988.

Quarrington, Paul. *Logan in Overtime*. Toronto: Random House, 1990.

Whitson, David, and Richard Gruneau, eds. *Artificial Ice: Hockey, Culture, and Commerce*. Toronto: Garamond, 2006.

Wong, John Chi-Kit. *Lords of the Rinks: The Emergence of the National Hockey League, 1875–1936*. Toronto: University of Toronto Press, 2005.

Stephen Hardy and Andrew Holman

Periodizing Hockey History
One Approach

In recent years, both scholars and journalists have analyzed the sweeping effects of globalization – on labour, small business and, especially, on culture. There is a sense that traditional local, regional and national forms of art and culture are both circulating and eroding in an era when information and products move with lightning speed across international borders. Sushi bars in Kansas City, McDonald's in Beijing, Salsa Week in Italy, Disneyland in France. If everything is everywhere, does anywhere matter anymore?

Sport has not been immune to this process; in fact, sport in the modern era (circa 1850–present) has been a particularly speedy vehicle for globalization. In soccer, the three biggest European leagues have siphoned the world's best talents from their homelands, threatening the stability of local teams and leagues. Jorge Valdano, who played for Argentina's 1986 World Cup champions and later served as sporting director of Real Madrid, put it this way: "Twenty years ago it was easy to say that Latin American football was about technique and talent, and European football was about organization, speed, and fighting spirit. But with television and player transfers, all these trends are coming together." In sport, the Local has been swallowed by the Global, or so it seems to some.[1]

While this process is remarkable, it is hardly new. Globalization is not just a recent phenomenon, it has happened before. And whenever this kind of cultural "coming together" in history has happened, it was never unidirectional or irreversible. Today's so-called global phase of sport is actually a second period of convergence in rules, patterns of play and perceptions about the meaning of "hockey."

Periodization is one of the most basic tasks that historians must consider when they research and conceptualize the past. Which events and personalities are useful and make sense to us? Which critical markers or signposts along historical highways should we give titles to and treat as important? Though it may seem at first glance a benign process – merely a necessary tool for "managing" the great expanse of past events and allowing historians to narrow their focus in time – modern historical periodization is anything but simple. Gone are the days when decades or centuries or millennia (the most arbitrary signposts) held legitimacy as appropriate points at which historians might start and stop their analyses.[2] In modern history, periodization has *in theory* assumed a much more meaningful role. Numerous historians have argued convincingly that their colleagues must be deliberate in the ways that they carve up the past and paint their periods with descriptive labels and metaphors, such as "the feminine fifties" or the "Jazz Age." As E. H. Carr wrote in 1961, periodization is not historical "fact," but rather "a necessary hypothesis or tool of thought, valid in so far as it is illuminating, and dependent for its validity on interpretation."[3] In short, periodization is something that all historians need to regularly revisit and, when warranted, change.

Oddly, we rarely consider periodization when reading or writing history. "It is part of our mental furniture," historian Ludmilla Jordanova has written recently, and we rarely give it "conscious inspection."[4] Too often, we are content to accept inherited periods and metaphorical labels and to shoehorn new research into old, sometimes ill-fitting, time frames. This inertia is only overcome occasionally, when it sparks interesting (but short-lived) debates about conventional practice and its underlying assumptions. For instance, in the 1970s ethnohistorians called for a new periodization of the Native American past, one that was separate from customary "white" time frames and spoke directly to the experiences of America's First Peoples.[5]

The same sort of inertia has been evident in the writing of sport history. Historians of sport have tended to accept the period markers outlined by works in national political, economic or military history, even when those markers had little direct impact on the sport's world. Barbara Schrodt expressed this ably in 1990: "We need to take a more critical approach to the dates we select, and not simply assume that the periodization used in one area of historical research is equally appropriate for all studies. Nor should we feel the necessity to work with a periodization developed for general Canadian history." More recently, Christiane Eisenberg pointed out that while it is important to consider sport in context, one must be careful not to swamp the history of an organization like FIFA in "alien categories and periods to such an extent that it is difficult to grasp satisfactorily its own pace of development, its own dynamics, and, above all, its own particular lasting influence."[6] These comments are well-taken and should be observed by all those who study sport as a national phenomenon, but the problem of periodization is compounded for those whose subject reaches beyond national borders. Historians of *global* sport face the task of identifying discreet turning points in a sometimes seemingly indefinite list of episodes, circumstances and events that have not just local and national but international contexts as well. This is precisely the challenge that we face in conceptualizing and giving order to an historical phenomenon as broad and complex as the sport of ice hockey. Here, periodization is an essential and early consideration that must reflect the global events that occurred.[7]

Adopting a global perspective of the game means considering hockey in all of its contexts, but still recognizing that the game resided, and still resides, more heavily and heartily in some places (especially Canada) than it has in others. Hockey has always been an imbalanced or asymmetrical global phenomenon, and hockey's heartland will command much of our attention. Still, as historians of any empire would argue, there is much to be learned about the sport by examining its hinterlands. The two-way relationship between the core of the Montreal game and its peripheries (be they in the United States, or Europe or Asia) is what has given the game its dynamism and what continues to provide its promise. It is this perspective – a global perspective that appreciates the roles of both core and fringe – that determines how we choose to periodize hockey's colourful past.

We suggest that hockey's history may be divided into four periods during which various elements and forms of the game – its culture and structure – converged, diverged and then re-converged. Scholars of world history have for some time fashioned models with long-term flows of divergence and convergence among peoples and cultures. Historian C. A. Bayly has described "archaic globalization" from 1400 to 1900 with slow but steady movement toward "uniformity" in language, food, dress, senses of time and, eventually, sport. Julie Stevens has employed the concepts of divergence and convergence in her fine analysis of the Canadian hockey organization over the last century. Convergence-divergence-convergence in rules, governance and tactics (among other things): just such a framework helps to periodize the wider world of hockey, beyond Canada, to the United States and Europe.[8]

It must be stressed from the outset that convergence and divergence are tendencies we discern from historical distance; they are ongoing, never complete and always subject to reversal, like a giant tide reconfiguring a world hockey market. Like hegemony, convergence is a tendency seldom fulfilled. While there may be a group or institution, such as the National Hockey League (NHL), seeking to diffuse and impose its values, convergence implies that the dominant group is quite willing to adopt the values and practices of others, such as the National Collegiate Athletic Association (NCAA) or International Ice Hockey Federation (IIHF). At the same time, our historical perspective suggests that the hockey world has had periods of aggregate convergence or divergence that provide boundaries for periodization.[9]

Part One. Imported Convergence: from Folk Games to the Montreal Game, 1700–1877

As J. William Fitsell and a committee of the Society for International Hockey Research (SIHR) have clearly shown, hockey was not "invented" so much as it emerged from a blend of old folk games played by native tribes and European immigrants. In short, hockey developed from the swirl of merging cultures, not unlike what Bayly has called "Archaic Globalization." While the first published set of rules (developed between 1875 and 1877 in Montreal) borrowed extensively from field hockey, the game as played and perceived owed just as much to hurling (or hurley), shinty, lacrosse and even rugby football. It is no stretch to say that a few centuries worth of folk games blended in the minds of a few Montrealers to create a new form of "hockey."[10]

Part Two. Exported Convergence: A Game Becomes The Game: 1877–1920

Over the next four decades, the Montreal version of hockey gradually emerged as the dominant stick/skate/ice game in North America and in many parts of Europe. What is more, many of hockey's apostles, such as George Meagher, who helped to spread its popularity in America and Europe, preached one basic set of rules – those of the Amateur Hockey Association of Canada (AHAC), the game's first real governing body, founded in 1886. When Americans in Baltimore and Washington, DC, first played hockey in 1895–96, they played under the rules of the AHAC. Hockey's first published guidebook – published by the Spalding empire in 1897 – included rules of the new Amateur Hockey League of New York, which were almost a verbatim copy of the AHAC rules. By 1920, when players, writers and fans in London, Zurich, Prague, Boston, St. Paul or Seattle used the term "ice hockey," they typically meant the Montreal game. To paraphrase sport sociologist Richard Gruneau, a version of stick and skate on ice became *the* version. But there is nothing to suggest that hockey's victory was inevitable. Montreal hockey faced strong competition from other hockey-like games, notably polo in America and bandy in Europe. In Russia and Sweden and other countries, the terms "bandy" and "hockey" were used interchangeably, and neither country adopted the Montreal game for years. Hockey's promoters had to skillfully position their product in the winter marketplace.[11]

By 1920, however, hockey had become the king of winter team sports. Why 1920? By this time, Canadian, American and European groups had developed viable hockey leagues and governing structures, such as the Ontario Hockey Association (1890), the NHL (1917), the Intercollegiate Hockey League (1900) and the Czech Hockey Union (1908). Representatives from four European countries (Britain, France, Belgium and Switzerland) had founded the *Ligue Internationale de Hockey sur Glace* (*LIHG*, 1908), which grew into the IIHF. Before World War I began, the *LIHG* had sponsored five European Championships. Their members had lobbied the International Olympic Committee to include hockey on the roster of Olympic competition, a drive that succeeded in 1920, when the *LIHG* held a tournament at April's Antwerp Games. At those Antwerp Olympics, the Swedes entered a team stocked largely with bandy players. They returned home as hockey apostles. Equally important, at Antwerp, both Canada and the United States entered teams and joined the *LIHG*. The web of hockey was now international and intercontinental.[12]

The year 1920 also marked a "return to normalcy" from the Great War that had brutally ended a crucial chapter in history. We must remember that Montreal hockey was not the only sport to sweep across continents and oceans between 1890 and 1914. There were particular economic conditions that promoted the circulation of baseball, basketball, soccer and rugby, as well as hockey. As economic historian Jeffry Frieden argues, the "Golden Age" of global capitalism occurred between 1896 and the start of the First World War. In Frieden's words, "the opening years of the twentieth century were the closest thing the world has ever seen to a free world market for goods, capital and labor. It took a hundred years before the world returned to that level of globalization."[13] Games such as soccer and hockey circulated with the clerks, merchants, engineers and missionaries who were the human faces of global capitalism.

Part Three. The Wide, Diverging World of the Montreal Game, 1921–1971

Hockey was lucky to circulate when it did, because the "Golden Age" did not last long.

In fact, the splintering of hockey's governance had started well before that age had ended, as John Wong, Julie Stevens and others have outlined. The creation of the OHA in 1890, the senior-level Canadian Amateur Hockey League (CAHL) in 1898, the professional International Hockey League (IHL) in 1904 and the National Hockey Association (NHA) in 1910 signified this change. Some of the fissures ran along the amateur-professional fault lines that crossed many sports at the time. Others simply represented fights over who would gain the glory from controlling a popular pastime. On the broader plane of political economy, World War I and the Depression ruptured the system of global capitalism. A new protectionism – economic and cultural – replaced the once-free movement of goods, capital and people. Following a window of free trade in the 1920s, the Depression brought an insularity to western nations that had far-reaching effects, even for a fledgling sport such as hockey. Within its several national and regional cocoons, hockey developed in different and divergent ways, along the two main lines mentioned above: the first having to do with power struggles within the sport; the second can be described as cultural self-sufficiency.[14]

A good example of the first type can be seen in the virtual firewall against Canadian-style fighting that developed in American college hockey in 1928–29. In 1928, the *Official Ice Hockey Guide* moved under the control of the National Collegiate Athletic Association (NCAA), becoming part of the association's "plan to issue rules on all sports participated in by college teams." The new editor of the rules was Rufus J. Trimble, a faculty member at Columbia University. For the next four decades, the NCAA Ice Hockey Rules Committee would consciously work to distinguish its game from other forms of hockey, especially the professional forms. Among its central goals, the NCAA committee wanted to promote "greater appreciation" of skill in contrast to the "approval, and even encouragement, of reprehensible rough play now sometimes unfortunately manifested by spectators." And in a jab at the NHL, the committee concluded that "the extension of professional hockey in the United States should not interfere with the improvement of intercollegiate play in this respect." And so the committee erected the great firewall that still distinguishes the American college game from the professional game – expulsion from the game for fighting. Rule 12–6 required a match penalty for "slugging, fighting, or fisticuffs, or attempting to hit or slug."[15]

When the Great Depression swept over the world's economy, it both spawned and reinforced regimes that declared their independence from western capitalism. Fascists, Socialists and Communists promised to go it alone and build their economies independently. Scholars call this "autarky," or what Jeffry Frieden describes as "forcible separation from the rest of the world." It is no surprise that the long disconnect from the Depression, World War II and, finally, the Cold War would also encourage sporting autarky. To be sure, the Depression did not hinder the expansion of international sporting competition. After all, the Olympics moved to true mass spectacle in 1932 and 1936. Instead, the era's geopolitics heightened awareness of a new tool for national identity. As Barbara Keys has argued in a recent book on international sport in the 1930s, once inside the Olympics or a sports federation, "each nation could claim that its participation in any international contest, though outwardly conforming to the same rules and conditions as every other nation's, was nevertheless fundamentally an expression of intrinsically national characteristics."[16]

Two sports seemed to manifest this separation more than the others: soccer and hockey. If Brazilians, Italians and Britons went their own ways in soccer, so did the Americans, the Swedes, the Canadians, the Czechs and the Russians in hockey. What is more, commentators and broadcasters in the six decades after World War I seemed to *look for* and accentuate the differences. Somehow, the ways that Canadians played hockey *had* to be different from the ways in which Europeans (especially the Socialists) played the game. Hockey was seen to reflect political economy. Americans and Canadians favored more individual play than the collectivists who skated on German, Soviet or Swedish rinks. Politics demanded it.

The development of Soviet and Swedish hockey in these years reflects this pattern clearly. As Soviet sport historian Robert Edelman has documented, in 1949 (at the time of NATO's formation), Soviet hockey's top referee, Sergei Savin, wrote negatively about the notion that his countrymen should embrace the Canadian version of hockey in order to compete on the international stage: "Hockey in our country develops by its own path and has nothing in common with foreign versions of the game. There, players follow the worst example of Canadian professional hockey, try always to fight, and replace technique with crude physical force." After 1945, the USSR embraced the wider world of international ice hockey, but only on its own terms.[17] Anatoly Tarasov, the "father of Russian hockey," took great pride in talking about "collective" hockey.

At the same time, Soviet teams were characterized by the Swedes and others teams as "robots" and "hockey machines," especially under Tarasov's successor, Viktor Tikhonov. And, in Swedish minds, if the Soviets were machines, the Canadians were brutes. A Swedish Hockey Federation official put it this way after the 1963 World Championships: "Canadians aren't hockey players – Canadians are murderers." Other characterizations were more subtle, such as the game program for the 1969 World Championships in Stockholm, which included two pages on hockey rules, using text and cartoon figures. While all of the text and most of the rule names were in Swedish, a few were amalgams (*offside i anfallszon*), and two penalty titles were starkly English: "cross-checking/spearing" and "but[t]-ending." More to the point, the cartoon figures for all penalties wore the plastic helmets so popular with the Swedes in that decade; that is, all but two. The perpetrators of cross-checking and butt-ending wore no helmets. Even a casual observer can see something different in this menacing player. No doubt, he was meant to be a Canadian.[18]

Part Four. Convergence toward the NHL and Corporate Hockey, 1972–2002

The "Rise of Corporate Hockey" refers to a period when the NHL's version of the game became more dominant worldwide. Here, convergence returns. We see three significant changes that define what we call "corporate" hockey. The first was part of a broader movement of grassroots and youth sports away from unorganized play toward highly structured, adult-dominated programs and leagues that sometimes seemed to exist more for the satisfaction of adult fantasies than for youth development. The introduction of "systems" into even the earliest ranks of minor hockey coaching, for example, epitomized this trend. Only recently, in the past decade, have coaches and parents bemoaned this trend and pushed back: let the kids play.[19]

The second aspect of corporate hockey was an increased willingness to embrace corporate partners who would underwrite costs in return for their ability to market their products through their affiliation with a team, a player, an arena or an event. These commercial intrusions would have been scandalous to hockey's earliest amateurs, such as James Creighton and Hobey Baker. By 1980, however, it would have seemed not just naive, but plain silly and suicidal, to reject corporate dollars and their related logos. In 1960, it would have been unthinkable for the Soviet Union to compete in anything but Socialist-made uniforms. But such notions would crumble like the Berlin Wall. By 1996, the IIHF gave Reebok the rights to supply all hockey competitors with Reebok brand uniforms. Two years later, Nike Bauer grabbed the rights. In 2006, the company would leverage its exclusive contract to roll out a space-age sweater. Except for colours, every uniform was the same – a nice advertisement for Nike Bauer.

The third aspect of corporate hockey involved the decisions of players, coaches and administrators at all levels of hockey to admit and even encourage tighter and tighter linkage to a giant hockey system where the most important roads led to the NHL, where the most important decisions rested directly or indirectly, but always consciously, on the interests of the NHL. This would have been inconceivable to American Olympic star Billy Cleary in 1960 or to Soviet Valery Kharlamov in 1970. Playing for their country was the pinnacle of success. By 1980, such views were quaint. The real test of ability had become the NHL. On all three of these levels, the era of corporate hockey has been one of convergence in the way hockey is organized, the way it is marketed and the way it is played.

Why 1972? That year serves as a watershed because of what it signaled or symbolized for the game itself. In Ken Dryden's words, "1972. It was the most important hockey year of the century." Among other things, 1972 was the year of the monumental series between Team Canada and the Soviet National Team, which began an era of "open" competition in tournaments and tours. And that year also began a reconfiguration of top-level professional hockey, triggered by the formation of the World Hockey Association. While the league's name reflected the bold and brash hucksterism of its founders, Gary Davidson and Dennis Murphy, the name also reflected a reality. In its war against the NHL, the WHA could not afford to sign too many top stars like Bobby Hull, Frank Mahovlich or Derek Sanderson. And so the WHA opened its doors to Swedes, Finns and Czechs. Also, 1972 was the year that Bruce Kidd and John Macfarlane published *The Death of Hockey*, a scathing critique of the game's organization and meaning that warned Canadians that they were losing "their" game to larger capitalist forces, most of which resided in the lower 48.[20]

Convergence happened both in the way the game was played and in the way that hockey was sold and consumed. Some of the causes were geopolitical. The Cold War softened, the Iron Curtain fell, the Soviet Union crumbled and the European Union grew. Money flowed to productive areas and industries and to cheaper labour. Products moved more readily. Some of these changes were linked to new technologies in information and communication. Computers, satellites and cable networks could move data and money at speeds undreamed of only decades earlier. Since the early 1970s, the world has opened up.[21]

At the same time, the increasingly wider net of global communications, beginning with satellite transmissions in the 1960s, allowed for the instant circulation of cultural performances and products, such as sports championships and stars. Some scholars have argued that this widening of consumer markets has "delocalized" sports fans, who eventually have succumbed to the onslaught of images and merchandise, forgotten their parents' or their childhood loyalties to the nearest franchise, and adopted some distant team or star as their most cherished brand. How long could a teenaged European defenceman rebuff the allure of Ray Bourque and the NHL? While this argument has compelling logic, historians must wait for more direct evidence – from the voices of the consumers – before accepting it as fact. In particular, there is need for evidence to show that fans gave up their local identities and loyalties.[22]

What is certain is that hockey's labourers and capitalists created a world much more fluid and connected than ever before. If players and fans did not renounce their local identities and loyalties, they appeared more willing to try out others. If coaches and administrators clung to beliefs that "their" system was the best, they accepted appeals from the NHL to make a few changes here and there, changes that were more fundamental than they may have first appeared. A couple of examples bear this out.

The first of these involves the internationalization of hockey. Canadians have always been accepted as hockey's experts. Even as the game was diverging from 1920–1972, European, American and Australian clubs often hired Canadian coaches. Australian and British teams stocked themselves with Canadian players. The latest period, however, has seen a much greater circulation of players from nation to nation, from system to system. One recent study reveals the controversies surrounding the importation of Canadians to America's eastern and Ivy League collegiate programs in the 1960s and '70s. Many pundits protested that a few coaches, such as Cornell's Ned Harkness and Boston University's Jack Kelley, were prostituting their programs. By the 1980s, only the University of Minnesota attempted to stay purely American. And by the 1980s, Europeans and Americans were moving into the NHL, its minor leagues and major junior hockey in increasing numbers. The lockout of 2004–05 demonstrated the full flow of this huge network, as NHL players moved to Europe to earn their paycheques.[23]

The second example involves the rising dominance of the NHL brand of hockey in terms of rules, tactics, violence and commercialism. The final third of the twentieth century was host to a top-down pressure exerted by NHL officials on those hockey organizations that acted as feeders to the big league. For example, during 1966–1967, the year of the NHL's expansion to twelve teams, Commissioner Clarence Campbell and Bruins' owner Weston Adams sent letters to the NCAA ice hockey committee recommending that the college game make two radical rule changes. One was to permit bodychecking all over the ice, rather than just the defensive half of the ice, a restriction in place since the late 1920s. The other was to adopt a restriction on "two-line" passes. The NCAA committee minutes of 1967 included a strong belief that such requests from the NHL should have "no influence" on the college game: "the sentiment was expressed many times that our game under the present rules is so much better than the professional game." The NHL also put pressure on the IIHF to make the same changes. By 1969, the IIHF rules allowed checking all over the ice. At their 1972 meeting, the NCAA Rules Committee followed suit, despite a "long, detailed, thorough discussion" about the potential for "more fights, more injuries, jamming, interference, retaliation." Despite these fears, both groups climbed onboard the NHL train.[24]

By the 1990s, the American Hockey Coaches Association (AHCA) formally recognized what had been implicit for more than two decades. The decision to allow checking in all zones had rendered NCAA hockey no longer an independent entity – a distinct and largely terminal choice for players. NCAA hockey was now part of a system that led inexorably to the NHL. In 1997, the AHCA developed a marketing brochure that stressed the effectiveness of NCAA play and coaching in developing future NHL stars. Fittingly, the cover's tagline – *Check It Out* – rocked with pictures of hard hits. Inside panels held one small picture of students studying on a lawn below the words "Alma Mater" tucked amid more action photos and inserts of ex-collegians Brett Hull, Adam Oates and Brian Leetch wearing NHL All Star jerseys (without mortarboards), and strong advertising pitches about NCAA hockey representing the "Best of Both Worlds" and a legitimate choice for "Staying in the Game." While college recruiters had for years used this kind of language to persuade Canadian players to come south, such an overt marketing brochure would have been unthinkable forty years earlier.[25]

What we have tried to map out here is a big picture, or panorama, for understanding hockey's long history in all its complexities. Periodization is, of necessity, a process that simplifies the past and artificially imposes boundaries on historical events, ideas and processes. What we must do is shoehorn complicated stories into neat boxes that we call periods. Naturally, we will never have a perfect fit.

Those well-versed in hockey history will doubtless think of historical episodes or events that just do not fit in the periods described above. We know of some, too. The NHL's and the Canadian Hockey League's thirst for European players, for instance, reflects a widespread belief that European clubs do a better job of youth development, which in turn reflects still-important differences in the nature of hockey from place to place. And how can one fairly characterize the quick rise of women's hockey in Canada and internationally since the 1980s? Is it a convergent pattern with a common, international appeal and base for recruitment? Or is it a divergent pattern: the women's game is vastly different from men's hockey, not just in rules, but in tenor and tone? Certainly there are other "outliers," or exceptions to our model.[26]

Our sense of periods – convergence, divergence and re-convergence in playing styles and governance – will also raise questions about what best fosters the "good of the game." Was hockey "better" during its decades of divergence, when the NCAA, the NHL, the CAHA, the IIHF and other national governing bodies lived in relative independence? Is hockey "worse" because governance, styles of play and rules have been converging in the last three decades? Many fans, players, coaches and scholars will have quick responses to these questions, but there is no easy answer. As one scholar of world history reminded his readers, we must be careful to avoid either excessive celebration or denigration of convergent or divergent forces, for "it is the complex interaction of these forces that need to be considered if we are to make sense of the past and present."[27]

1   Walter LaFeber, *Michael Jordan and the New Global Capitalism* (New York: W. W. Norton, 2002). "Passion, pride, and profit: a survey of football," *Economist*, June 1, 2002. For other balanced views of global sport see the special issue of the *Sociology of Sport Journal* 11, no. 4 (December 1994); Grant Jarvie, "Internationalism and Sport in the Making of Nations," *Identities: Global Studies in Culture and Power* 10, no. 4 (June 2003): 537–51; Alan Bairner, *Sport, Nationalism, and Globalization: European and North American Perspectives*, SUNY Series in National Identities (Albany: State

University of New York Press, 2001); Toby Miller, Geoffrey Lawrence, Jim McKay and David Rowe, *Globalization and Sport* (London: SAGE, 2001).

2   This is what David Hackett Fischer calls "hectohistory ... when history is neatly chopped into Procrustean periods." See David Hackett Fischer, *Historians' Fallacies: Toward a Logic of Historical Thought* (New York: Harper & Row, 1970), 145.

3   E. H. Carr, *What is History?* (London: Macmillan, 1961), 60. See also Fischer, *Historians' Fallacies*, 144–46; John Tosh, *The Pursuit of History*, 3rd ed. (London: Pearson, 2002), 219–21; Richard J. Evans, *In Defense of History* (New York: W. W. Norton 1999), 131–34. On the theory and historical practice of periodization, see Jason Scott Smith, "The Strange History of the Decade: Modernity, Nostalgia, and the Perils of Periodization," *Journal of Social History* 32, no. 2 (Winter 1998): 263–85; and Ann Douglas, "Periodizing the American Century: Modernism, Postmodernism, and Postcolonialism in the Cold War Context," *Modernism/Modernity* 5, no. 3 (September 1998): 71–98. For one attempt at periodizing the global spread of sports between the sixteenth and twentieth centuries, see Joseph Maguire, *Global Sport: Identities, Societies, Civilizations* (Cambridge: Polity Press, 1999), 75–94.

4   Ludmilla Jordanova, *History in Practice* (London: Arnold, 2000), 114.

5   More recently, North American social historians have questioned the legitimacy of "the Gilded Age" and the "Progressive Era" and the logic of conventional periodization in Quebec historiography. They have debated the stages of childhood in the United States, and proposed a new periodization for the history of consumerism. See Martin J. Sklar, "Periodization and Historiography: Studying American Political Development in the Progressive Era, 1890s–1916," *Studies in American Political Development* 5, no. 2 (Fall 1991): 173–213; Robert Rutherdale, "Generations, Narration, and Periodization: Epochs and Applications in Historical Practice," *Canadian Review of American Studies* 28, no. 1 (1998): 105–19; John A. Dickinson and Brian Young, "Periodization in Quebec: A Reevaluation," *Québec Studies* 12 (1991): 1–10; and Peter N. Stearns, "Stages of Consumerism: Recent Work on the Issues of Periodization," *Journal of Modern History* 69, no. 1 (March 1997): 102–17.

6   Barbara Schrodt, "Problems of Periodization in Canadian Sport History," *Canadian Journal of the History of Sport* 21, no. 1 (May 1990): 65–76; Christiane Eisenberg, "From Political Ignorance to Global Responsibility: The Role of the World Soccer Association (FIFA) in International Sport during the Twentieth Century," *Journal of Sport History* 32, no. 3 (Fall 2005): 380. A similar (but less systematic) critique and proposal for revision for American sport history can be found in Nancy L. Struna, "Conceptualizing and Questioning in Undergraduate Sport History" (paper presented at the North American Society for Sport History convention, University of Wisconsin–La Crosse, La Crosse, WI, May 1985); and in Struna, "Beyond Mapping Experience: The Need for Understanding in the History of American Sporting Women," *Journal of Sport History* 11, no. 1 (Spring 1984): 129.

7   Of course this challenge is not new. Practitioners (and teachers) of world history have had to grapple with the problem of periodizing the global past for some time now. See, for example, William A. Green, "Periodizing World History," *History and Theory* 34, no. 2 (May 1995): 99–111.

8   David Northrup, "Globalization and the Great Convergence: Rethinking World History in the Long Term," *Journal of World History* 16, no. 3 (September 2005): 254; C.A. Bayly, *The Birth of the Modern World: 1780–1914*, Blackwell History of the World (Oxford: Blackwell, 2004), 12–19; Julie Stevens, "The Development of the Canadian Hockey System: A Process of Institutional Divergence and Convergence," in *Putting It On Ice*, vol. 2, *Internationalizing "Canada's Game,"* ed. Colin D. Howell (Halifax: Gorsebrook Research Institute, St. Mary's University, 2003), 53.

9   On market convergence, see Raymond Williams, *The Sociology of Culture* (New York: Schocken Books, 1981), 103–109.

10 The first person to look carefully at the origins of hockey was Fitsell in his groundbreaking book, *Hockey's Captains, Colonels, and Kings* (Erin, ON: Boston Mills Press, 1987). All hockey historians are indebted to Bill for his dogged research. See also Society for International Hockey Research, "The Origins of Hockey," July 10, 2008, www.sihrhockey.org/origins_main.cfm.

11 J. A. Tuthill, ed., *Spalding Ice Hockey and Ice Polo Guide, 1898* (New York: American Sports Publishing Company, 1897), 61–70; C. G. Tebbutt, "Bandy," in *Skating and Figure-skating*, ed. J. M. Heathcote and C. G. Tebbutt (London: Longmans, Green, 1894), 441–2; Peter Patton, *Ice-Hockey* (London: George Routledge & Sons, 1936), 4–5. For a history of polo, see Stephen Hardy, "'Polo at the Rinks': Shaping Markets for Ice Hockey in America, 1880–1900," *Journal of Sport History* 33, no. 2 (Summer 2006): 156–74. For a compelling discussion of institutionalization in sport – how a way of playing becomes the way of playing, see Richard Gruneau, *Class, Sports, and Social Development* (Champaign, IL: Human Kinetics, 1999), 3.

12 Our thanks to Tobias Stark for his kind review of an earlier draft of this paper, which led us to rethink the date for dividing part two and part three. For insight on governing bodies, see John Chi-Kit Wong, *Lords of the Rink: The Emergence of the National Hockey League, 1875–1936* (Toronto: University of Toronto Press, 2005); Karl Adolf Scherer, *1908–1978: 70 Years of LIHG/IIHF* (Zurich: International Ice Hockey Federation, 1978); Igor Kuperman, "From Andora to Yugoslavia: The History of Hockey and is Structure Today in Each IIHF Nation," in *Total Hockey*, 1st ed., ed. Igor Kuperman (New York: Total Sports, 1998), 447; Andrew Podnieks and others, *Kings of the Ice: A History of World Hockey* (Richmond Hill, ON: NDE Publishing, 2002), 155. For Sweden's early bandy-hockey history, see Bill Sund, "The Origins of Bandy and Hockey in Sweden," in *Putting It On Ice*, vol. 2, *Internationalizing "Canada's Game,"* ed. Colin D. Howell, 15–20; and Kenth Hansen, "The Birth of Swedish Ice Hockey – Antwerp 1920," *Citius, Altius, Fortius* 4, no. 2 (May 1996): 5–27.

13 Jeffry Frieden, *Global Capitalism: Its Fall and Rise in the Twentieth Century* (New York: W. W. Norton, 2006), 16.

14 Wong, *Lords of the Rinks*; Frieden, *Global Capitalism*, 128; Bruce Kidd, *The Struggle for Canadian Sport* (Toronto: University of Toronto Press, 1996), chap. 5.

15 Rufus Trimble, ed., *Official Ice Hockey Rules of the NCAA, 1928–29* (New York: American Sports, 1928), Foreword, 26, 30–1.

16 Frieden, *Global Capitalism*, 191; Barbara J. Keys, *Globalizing Sport: National Rivalry and International Community in the 1930s*, Harvard Historical Studies (Cambridge: Harvard University Press, 2006), 188.

17 Robert Edelman, *Serious Fun: A History of Spectator Sports in the USSR* (New York: Oxford University Press, 1993), 116. See Brian McFarlane, *Tarasov's Hockey Technique: Anatoli Tarasov*, trans. Verner Persson (Toronto: Holt, Rinehart and Winston of Canada, 1972). Hockey was only one sport in which the Soviets sought not just individuality, but domination. Stalin's 1948 directive was clear: "Soviet sportsmen, in upcoming years, will surpass the world records in all major sports." See also Hart Cantelon, "Revisiting the Introduction of Ice Hockey into the Former Soviet Union," in *Putting it On Ice*, vol. 2, *Internationalizing "Canada's Game,"* ed. Colin D. Howell, 30.

18 Quoted in Markku Jokisipilä, "Maple Leaf, Hammer, and Sickle: International Ice Hockey During the Cold War," *Sport History Review* 37, no. 1 (May 2006): 47. See also Tobias Stark, "The Pioneer, the Pal, and the Poet: Masculinities and National Identities in Canadian, Swedish, and Soviet-Russian Ice Hockey during the Cold War," in *Putting It On Ice*, vol. 2, *Internationalizing "Canada's Game,"* ed. Colin D. Howell, 39.

19 Ed Arnold, *Whose Puck is it, Anyway?: A Season with a Minor Novice Hockey Team* (Toronto: McClelland & Stewart, 2003).

20 See Ed Willes, *The Rebel League: The Short and Unruly Life of the World Hockey Association* (Toronto: McClelland & Stewart, 2005); Bruce Kidd and John Macfarlane, *The Death of Hockey* (Toronto: New Press, 1972).

21 See Frieden, *Global Capitalism*, 416–17.

22 For this argument, see Julian Ammirante, "Globalization and Professional Sport: Comparisons and Contrasts between Hockey and European Football," in *Artificial Ice: Hockey, Culture, and Commerce*, ed. David Whitson and Richard Gruneau (Toronto: Garamond Press, 2006), 237–61.

23 Andrew C. Holman, "The Canadian Hockey Player Problem: Cultural Reckoning and National Identities in American Collegiate Sport, 1947–80," *Canadian Historical Review* 88, no. 3 (September 2007): 439–68.

24 Minutes of the Annual Meeting of the NCAA Ice Hockey Rules Committee, 1967, 1972, Charles Holt Archives of American Hockey, Series 5: NCAA Box 1, Folders 4 and 5 Dimond Library, University of New Hampshire.

25 American Collegiate Hockey Association brochure (Union Lake, MI: American Collegiate Hockey Association, 1997).

26 Szymon Szemberg, "IIHF Study on European Players Going to North America" (Zurich: International Ice Hockey Federation, September 2006), 13–14; Fluto Shinzawa, "Will collegians again receive golden opportunity?," *Boston Globe*, March 8, 2006.

27 Northrup, "Globalization and the Great Convergence," 266.

Michael P. Buma

"Save Our Team, Save Our Game"

Identity Politics in Two Canadian Hockey Novels

Many Canadians see hockey as their game, as an expression of national identity and as an important mark of cultural distinction from other nations, especially the United States. However, for almost as long as Canadians have seen themselves as the rightful owners of hockey, the inherent Canadianness of the game has also been thought to be threatened by American involvement, or, more precisely, by what America represents, "the values of modernity in national form" (Szeman, 161). The fear that modernity – "the aspiration of progress ... [toward] a universal and homogenous state" (Grant, 67) – has made Canadian particularities unnecessary or obsolete has perhaps been most famously expressed in George Grant's *Lament for a Nation: The Defeat of Canadian Nationalism*, the essence of which is that "branch-plant economies will have branch-plant cultures" (56). For Grant, Canadian distinction from the United States is an impossibility in an age in which "everything is made relative to profit-making, [and] all traditions of virtue are dissolved, including that aspect of virtue known as love of country" (61).

Grant's complaint about the loss of patriotism to international capitalism is effectively the grievance of many Canadian hockey fans against American involvement in "Canada's game." Seven years after Grant's *Lament for a Nation*, Bruce Kidd and John Macfarlane's *The*

Death of Hockey suggested the importance of reclaiming the game from American corporate capitalism. Dedicated to "the rightful owners of hockey, the Canadian people," *The Death of Hockey* sees the game as "the Canadian metaphor," "something most of us share from birth," a "unique expression of our culture," and the one indisputable symbol of "national identity" in "a country we no longer own … [but] merely lease … from the Americans" (4–5, 16). Kidd and Macfarlane see this final remaining marker of Canadian difference as having been systematically eroded by the economic bottom line and – following Grant – by "our cheap faith in free enterprise" (19). In other words, "because the Americans could afford to pay more for hockey than we could, they got it" (Kidd and Macfarlane, 19). To address this issue Kidd and Macfarlane propose the creation of an all-Canadian hockey league founded on reasonable player salaries, community-based franchise ownership and government subsidies to help cover operating costs.

What is most striking about *The Death of Hockey* is its continued resonance with Canadian hockey culture. Although Kidd and Macfarlane's facts and illustrations are now thirty-five years out of date, their central claim remains remarkably current. Globalizing processes have continued to efface the idea of a distinctly Canadian identity and have increasingly contributed to a continental monoculture in the years since *The Death of Hockey*, and many Canadians have remained invested in the idea that hockey defines their national identity. Hockey, then, is often seen to ensure our cultural distinction from the United States, which, in turn, appears to justify our continued political distinction. At the same time, Canada's symbolic possession of hockey is still often seen as threatened by the globalizing and Americanizing processes that the game is often mobilized to oppose. As I write this, debates about Canadian possession and American infringement have again been brought to the fore by Kitchener-Waterloo, Ontario-based billionaire Jim Balsillie's successive failures to acquire the Pittsburgh Penguins in December 2006, the Nashville Predators in July 2007 and apparently, although the issue remains ongoing, the Phoenix Coyotes in the summer of 2009. All of Balsillie's purchases have allegedly been opposed by NHL management because of his intent to relocate the teams to Southwestern Ontario, prompting rumours of bureaucratic collusion and conspiracy in Internet hockey chat rooms and accusations of neglect and discrimination from the mainstream Canadian media. Charlie Gillis and John Intini, for instance, wondered in *Maclean's* whether "the NHL [has it in] ... for Canada," while the CBC's Elliotte Friedman suggested in a blog that "[NHL commissioner] Gary Bettman doesn't care about Canada."[1]

When the NHL hired Gary Bettman as commissioner in 1992, it did so with the idea of expanding its presence in the American market. To this end, Bettman's "first years in office saw new expansion franchises and relocations of existing teams, as well as new television contracts and merchandising initiatives" (Mason, 181). As Bettman and the NHL pushed to attract high-profile buyers for new markets such as Miami and Anaheim, existing small-market teams in Quebec City and Winnipeg were struggling. Quebec and Winnipeg's troubles stemmed from their inability to tap into the NHL's expanding media efforts, the lack of a league-wide revenue sharing plan at the time, their outdated arena facilities and the declining Canadian dollar. Despite massive public outcries and grassroots fundraising campaigns both teams eventually relocated south.[2] The Quebec Nordiques moved to Colorado and became the Avalanche in time for the 1995–96 NHL season (in which they won the Stanley Cup), while the Winnipeg Jets held out one year longer before moving to Phoenix and becoming the Coyotes. After the loss of Quebec and Winnipeg, teams such as Edmonton and Ottawa also struggled to survive in the economic climate created by the NHL's drive for American expansion.

Among the reader responses to Friedman's reproach of Bettman over the Balsillie affair were several posts echoing Kidd and Macfarlane's proposal in *The Death of Hockey* to repatriate the game by creating a Canadian professional league. Others expressed frustration about NHL expansion in the United States. Michelle from Winnipeg, for instance, wrote that "as a true, proud, hockey-loving Canadian, my heart feels like it is being ripped out and thrown to the ground every time I hear about the USA getting another team" (response to Friedman, July 15, 2007). What this post and others like it indicate, along with the broader reaction to the Balsillie affair in general, is the unsurprising belief that Canada's perceived symbolic possession of hockey entitles the nation to literal possession as well. Many Canadians continue to express outrage at the fact that Sunbelt cities with no "natural" connection to the game such as Anaheim, Atlanta, Miami, Dallas, Tampa Bay, San Jose, Raleigh and Phoenix should have NHL franchises while Canadian hockey hotbeds such as Winnipeg, Quebec City and Hamilton have none. As Kidd and Macfarlane put it in *The Death of Hockey*, "hockey may be [Canada's] national religion, but the services are held in the United States" (17).

In the context of this ongoing discussion about hockey's "Canadianness" let's consider the issue of identity politics in Canadian hockey novels.[3] The majority of Canadian hockey novels aimed at adults and young adults have been written since 1990, and it is striking how Canadian these novels attempt to be in an age that has been characterized as distinctly post-national. Hockey novels tend to participate in the nationalistic backlash against continental monoculture that has characterized the discussion of Canadian hockey for the last thirty-five years. Bill Gaston's *The Good Body*, Ray Robertson's *Heroes* and Mark Anthony Jarman's *Salvage King, Ya!*, for instance, all portray American fans as ignorant and unappreciative of hockey in some way, symbolically questioning the American right to possess the game and legitimizing Canada's claim. Roy MacGregor's *The Last Season* and Steven Galloway's *Finnie Walsh* extend such pictures of American unworthiness to include southernness as well, questioning whether cities without naturally occurring ice have a right to professional hockey and proving Canadian possession of the game by virtue of northernness and geography. Another way in which Canadian hockey novels establish the Canadianness of the game is by the symbolic importance they place on the small town. Adrian Brijbassi's *50 Mission Cap*, F. G. Paci's *Icelands*, Eric Zweig's *Hockey Night in the Dominion of Canada* and Don Reddick's *Dawson City Seven*, for instance, all work in various ways to render the small-town as a preserve of innocence, authenticity and pastoral purity in contrast to big-city corruption, artificiality and greed. Several of these novels apply similar characterizations to the relationship between

Canada and America as well. In this reading the essence of Canadian hockey is the love of the game, which is constantly under threat from the supposedly American tendencies toward selfishness and greed. This duality is a key part of two novels which are centred on the small-town purity versus big-city corruption relationship between Canada and America, Robert Sedlack's *The Horn of a Lamb* and Steve Lundin's *When She's Gone*, both published in 2004. Both these novels respond to an event that they see as characteristic of American capitalism ruining Canada's game: the relocation of the Winnipeg Jets to Phoenix, Arizona.

The Horn of a Lamb is the story of Fred Pickle, a thirty-eight-year-old man who suffered a brain injury during a hockey accident when he was nineteen. Fred's two passions in life are to build an outdoor rink for the entire neighbourhood to skate on every winter and to watch the local NHL team play. Although the local team is never mentioned by name, they are clearly meant to resemble the Jets. *The Horn of a Lamb* addresses a hockey climate in which conversation at the arena focuses on "dwindling attendance, high taxes on the team, the Canadian dollar, [and] the possibility that the team might move" (40). Fred first becomes worried about the fate of the team when he hears rumours that Andrew T. Madison, the team's American owner, is thinking about "moving the team south after the season" (14). For Fred, the conflict is framed in nationalistic, ideological and economic terms:

> [Andrew Madison] had been quoted in a newspaper as having called Canada a socialist country. In another interview he had called Canada the fifty-first state. He had brought in a larger American flag to fly beside the now-smaller Canadian flag at the arena. After enough fans complained, he said it had been an honest mistake and replaced it ... Fred had been told of some words of wisdom that Madison kept framed in his office: *The American system of ours, call it Americanism, call it capitalism, call it what you like, gives each and every one of us a great opportunity if we only seize it with both hands and make the*

most of it. The name below the quote was Al Capone. (48, italics original)

The identification of American capitalism here with the gangster virtues of Al Capone is certainly no compliment. When rumours about the team's possible move become a frequent topic of conversation at the rink, Fred's friend Badger, an aging lawyer and political activist, makes an impassioned speech about the threat of American cultural imperialism:

> Today it's the hockey team. Next week it's the airlines, the railroads. And then the trees and water. And a week after that we're walking around with American money jingling in our pockets, stuffing our faces with Big Macs and singing the "Star Spangled [sic] Banner." (87)

Badger fears that the loss of the hockey team is merely the first step toward the wholesale Americanization of Canada. The gradations of the conquest, as Badger outlines them, begin with hockey as an ostensible marker of cultural distinction but move quickly to the appropriation of actual binding forces such as infrastructure (airlines and railroads) and natural resources (trees and water). The loss of these, as Badger tells it, would lead to a total dissolution of Canadian culture (Big Macs as a marker of US imperialism), economic union (the loss of national currency) and, indeed, the collapse of the Canadian identity itself (the loss of the national anthem). For Badger, hockey is the first domino in this long chain reaction: knock over hockey, and the Canadian nation itself will eventually fall. Badger's speech goes on for almost a full page, and lays the groundwork for what will later become a campaign to save the team. Before this campaign gets underway, however, an interesting incident on Fred's uncle's farm (where Fred lives) foreshadows the novel's thematic conclusion.

Fred's Uncle Jack has been clearing brush behind his house, and has amassed a great deal of firewood as a result. Jack arranges for a rich American lodge owner to buy the wood for several thousand dollars, a good deal of money for Jack's struggling-to-break-even sheep farm. When the American buyer comes to complete the sale, he behaves like the stereotypical "ugly American": "He poked fun at Canadian money and how Canadians were always comparing themselves to Americans when Americans didn't care one way or the other" (138–9). Fred is outraged by this, and launches into a long diatribe against American history and culture. After the incident, the narrator explains that "the American had left shortly after the slaves were hanging from the trees [in Fred's speech]" (142). Meanwhile on Fred's rink, "a puck was slapped … [and] somebody shouted after they scored" (142). This relatively innocuous passage both mobilizes hockey as a preserve of Canadianness against the threat of Americanization and foreshadows the thematic victory of Canadian hockey by the novel's end. The play-for-fun pond-hockey ethos of the goal on Fred's outdoor rink triumphs over the arrogant capitalism of the American lodge owner, simultaneously celebrating his defeat and symbolically participating in it.

When the news that the team will be sold is made public, Fred and Badger begin their campaign in earnest. Badger makes another impassioned public speech against the American attempt to buy Canadian identity and difference. He tells the crowd:

> You didn't come here to save your hockey team. You came here to save your country … A lousy hockey team has brought us together in this cold parking lot to mark a turning point in our destiny. This is a great day to be alive. The country is watching … What is the price of a nation's soul? Is it one hundred million dollars? Is it five billion? Three trillion? Is everything for sale? (159–60)

In order to buy back the nation's soul, as Badger puts it, the city will have to raise eighteen million dollars in thirty days. To make matters worse, Andrew Madison has worked out a legal provision whereby he gets to keep twenty percent of any failed bid. Nevertheless, the campaign begins in earnest. Money starts to flow in from all sectors of the community, including young children, but Fred is frustrated that big companies "couldn't dig as deep as most of the children were doing when they donated their life savings in their piggy banks" (167). Determined to do his part, Fred rides his bicycle from farm to farm outside the city to solicit contributions. As the money continues to roll in, hope flourishes. Fans hold up signs condemning Andrew Madison, and chant during games: "Save our team, save our game" (156). These events mirror the actual campaign to save the Winnipeg Jets, in which a public group that became known as the "Spirit of Manitoba" made a bid to purchase controlling partnership in the franchise that would keep it in Winnipeg. In the end, however, both campaigns failed, the fictional rendering of this event in *The Horn of a Lamb* falling short by a mere million dollars after the local newspaper 'discredits' Badger by revealing his extremist past. Badger vows an ominous revenge on Andrew Madison, which he plans to enact during the team's last home game. The nature of the plot is never revealed, and whatever Badger had in mind is foiled when Fred inadvertently lets slip that something is afoot. Badger does manage to grab the puck from the last game, however, and gives it to Fred with a note that says "the last puck for the last fan" (195).

As the story continues, Badger and Fred scheme about travelling to the team's new American city to enact their revenge on Andrew Madison. When Badger dies unexpectedly, Fred decides that despite his handicap he must make the trip alone. The narrative strategy surrounding Fred's plan is one of ambiguity and delay, resulting in a suspenseful climax where the reader has been led to believe that Fred is going to kill Andrew Madison. The revenge, however, turns out to be more benign: Fred hits Madison in the face with a boysenberry pie. The significance of this turn from expectation is to enforce the stereotype that Canadian society is kindler and gentler than that of America; to kill Madison, *The Horn of a Lamb* seems to suggest, would not be the Canadian way. In other words, when "the beaver bites back" (to quote one recent examination of American popular culture in Canada), it does so quite harmlessly. When Fred travels through America on his quest to get to Madison, his presuppositions about Americans are confirmed:

> He encountered many Americans, Americans he thought would annoy and provoke him. But the only feeling that the worst of them instilled was pity. They seemed spoiled. And

angry. Because deep in their hearts they knew it wasn't okay to be so spoiled ... This was, after all, Babylon, where the snobby, money-hungry people lived. (338–9)

When Fred arrives at the team's new city, he plans to attend a game and try to confront Madison for an apology before enacting his revenge. Being a devoted fan, however, Fred can't help but watch some of the game first. When Fred takes his seat he is shocked by the ignorance and indifference of the American fans: "He tried to explain what constituted an offside penalty, what a two-line pass was, why one play was tripping and another wasn't. But nobody listened" (344–5). After this Fred has the epiphany that:

> [hockey] wasn't the game he remembered. In fact, it wasn't a game at all any more. It was a business. A business that had pulled his team out from under his nose because fans had stopped supporting mediocre hockey at prices they could no longer afford. A business that pulled players from one city to the next in search of bigger contracts and U.S. dollars. A business that paid no attention to the time-honoured traditions of hockey: loyalty and respect. In fact, it was a business that now trampled those ideals. This was no longer a game Fred knew at all. This was garbage. (345)

Motivated by his new perspective on the professional game, Fred manages to track down Andrew Madison. Madison, eager not to cause a scene, tries to placate Fred but eventually loses his patience and tells him that moving the team was "simple economics" and "if you don't understand that then you are as dumb as you look" (350). It becomes clear to Fred that Madison is beyond any hope of forgiveness or redemption, and after the game Fred arrives to deliver his boysenberry pie.

When Fred makes his way back to Canada after the pie incident he is greeted as a conquering hero. He is eventually hired by his old junior team, the Brandon Wheat Kings, and honoured with the opportunity to go for a warm-up skate with the team and to drop the puck in one of their games. When Fred is announced at the game, the crowd cheers and miniature Canadian flags are waved. Several fans are dressed in costume to parody Andrew Madison and honour Fred's triumph over hockey capitalism. When Fred drops the puck for the ceremonial faceoff at centre ice, he uses the "last puck" that Badger had salvaged for him from the professional team's last game: "nobody but Fred knew the significance of the puck. It said that no owners, no amount of money or greedy players were greater than the game itself" (385). This is the central thematic conclusion of *The Horn of a Lamb*: that the essence of Canada's game – the pond-hockey purity and natural overtones of the homemade rink, the untainted passion that powers shinny games and junior hockey – can't be bought for any amount of money. Canadian hockey is characterized by its small-town pastoral virtues as opposed to the big-city American values of selfishness and greed. As Fred becomes accustomed to life in Brandon, it takes him "no time at all to see that junior hockey was every bit as good as the professional game, minus the snobby, money-hungry players and owners" (392). In other words, amateur, junior and recreational hockey are seen as preserving the purity and Canadianness of the game. Because the love of hockey can't be bought, *The Horn of a Lamb* seems to say, the cultural and political distinctiveness of Canada are ultimately safe.

When She's Gone also works to recuperate hockey's Canadianness by appealing to the pastoral. It is the story of two hockey-loving brothers from Winnipeg, Mark and Jack, who embark on a canoe trip across Britain in order to deliver Mark to a tryout for a professional hockey team in Cardiff. Along the way the family's story unfolds, and the brothers' various philosophies on life, love, history and hockey are shared. Much of this involves Mark and Jack trying to come to terms with the relocation of their beloved Jets, as well as with the underlying selfishness and greed that they perceive to be destroying Canadian hockey in general.

Interspersed throughout the plot of *When She's Gone* are several fantasy sequences that retell Canadian history as hockey and invent various hockey creation myths that attempt to recuperate a lost or inaccessible "pure" essence of the game (the origins of skating, sticks, etc.). The ultimate thematic goal of *When She's Gone* is to access the perfect essence of hockey, the "memory that Plato talked about, the ghost world of perfection we all use as a reference" (189). Much of this work is diagnostic. Mark and Jack go on for pages and pages about what is wrong with hockey, much of which can be summarized by the word "greed." An incident in which Mark remembers Jack being arrested for breaking into a movie-theatre projection-booth to try to steal the reel-to-reel copy of a certain film is particularly illustrative. Mark recalls that it was "the year of the Mighty Ducks, the final humiliation of Canada's game, the theft of our myth nearly as horrendous as some Canadian blathering on about baseball" (74). It is "the theft of our myth" that Mark and Jack are so upset about and their own exercises in narrative myth-making attempt to stem this loss. The Mighty Ducks were "a classic example of a cross-marketed sport franchise – an NHL franchise owned by a major corporation (Disney), named after a fictional team from a Disney movie, and purchased in hopes of promoting a variety of Disney-related products and services (including the theme parks located around Anaheim)" (Wilson, 61).[4] For Jack, the Mighty Ducks represent the ultimate trivialization of Canada's game:

> Everything's in reduction, Mark. Pare away the crap and you come down to a single word: money. The world's poison rotting every soul there's no beating it. Some Hollywood execs got together and walked all over another country's heart, nothing new in that but they stole it from us and we take kids to the show, line up to buy tickets, are we stupid or what… it's not just sport, Mark. Money's poisoned everything. It bids for dreams, turns them into euphemisms for greed, every aspiration these days is just another facet of greed and success turns the soul rotten. (74–5)

This culture of hockey greed, which is closely identified with the "American" commodification of the game represented by the Mighty Ducks, is suggested most pervasively by the loss of the Winnipeg Jets. When it is revealed that the Jets will be leaving, Mark reflects that the "NHL was delivering Winnipeg its message: Winnipeg you're nothing in the scheme of hockey, nothing in the eyes of the NHL, your fans are a drop in the ocean, who gives a shit about your loss, who really gives a shit" (112). Worse than the loss of the team or the cruel indifference of the league, however, is the fact that "the south tugged at our myth" (112). Mark notes earlier in the narrative that "when greed became a right worth fighting for" and "television brought Hollywood into professional sports" the "core of [hockey's] worth got bought out, never stood a chance against money but the myths kept [it] alive for a long time, struggling against the tide but now even the myth's dead, the withered roots of a starved tree" (85). By underscoring the importance of myth, Mark helps to explain the presence of the fantasy and creation myth sequences that pepper the novel as a way of getting back to the pure, Platonic and, again, notably Canadian, form of hockey.

When She's Gone, however, holds Canadians at least partially responsible for allowing the theft of their myth. Jack complains that "we take the sacred blade and deliver our own cuts and everybody smiles and nods like it was the right thing to do, smiles and nods because some things are beyond even questioning, some prairie boy's got a chance to earn twenty-six million U.S. over seven years and we say 'hey boy you've done it now go for it'" (40). For Jack, Canadians are complicit in the American culture of greed because they have allowed and even encouraged hockey to be profaned by it. During a discussion of British history Mark tells Jack that "rape is rape even if you take it with a smile" (20). Jack responds that Mark has "spoken like a true Canadian hockey fan" (20). The American assault on Canadian hockey, then, is characterized as a rape, and Canadian fans are seen as accepting it without struggle or resistance. According to Jack, Canadians have "made cowardice a national trait, getting stepped on a way of life" (75). What is ultimately called for, then, is a sort of hockey revolution, a "night when cynicism's put aside and all things are possible. The fans say no more, you're killing us, you're killing our love you fucking vampires, here's your empty arenas [and] switched channels, we've turned our back" (52). In other words, Canadian fans have the power to reclaim hockey by refusing to support the big-money professional game. In a way, this is the same conclusion that Fred Pickle arrives at in *The Horn of a Lamb* when he decides to give up his interest in the NHL in favour of the "play for the right reasons" ethos of the junior game. *When She's Gone* concludes with a final fantasy sequence, in which a young boy plays hockey on a frozen pond "somewhere in the Canadian bush," an example of "sport without a coin to its name" and, as such, played purely for the love of the game (189). This pastoral scene represents the Platonic essence of hockey that *When She's Gone* gestures toward throughout, notably maintaining the explicit Canadianness of the sequence. It is a symbolic vision of hockey as it "should" be played, purely for the love of the game and in close connection with nature. Both *When She's Gone* and *The Horn of a Lamb*, then, ultimately, see professional hockey as spoiled by American selfishness and greed while maintaining the amateur/recreational game as a symbolic preserve of purity, authenticity, innocence and, most importantly, Canadianness.

Although *The Horn of a Lamb* and *When She's Gone* put forward the hockey nationalist position as it has often been articulated in the thirty-five or so years since *The Death of Hockey*, their solutions to the diminishing Canadianness of the game don't involve repatriating professional hockey or the creation of new NHL franchises in Canadian cities. Rather, *The Horn of a Lamb* and *When She's Gone* surrender these options as lost or impossible, echoing Grant's belief that any significant Canadian difference must exist apart from capitalism's devotion to profit and the political liberalism by which this is made possible. By situating the true Canadianness of hockey in the play-for-fun ethos of the recreational and amateur games, as well as in the pastoral innocence of "the pond," these novels attempt to "see hockey as it was before it became complicated by economics, corporate lust, [and] the ravages of progress … a game of passion, of the people" (Bidini, xviii). As Mark concludes in *When She's Gone*, "there are just some things money can't buy" (189). But by propounding this idealized version of Canada's democratic love for hockey, *The Horn of a Lamb* and *When She's Gone* come dangerously close to what Richard Gruneau and David Whitson call "the marketing of nostalgia" (283). As Gruneau and Whitson point out, while Canadian hockey "is flourishing both as a form of recreation and community entertainment, the game simply does not have the same claim on the time of Canadian children that it had for the generation of boys who grew up between the 1940s and 1980s" (283). Furthermore, the pastoral ambitions of *The Horn of a Lamb* and *When She's Gone* are increasingly inapplicable as well. Already in 1983, well before the publication of either of these novels, Ken Dryden had recognized the separation of Canadian hockey from the outdoor rink: "a game we once played on rivers and ponds, later on streets and driveways and in backyards, we now play in arenas, in full team uniform, with coaches and referees, or to an ever-increasing extent we don't play at all" (134).

The connection between hockey and Canadianness, of course, is arbitrary and artificial rather than natural and inevitable. As Andrew Holman has shown, hockey actually served as "a link between ordinary Canadians and ordinary Americans" (35) living in regions near the Canada-US border around the turn of the twentieth century. In other words, hockey "bound Canadian and American borderland dwellers [together], even as the border was supposed to keep them apart," a fact which calls into question the "nature of identity formation ... and the meaning of the international border itself" (35). More contemporary in their focus are Jeff Klein and Karl-Eric Reif in *The Death of Hockey: Or, How a Bunch of Guys With Too Much Money and Too Little Sense Are Killing the Greatest Game on Earth*. It can be inferred from their title – an update of Kidd and Macfarlane's eponymous manifesto – that Klein and Reif oppose the culture of hockey greed that *The Horn of a Lamb* and *When She's Gone* characterize as American. What their title doesn't reveal, however, is the fact that Klein and Reif themselves are Americans who, while opposing this alleged culture of greed, challenge the inherent Canadianness of hockey and celebrate the sport's global gains in recent years. Although hockey continues to enjoy a prominence in Canada that it undeniably doesn't in the United States, it is an oversimplification to suggest the game as an overarching marker of Canadian cultural difference. The ideological work of *The Horn of a Lamb* and *When She's Gone*, then, is to render this oversimplification as both believable and desirable. In effect, these novels distil the complex realities of North American hockey and identity into usable sound-bite endorsements of Canadian cultural nationalism. In an age that has been "more likely to speak in terms of the interwoven and overlapping play of identities and differences" than about any one "unified and coherent" identity (Kernerman, 6), *The Horn of a Lamb* and *When She's Gone* swim stubbornly against the current, attempting once and for all to offer Canadians that one elusive commonality on which to hang their sense of collective and national belonging.

1. Balsillie's initial bid to buy the Penguins prompted an outbreak of rumours that the team would relocate to Hamilton or Kitchener–Waterloo, and many suggested the inherent Canadianness of hockey as a rationale for the move. While Balsillie denied any intention to move the Penguins to Canada, he eventually walked away from the deal after Gary Bettman reportedly insisted on a no-movement clause. When Balsillie put in his second offer, this time on the Predators, he publicly announced his intention to move the team by securing a twenty-year lease for Hamilton's Copps Coliseum and opening season-ticket sales on the "Hamilton Predators." Balsillie's brazenness was greeted with incredible enthusiasm by Canadian fans, many of whom saw the deal as fulfilling Canada's right to another NHL franchise, especially one which had clearly struggled in a relatively disinterested American market. The deal fell through, however, when Predators owner Craig Leipold unexpectedly rejected Balsillie's offer in favour of another nearly fifty-million dollars lower. Balsillie's latest attempt to bring another NHL franchise to Southwestern Ontario involves a bid to purchase the bankrupt Coyotes under the condition that they be relocated to Hamilton. The matter is currently being decided in an American bankruptcy court, although the NHL Board of Governors has unanimously rejected Balsillie as an owner.

2. In both cases, it was the arena issue that eventually brought about the team's relocation. In the NHL of the 1990s, teams were increasingly relying on amenities such as luxury boxes and priority seating to generate operating revenue. Both Quebec and Winnipeg launched bids to receive new publicly-funded arenas similar to those being built in many American expansion cities at the time, but both campaigns ultimately failed.

3. I propose the term "hockey novel" as a generic distinction that delineates commonality of subject rather than reliance on convention; in other words, hockey novels are not shaped by specific structural expectations in the ways that, say, detective or romance novels are. Rather, hockey novels are quite simply novels in which hockey contributes significantly to plot action or character development, or in which hockey assumes noteworthy thematic importance.

4. Disney no longer owns the Anaheim team, whose name has been changed simply to The Ducks.

Works Cited

Bidini, Dave. *Tropic of Hockey: My Search for the Game in Unlikely Places*. Toronto: McClelland & Stewart, 2000.

Friedman, Elliotte. "Gary Bettman doesn't care about Canada." From the Pressbox. CBCSports. CBC.ca, July 13, 2007. http://www.cbc.ca/sports/sportsblog/2007/07/gary_bettman_doesnt_care_about.html (accessed August 3, 2007).

Gillis, Charlie and John Intini. "Shut out of the NHL." *Maclean's*, July 23, 2007. http://www.macleans.ca/culture/sports/article.jsp?content=20070723_107266_107266&page=3 (accessed August 3, 2007).

Grant, George. *Lament for a Nation: The Defeat of Canadian Nationalism*. Ottawa: Carleton University Press, 1997.

Gruneau, Richard and David Whitson. *Hockey Night in Canada: Sport, Identities, and Cultural Politics*. Toronto: Garamond Press, 1993.

Holman, Andrew. "Playing in the Neutral Zone: Meanings and Uses of Ice Hockey in the Canada-U.S. Borderlands, 1895–1915." *American Review of Canadian Studies* 34 (2004): 33–57.

Kernerman, Gerald. *Multicultural Nationalism: Civilizing Difference, Constituting Community*. Vancouver: UBC Press, 2005.

Kidd, Bruce and John Macfarlane. *The Death of Hockey*. Toronto: New Press, 1972.

Klein, Jeff and Karl-Eric Reif. *The Death of Hockey, Or: How A Bunch of Guys With Too Much Money and Too Little Sense Are Killing the Greatest Game on Earth*. Toronto: Macmillan, 1998.

Lundin, Steve. *When She's Gone*. Winnipeg: Great Plains Publications, 2004.

Flaherty, David and Frank Manning, eds. *The Beaver Bites Back: American Popular Culture in Canada*. Montreal and Kingston: McGill-Queen's University Press, 1993.

Mason, Dan. "Expanding the Footprint? Questioning the NHL's Expansion and Relocation Strategy." In *Artificial Ice*, edited by David Whitson and Richard Gruneau, 181–199. Toronto: Garamond Press, 2006.

Sedlack, Robert. *The Horn of a Lamb*. Toronto: Random House, 2004.

Szeman, Imre. *Zones of Instability: Literature, Postcolonialism, and the Nation*. Baltimore: Johns Hopkins University Press, 2003. See esp. chap 4, "The Persistence of the Nation: Literature and Criticism in Canada."

Wilson, Brian. "Selective Memory in a Global Culture: Reconsidering Links between Youth, Hockey, and Canadian Identity." In *Artificial Ice*, edited by David Whitson and Richard Gruneau, 53–70.

Andrew Holman

Frank Merriwell on Skates:
Heroes, Villains, Canadians and Other Others in American Juvenile Sporting Fiction, 1890–1940

In a winter 2006 essay in the *New York Times Book Review*, writer Keith Gessen posed a couple of interesting, but seldom considered questions about "Canada's game" and American literature: "What accounts for the marginal place of hockey in the world of American professional sports? Might it not, in the end, have something to do with its marginal place in American letters?" Indeed, American writing on the country's more central sports – baseball, boxing and football – has achieved not just a critical mass of "classic texts" but a broader legitimacy, too. These games are recognized by writers and readers as pastimes and pursuits whose forms and functions have much to say about the meanings of American life, the American *condition*. Provocatively-titled "In Search of the Great American Hockey Novel," Gessen's editorial floated a few ideas as to why this game, played and watched for over a century in the United States, has significantly less literary purchase. It "can be gruesomely violent" he argued, and it is almost wholly white. "It does not look like America." But, to Gessen, most damning is its origin: "from an American perspective, hockey is an import from Canada."[1] These musings are interesting because they give voice to looming, enduring impressions about the role of literature in equating sports with national character. In this view, hockey remains sparse in American writing because its origin makes it an imperfect vessel for the carriage of American values.

The Great American Hockey Novel may never be written, but this twenty-first century discussion is interesting because it echoes the themes expressed in an earlier generation of American sporting literature. Hockey *has* been a subject of American literary interest in the past, and long before the publication of Cleo Birdwell's (that is, Don DeLillo's) *Amazons* or Jack Falla's *Saved*.[2] In fact, between the 1890s and 1940s, hockey had a conspicuous place among the subjects examined in American juvenile sporting literature, the novels and short stories that fed the imaginations of two generations of American youth.

The scores of sports novels and short stories for boys produced during the age of the school story, 1890s–World War I, and heyday of the "pulps," 1920–1940, provide a rich and underused source for examining the literary construction of the national character in North America. Scholars have identified this popular literature as a vehicle celebrating quintessential American traits; but boys' sports fiction simultaneously constructed otherness, articulating differences from the American ideal. In those stories that involved winter settings and the sport of ice hockey, Canada and Canadians appear quite often, in conspicuous and discriminate ways. In American hockey stories, the game acted as a canvas to illustrate national cultures, even cultures as outwardly similar as those in Canada and the US. Though fictional, these accounts betray an ambivalence that American writers and readers had about hockey (and by allegorical extension, Canadian culture) and its capacity for instilling "American" values. Then, as now, as a means for carrying American values, hockey was an imperfect one.[3]

Until fairly recently, North American scholars in literature and cultural studies ignored juvenile fiction, perhaps considering it too simple and unsophisticated to yield much of interest. In the past twenty years, new light has been cast on this genre, and in particular on juvenile sporting novels. As cultural historian Michael Oriard has noted, "Juvenile sports novels ... figured importantly in the childhood of millions of Americans." They defined "patterns and polarities in American thought ... [and] provide an important index to American culture." Sporting fiction both mirrored American social ideals and prescribed proper behavior in society. Though often escapist and fantastic, as historian Steven Mintz has observed, youth novels and stories like these preached selflessness, teamwork, pride in family and school, perseverance, fair play, moderation in all things and respect for authority.[4] Indeed, youth sports novels prescribed to millions of youthful readers the norms for masculinity and gender roles and preached upright behaviour and attitudes. They celebrated these elements as quintessential *American* traits and argued that sport was a critical part of boys' lives where these traits could be nurtured. Sport, in these stories, had invariably a cathartic power that helped to make red-blooded American boys even more red-blooded and even more American.

The sheer volume of juvenile sports fiction in the United States from the late nineteenth to the mid-twentieth century is quite staggering. In these years, thousands of novels and serialized stories were produced and sold to a booming mass market in the United States. Taking advantage of the transatlantic success of Thomas Hughes' British school story, *Tom Brown's School Days*, publishers such as Beadle & Adams, Street & Smith and Grosset & Dunlap produced entertaining and edifying materials for at least two generations of American boys. Authors of these books included: Gilbert Patten, Ralph Henry Barbour, Owen Johnson, Arthur Stanwood Pier, Graham Forbes, William Heyliger, Harold Sherman and John R. Tunis. Of these writers, the most influential was Patten who, under the pseudonym Burt L. Standish, created the mould for American juvenile sporting fiction with the boy-hero Frank Merriwell, an "all-rounder" whose escapades at Fardale Academy and Yale first appeared in serial form in *Tip Top Weekly* in 1896 and continued to thrill American boys until 1916.[5] Patten opened this literary door for dozens of other serious writers and some hacks, those who could piece together thrilling narratives about pluck and courage and, ultimately, success in sporting endeavors. Among Patten's followers were writers such as Barbour, Harold Sherman and Leslie McFarlane, whose work was as prolific if not as popular. Between 1899 and 1943, Barbour published one hundred and sixty books of fiction for boys, on sports as wide-ranging as tennis and golf, football and hockey.[6] Sherman published twenty-three books of juvenile sporting fiction and many short stories featuring a wide variety of sports, largely in the 1920s and '30s.[7] McFarlane, using the *nom de plume* Franklin W. Dixon, wrote most of the popular Hardy Boys books. Under his own name, he wrote dozens of sporting short stories that appeared in pulp magazines such as *Sport Story, Thrilling Sports and Ace Sports*.[8] Presumably, the stories written by this group of writers were read by hundreds of thousands of boys and, perhaps, influenced the way they saw the role of sports, the meaning of character and the depiction of "others" – women, non-whites and foreign nationals.

Ice hockey, it should be noted, was hardly the most frequent setting for American juvenile sporting fiction from 1890 to 1940.[9] Four or five times as many football, boxing or baseball stories were published in American books and magazines in this era.[10] Still, hockey stories were not few, by any measure. An initial count reveals more than fifty boys' novels and more than two hundred and fifty short stories that used ice hockey as a central vehicle.[11] During this time, hockey was being rapidly exported to the United States and so the presence of hockey and Canadians was reflected in this literature.

Much of this early juvenile fiction was constructed around a conflict between the protagonist and an "other," often an outsider, who operates as a foil, a way to distinguish and separate the body of values being prescribed from those being cautioned against. Women and girls, the working class, the idle poor, the "criminal class" and foreign nationals were often cast as the "other" in books and stories aimed at boys.[12] This is the role in which Canadians sometimes appear. Most often Canadians were stock characters from the North: ruddy and rectified Mounties, sly fur trappers, rustic lumberjacks or lovable but simple-minded French-Canadian farmers.[13] In youth sporting novels and stories, however, Canadians appear most often when the game of ice hockey is used as the central subject. These texts provide a series of simple but fascinating glimpses into the popular thinking of Americans at this time about their neighbours to the north.[14]

The hockey stories differ only slightly in plot, characterization and message. Almost all of these stories are set in leafy New York state or New England prep schools, high schools or colleges (with names like Hillton Academy, Oak Hall, Yardley Hall School and St. Timothy's School). And almost all of the school-based stories follow closely the formula that Walter Evans observed in his 1972 article, "The All-American Boys." The classic sports story focuses on one boy's integration into school life or into acceptance as part of a team. "The typical school story is some variation on a fairly standard but flexible pattern of introduction / bully attack / proof / bully regeneration / apotheosis." In all of these stories, conformity to a "sportsman's code" is expected. The stories often feature characters' struggles to adopt a standard of morality; to overcome bad habits and become "manly" by adopting disciplined, modest, polite and self-reliant behaviour.[15] And all of this happens just in time for the central character to lead a struggling school sports team to victory against a perennial rival.

Put together, the importance of these stories can be seen in three main ways. The first is perhaps simple, but worth saying: there is much to be gained from seeing these texts as *historical* documents; that is, as texts that reflect the times and places in which they were created, records that literally reflect change over time. More specifically, these stories reflect the newness of the sport of ice hockey in the United States in this period and the rather "experimental" nature of the rules of the game. The modern rules of ice hockey were first established in Montreal in 1877, but it was not until about 1895 that American players and schools began to adopt the Canadian game very noticeably, abandoning their "ice polo." And it was Ivy League colleges and New England prep schools (the schools after which juvenile fiction authors fashioned their settings) where the Canadian game first took root and the game expanded impressively to high schools and youth leagues in the Northeast and the Midwest by the 1920s.[16]

Several of the earlier books describe the formation of schools' first-ever hockey teams.[17] In books published in the 1890s and 1900s, authors clearly used their characters to explain the game of hockey to an audience made up largely of the uninitiated. "What are the rules about hockey?" Arthur Stanwood Pier has one of his characters ask another in one 1904 story: "You can't swing your hockey [stick] above your waist, and you can't throw the puck with your hands, and you can't kick it with your skates. You've got to be on side, and you can't trip a man up; but you can butt him all over the rink if you want to … A hockey game is not like a football or baseball game," the author continued. "It is just as good in its way to watch, but it is not one at which you can cheer. The play is too rapid and incessant, and the most spectators can do is give a sharp yell when anything sensational happens."[18]

In addition to hockey's novelty, these stories reflect the gradual change in the games rules and the general dynamic of the sport in these years. A few examples show this. These novels and stories document the adoption of the goal net in 1900, the decline of seven-man hockey by 1922, the change in hockey as an "on-side" game, the use of the forward pass and the archaic practice of referees calling penalties for slow play, or "loafing." Changing strategies are depicted, too. In one passage in Barbour's *Guarding His Goal*, the author refers to an opposing coach "adapting the Canadian scheme of playing three forwards abreast and a fourth behind." There is truth to this distinction. By 1919, most seven-man teams in the Northeast United States preferred a system that played four forwards abreast. This was something known at the time as the "American system" or the "Winsor" system, after Ralph Winsor, hockey coach at Harvard (1902–17) and the first to adopt the strategy.[19]

It is also interesting to note that these stories reflect the historical *periodization* of Canadian influence in American hockey. Despite the fact that the rules described by these authors derive directly from the Montreal rules of 1877, no mention of the Canadian influence on or origin of hockey appears in these stories until after the First World War. To a Canadian reader, the books by Barbour, Pier and Edward Stratemeyer and others before 1919 are conspicuous in their depiction of ice hockey as a home-grown, indigenous *American* product. It is only after World War I and, especially by the mid-1920s, in the works by Barbour, Sherman, Rex Lee and others that the Canadian connection appears.

One of the first mentions of the Canadian connection comes in Barbour's 1919 hockey novel, *Guarding His Goal,* a story about a hockey novice, one Toby Tucker, who through pluck and determination works his way into the role of starting goaltender on the Yardley Hall School varsity. In one dorm-room discussion about the best sort of hockey skate to choose, the author makes one character declare to Tucker: "Look at the Canadians. You don't deny that they know more hockey than we do, do you?"[20]

Explaining this pattern is difficult, but it seems likely that American authors identifying hockey as a Canadian game by the 1920s had much to do with the massive commercial exportation of hockey to the US at that time. Though the National Hockey League (NHL), the highest-calibre professional vessel of the sport, had been in existence in Canada since 1917, NHL teams were first located in the US in 1924, with the Boston Bruins and in 1925, with the New York Americans. By 1929, fully six of the ten NHL franchises were located in the United States. This migration of the best Canadian teams and players was accompanied by massive public relations campaigns – through print and radio media – in order to sell tickets, "brand" the product and create an American market.[21] In all of this, the Canadian connection was undeniable. The presence of Canadian professionals (and their faster and more violent version of the game) seemed now to colour the way authors wrote about hockey: the Canadian connection began to compete with earlier constructions of ice hockey as a wholly *American* game.[22]

The second point from an initial examination of these stories concerns an interesting pattern: in all of these stories, the sport of hockey is characterized as wild, chaotic, savage – a product of a frontier society and game that reflects an elemental or "natural" rusticity. Weather, of course, is important. In all of these stories hockey is played outdoors on either frozen rivers or hastily constructed rinks, with players exposed to the harsh elements of winter. The game depends on ample snow and low temperatures. Mother Nature owns the rink.

The harshness of required conditions for play was matched by the harshness of play itself. In these stories the game is characterized as a violent, seemingly chaotic struggle, but one that has a "natural order": the fittest players and teams survive and thrive. The descriptive language these authors use is telling. In these hockey games, there are clashing and slashing sticks, reckless charges, exchanges of blows, melees, bruising falls, mad-travelling pucks, goalmouths being besieged and goaltenders being "hammered at savagely." In *Guarding His Goal*, Toby Tucker is made to wonder: "How can a fellow stay cool, when nine or ten wild Indians are banging into the net and slashing his feet with their sticks!" In Harold Sherman's 1932 story "Down the Ice," the rink is a "bedlam of sound" and one player "a madman on the loose." Players in Barbour's *The Crimson Sweater* fight "tooth and nail to drive back the invader."[23]

In much of this writing, the boys who excel at hockey, the ones who have a natural affinity for it, are country boys whose rustic nature suits them to a frontier game. This is a theme in adult sporting literature of the era (i.e., Jack London's *The Abysmal Brute*) that gets expressed in juvenile literature as well.[24] Among the stories in Arthur Stanwood Pier's collection, *The Boys of St. Timothy's*, for example, is one titled "The Young Savage." The story is a typical tale of integration involving John Hull, the son of an "old lumberman" from the Michigan woods who is an outcast at the school but is gradually embraced by it after he joins the hockey team, learns to master his anger and make friends, and develops a sense of fair play on the ice. Nicknamed "Darwin" by his classmates, Hull evolves into a new boy, but not one wholly divorced from his rustic self. Even after his transformation, at least one classmate dismisses Hull's candidacy for the captaincy by saying: "He's just an Indian!"[25]

This connection between rusticity and hockey is most clearly drawn in the stories after World War I that introduced Canadian characters. In these depictions "Canadian as rustic" is clear to see. In Barbour's 1932 novel, *Skate Glendale!*, an ice hockey team made up of newcomers led by newcomer goalie Tom Garvin begins to enjoy success on the ice only after Sam McLeod, a Canadian and former professional hockey player, is recruited to help coach the team. As a character, McLeod, the manager of the local ice house and a "huge, bear-like figure," is pure bumpkin: kind-hearted, honest, generous; but fierce and serious when it comes to teaching others how to play the sport he loves. Barbour relates this in McLeod's role but also in his language; an otherly accent. Here is McLeod teaching Garvin the basics about hockey goaltending:

> '[T]is [sic] knees bent and two fists on the stick that makes a hockey man, my lad. Remember that. Do you practice skating so, the blade of your stick flat an' your two hands on the handle, an' 'twill be as natural as natural before you know it. Some afternoon I'll be comin' up there to see you play, an' if I catch you with one hand in your pocket I'll be over the boards and wearin' your hide off!'[26]

When it was occasionally referenced, Canada itself was further depicted by these authors playfully as uncultivated wilderness; a natural incubator for rustics. Harold Sherman's 1929 novel, *Flashing Steel*, follows the trials of the Yankville High School hockey team, whose sterling record earns it the title of US National Champions and the right to travel to Canada to play against By-Town High School, the Canadian champs. The book is full of overwrought stereotypes, but one example makes the point. The prospect of playing hockey in Canada strikes Yankville's right winger, Toot Hadley, as something right out of the Wild West: "I'll bet we'll find the rink surrounded by Indians and a bunch of mounted police! And the minute we start down the ice toward By-Town's goal – plink! plank! And somebody shoots the hockey sticks out of our hands!"[27]

The final point about these stories is perhaps the most meaningful one. Hockey and nation were strangely constructed in this literature. There is an ambivalence or duality (if not an outright contradiction) here. Hockey was alternately claimed as a quintessential American sport that, like football and baseball, bred American traits. At the same time, hockey's Canadian roots were increasingly alluded to and characters' Canadian connections established them as authorities in the game. In these years, sport had become an arena for the expression of national character. The problem here was that hockey seemed to speak for two nations.

On one hand, hockey manifested American values. As Griffith Ogden Ellis wrote in his foreword to the 1929 collection *American Boy Sports Stories:* "Football and baseball, swimming and hockey, basketball and the rest set American blood racing and brings out at their best what we like to call typical American qualities. The book ... [is] a handbook of the vitality of American youth."[28] In Donald Ferguson's *The Chums of Scranton High at Ice Hockey*, the sport is claimed as "perhaps, the most cherished winter sport among youthful Americans."[29]

But after World War I, the "Canadianness" of hockey was introduced into these novels and short stories in auspicious ways. The Canadian connection was a trump card that was used to elevate fictional hockey players in skill and status. "I should be able to skate," Frederick Barker declares in Harold Sherman's 1932 story, "The Ice Cyclone," "my folks spent a couple years in Canada and, you know, babies are born with skates on their feet up there." Professor Dean Hogart, coach of Parker High's team in Sherman's "The Penalty Box," had developed his "knowledge and appreciation of the game through observation during years he had spent in Canada." Mr. Leonard, coach to the Scranton High Chums says at one point: "[S]plendid work, fellows ... the way you played this afternoon was worthy of any Montreal Seven that ever toured the East to show how they do things up there in Canada at their favorite winter sport" (Ferguson). In this story, even the game officials recruited for the final match are men whose authority over and mastery of the rules is established in the fact that they "had been members of famous [hockey] clubs in Canada."[30]

Still, the Canadian card seems to have had an important proviso: authors were careful not to celebrate characters' Canadianness unreservedly. The best Canadians were those who were in transition; those who culturally or legally were becoming Americans and for whom the Canadian connection was either distant or past. The best example of this can be found in Barbour's *Skate Glendale!* Glendale High's coach, Sam McLeod, a resident of New York for six years, is arguably more culturally acceptable because he no longer thinks of Canada as "back home." At one point, he says: "... Canada, I mean, ... 'tis [sic] no longer home, bein' as I'm naturalized an' a good citizen of the uncle I was named for."[31]

Similarly, Rex Lee's 1929 "Clashing Skates" relates the story of brothers Jerry and Bob Drummond, two Canadian recruits studying and playing at leafy Stanton College, where the hockey team underachieves all season because it lacks team spirit and because the most talented Drummond, Bob, fails to "give it his all." A late-in-the-season reckoning readjusts attitudes and Stanton defeats Princeville College in Madison Square Garden in the final game on the heroics of a new, now focused Bob Drummond. The brothers are the sons of "Bearcat" Drummond, one of Canada's greatest amateur hockey players, a player on "Montreal's world champions, after that on three Olympic teams." As the team begins to find success, Jerry and Bob hark back to "their days as forwards on the school team in Canada." Importantly, the author characterizes Bob's change as a sort of *Americanization*. In shedding his selfishness and becoming a team man, he had become an *American* hockey hero. Bob's change represented, to use the author's words, "the birth of the greatest collegiate hockey player since the day of Hobey Baker."[32] Hobey Baker? In hockey terms, that literary equation in the early twentieth-century United States would have been profound. As a skater, scorer and passer, the real-life Hobart Amory Hare Baker (1892–1917) dominated the games he played in as a schoolboy at St. Paul's School in Concord, New Hampshire, and later as a student at Princeton. His athletic prowess, his sterling character and his early, heroic death in World War I made him a living model of the "gentleman amateur." To contemporaries, he was about as American as one could get.[33] Still, Bob Drummond's conversion was a rare sort in these stories and the introduction of Canadian references after 1919 must have disturbed (or at least complicated) the connection between hockey and nation among American readers.

American juvenile sporting fiction of the early twentieth century provides an interesting series of texts that students of sporting literature and sport history should take seriously. This body of literature provides us, first, with a meaningful (though figurative) historical record; in particular, it shows us that hockey grew in form and following in the years between the 1890s and the 1930s. Second, these stories demonstrate the characterization of ice hockey as "natural," "wild," chaotic and rustic. Third, they tell us something about the images that American writers (and presumably readers) believed about Canada, Canadians and Canada's game. And here, in this last point, lies a significance that resonates even today. These simple, morality-driven stories betrayed ambivalence about ice hockey, especially after the First World War. In recognizing the game's Canadian roots, in alluding to Canada as the gold standard for the sport, these writers made less credible the idea that this sport could instill "American" values, in the same ways as baseball, boxing and football. Even in the game's early years, hockey was cast in literature as a marginal game that could hardly express the challenge and fruits of being and becoming *American* for their youthful readers. That marginality, if Gessen is correct, has remained in place ever since in American life and letters.

1   Keith Gessen, "In Search of the Great American Hockey Novel," *The New York Times Book Review*, February 19, 2006.

2   Cleo Birdwell, *Amazons: An Intimate Memoir by the First Woman Ever to Play in the National Hockey League* (Austin: Holt, Rinehart and Winston, 1980). The book is now publicly recognized as having been authored by renowned sport novelist Don DeLillo; Jack Falla, *Saved* (New York: Thomas Dunne Books, 2008).

3   The argument presented here is part of a larger, book-length study in progress, which I have tentatively titled "The Hockey Boys: A Study in the History of Juvenile Sporting Fiction."

4   Michael Oriard, *Dreaming of Heroes: American Sports Fiction, 1868–1980* (Chicago: Nelson-Hall, 1982), 17, 23. Oriard is to be commended for first suggesting in this book that juvenile literature (and "popular fiction") be considered an important, integral part of the canon of American sports fiction. More recently, he has taken up his own call. See Michael Oriad, "Wanted: A New History of American Sport Fiction," *Aethlon: The Journal of Sport Literature* 25, no. 1 (Fall 2007/ Winter 2008): 27–32. On this point, see also Chris Crowe, *More than a Game: Sports Literature for Young Adults* (Lanham, MD: Scarecrow Press, 2003), chaps. 1 and 2; and Steven Mintz, *Huck's Raft: A History of American Childhood* (Cambridge: Harvard University Press, 2004), 185–86.

5   On Patten (and Merriwell) see Robert H. Boyle, "The Unreal Ideal: Frank Merriwell," in *Sport: Mirror of American Life* (Boston: Little, Brown, 1963), chap. 7. Boyle claims that, on the strength of the Merriwell stories, the circulation of Tip Top Weekly eventually reached an amazing three hundred thousand. The Merriwell stories were later serialized as radio shows as well. See also John Levi Cutler, *Gilbert Patten and his*

Frank Merriwell Saga: A Study in Sub-Literary Fiction, University of Maine Studies, 2nd ser., no. 31 (Orono: University of Maine Press, 1934) and Gilbert Patten [Burt L. Standish, pseudo.], *Frank Merriwell's "Father": An Autobiography by Gilbert Patten ("Burt L. Standish")* (Norman: University of Oklahoma Press, 1964). On the genre's new elevation in scholarly estimation, see Oriard, *Dreaming of Heroes*.

6 On Barbour, see Christian K. Messenger, *Sport and the Spirit of Play in American Fiction: Hawthorne to Faulkner* (New York: Columbia University Press, 1981), 171–73; Fred Erisman, "The Strenuous Life in Practice: The School and Sports Stories of Ralph Henry Barbour," *The Rocky Mountain Social Science Journal* 7, no. 1 (1970): 29–37; William R. Gowen, "Ralph Henry Barbour: Boys' Books and Much More," *Newsboy* (November–December 1993): 15–24.

7 Sherman's work awaits serious study, but unlike other juvenile writers, sources for such a study exist. Sherman's papers (all one hundred and thirty cubic feet of them) are available for consultation at the Torreyson Library, University of Central Arkansas.

8 See Leslie McFarlane, *Ghost of the Hardy Boys: An Autobiography* (Toronto: Methuen, 1976); Marilyn S. Greenwald, *Secret of the Hardy Boys: Leslie McFarlane and Stratemeyer Syndicate* (Athens: Ohio University Press, 2004) and, especially, Karen E. H. Skinazi, "The Mystery of a Canadian Father of Hockey Stories: Leslie McFarlane's Break Away from the Hardy Boys," in *Canada's Game: Hockey and Identity*, ed. Andrew C. Holman (Montreal: McGill-Queen's University Press, 2009), 98–124. Recently, some of McFarlane's best-read hockey stories have been reprinted in *Leslie McFarlane's Hockey Stories*, ed. Brian McFarlane (Toronto: Key Porter Books, 2006) and *McGonigle Scores!* (Toronto: Key Porter Books, 2006). McFarlane's papers are deposited at the Ready Archives, Mills Library, McMaster University.

9 This first book of this sort to feature hockey actually predated the Merriwell phenomenon and clung more closely to the model of Tom Brown's School Days. See Robert Lowell, *Antony Brade* (Boston: Roberts Brothers, 1874). See esp. chap. 35, "The Match on the Ice."

10 See, for example, the counts listed for *Sports Story Magazine* in John Dinan's useful study, *Sports in the Pulp Magazines* (Jefferson, NC: McFarland, 1998).

11 The working bibliography on which this estimate is made is in the author's possession and available upon request.

12 For the foreign national as "other," see J. Frederick MacDonald, "'The Foreigner' in Juvenile Series Fiction, 1900–1945," *Journal of Popular Culture* 8, no. 3 (1974): 534–48. Of course "otherness" in juvenile fiction was used to characterize other, "exotic" parts of the United States. See Peter A. Soderbergh, "Florida's Image in Juvenile Fiction, 1909–1914," *Florida Historical Quarterly* 51, no. 2 (1972): 153–65.

13 See for example James Oliver Curwood, *Steele of the Royal Mounted: A Story of the Great Canadian Northwest* (New York: A.L. Burt, 1911); J.W. Duffield, *The Radio Boys in the Thousand Islands or the Yankee-Canadian Wireless Trail* (Chicago: M.A. Donohue, 1922).

14 These stereotypes were echoed in later decades in the depictions of Canada and Canadians in Hollywood films. See, for example, Pierre Berton, *Hollywood's Canada: The Americanization of Our National Image* (Toronto: McClelland & Stewart, 1975).

15 Walter Evans, "The All-American Boys: A Study of Boys' Sports Fiction," *Journal of Popular Culture* 6, no. 1 (1972): 107.

16 On the origins of ice hockey in the United States, see Stephen Hardy, "Memory, Performance, and History: The Making of American Ice Hockey at St Paul's School, 1860–1915," *International Journal of the History of Sport* 14, no. 1 (1997): 97–115; and S. Kip Farrington, *Skates, Sticks, and Men: The Story of Amateur Hockey in the United States* (New York: David McKay Company, 1972).

17 In Barbour's *The Crimson Sweater*, for example, students at Ferry Hill Academy resolve to form their own hockey club because their rivals at Hammond Academy had had one for five or six years. "If Hammond has a team we ought to have one too," hero-in-the-making Roy Porter stated. Barbour, *The Crimson Sweater* (New York: Century Book Company, 1906), 170.

18 Arthur Stanwood Pier, *Boys of St. Timothy's* (New York: Charles Scribner's Sons, 1904), 92, 100. Pier authored several sport novels about St. Timothy's, including *Harding of St. Timothy's* (Boston: Houghton Mifflin, 1906) and *Grannis of the Fifth* (New York: Grosset & Dunlap, 1914). St. Timothy's was a thinly-veiled rendering of St. Paul's School in Concord where Pier himself was educated and where, as Hardy argues, American hockey was born. See Hardy, "Memory, Performance, and History"; and Messenger, *Sport and the Spirit of Play in American Fiction*, 342–43. For other instances of authors "teaching" boys hockey through their fiction, see Ralph Henry Barbour, *Guarding His Goal* (New York: D. Appleton, 1919), 28, 122–3; and Donald Ferguson, *The Chums of Scranton High at Ice Hockey* (Cleveland: World Publishing, 1919), 169–70.

19 See for example, "American Hockey is Superior to Canadian," Boston Herald, January 7, 1918. This is described also in Barbour, *The Crimson Sweater*, 201. On Winsor, see Stephen Hardy, "Long Before Orr: Placing Hockey in Boston, 1897–1929," in *The Rock, the Curse and the Hub: A Random History of Boston Sports*, ed. Randy Roberts (Cambridge: Harvard University Press, 2005), 253–55.

20 Barbour, *Guarding His Goal*, 94.

21 On this process, see John Chi-Kit Wong, *Lords of the Rinks: The Emergence of the National Hockey League, 1875–1936* (Toronto: University of Toronto Press, 2005); Richard Gruneau and David Whitson, *Hockey Night in Canada: Sport, Identities and Cultural Politics* (Toronto: Garamond, 1993), chap. 4; Bruce Kidd, The Struggle for Canadian Sport (Toronto: University of Toronto Press, 1996), chap. 5; and Hardy, "Long Before Orr."

22 It is ironic, perhaps, that Canadians lamented this process, concerned that it constituted the Americanization of their game and the stealing of their collective birthright in pursuit of private commercial gain. See John Herd Thompson with Allen Seager, *Canada 1922–1939: Decades of Discord* (Toronto: McClelland & Stewart, 1985), 188–89; Archibald MacMechan, "Canada as a Vassal State," *Canadian Historical Review* 1, no. 4 (December 1920): 347–53; and Kidd, *The Struggle for Canadian Sport*, chap. 4.

23 Barbour, *Guarding His Goal*, 29; Harold M. Sherman, "Down the Ice!" in *Down the Ice! And Other Winter Sport Stories* (Chicago: Goldsmith Publishing, 1932); Barbour, *The Crimson Sweater*, 233.
24 Jack London, *The Abysmal Brute* (New York: Century Book Company, 1913). On the themes in this work, see Oriard, *Dreaming of Heroes*, 82–85.
25 Pier, *Boys of St. Timothy's*, 106.
26 Ralph Henry Barbour, *Skate Glendale!* (New York: Farrar & Rinehart, 1932), 148–9.
27 Harold M. Sherman, *Flashing Steel* (New York: Grosset & Dunlap, 1929), 8.
28 Griffith Ogden Ellis, ed., *American Boy Sports Stories* (Garden City, NY: Doubleday, 1949), v.
29 Ferguson, *The Chums of Scranton High*, 10.
30 Sherman, "The Ice Cyclone" in *Down the Ice! And Other Winter Sport Stories*, 42; Sherman, "The Penalty Box" in *Down the Ice! And Other Winter Sport Stories*, 184; Ferguson, *The Chums of Scranton High*, 96, 117.
31 Barbour, *Skate Glendale!*, 224–5.
32 Rex Lee, "Clashing Skates" in *American Boy Sports Stories*, ed. Ellis, 187.
33 Baker was also inspiration for more than one athletic character in his Princeton classmate F. Scott Fitzgerald's novels. He was often referred to in juvenile fiction as well. See, for example, Harold Sherman, "Whiskers" in *Flying Heels* (New York: Grosset & Dunlap, 1930), 23–4. In Sherman's *Flashing Steel*, the Yankville team's star is named "Jolly Baker." On Fitzgerald's use of Baker, see John Davies, *The Legend of Hobey Baker* (Boston: Little, Brown, 1966); Messenger, *Sport and the Spirit of Play in American Fiction*, chap. 8; and Robert J. Higgs, *Laurel & Thorn: The Athlete in American Literature* (Lexington: University Press of Kentucky, 1981), 39.

Richard Harrison

Stanley Cup/Superman

Every time I tell my father, whose memory is failing, the title of this essay, he says, "Gordie Howe." I don't argue. If his mind holds on to that, it must be true. Every year the Stanley Cup produces a Superman the fans remember for the rest of their lives. In one way, I am writing about the trophy's effect on those it touches, but instead of considering individuals turning into playoff superheroes, this is about the Cup itself, and how it can make the culture that created and sustains it heroic.

Here are two poems, written fifteen years apart, about concepts I never thought I would find together. "Stanley Cup" is a poem about the love of the victorious moment, "Superman" about the love found in defeat.

Stanley Cup
At the centre of the circle of the Champions of the
World, Mario Lemieux hoists the Cup, kisses its silver
thigh, the names of men where *his* will soon be cut
with a finish pure as a mirror; around him, the
tumult. And Scotty Bowman, the winningest coach
in the NHL, named his first son Stanley when his
Canadiens won it in '73 with a stonewall blueline and
a dizzying transition game. Every player on every
team who ever won the Cup gets to take it home; it
has partied on front lawns, swimming pools and in
the trunks of cars, and even the guy who left it by

the side of the road and drove away, still he thinks
of it as holy. And that word – *holy* – appears most
in the conversation of veterans who know how the
touch fades, the shoulder takes longer between days
of easy movement, how Bobby Hull passed on his
chance to drink champagne from its lip when the
Hawks won it '61 because he thought there'd be so
many in his life. Some take the Cup apart, clean the
rings, make minor repairs in their basements, and
then inscribe on the inside of the column the unofficial log of their intimate knowledge: This way
I have loved you.

        (*Hero of the Play*, 1994)

Superman
After the stroke
had done its work,
my father did not know
when his stomach was full,
and eating a meal
was the same to his brain
as closing his eyes on the table.
What an image this is –
my commanding father, whose
finger once imitated the thump
of a bullet striking my chest
so I might be educated in the way
power makes a hammer
from a nail, raiding
the fridge in the middle
of the day like he was a teen,
or toddler, and growing all over again
the body of his youth: ahead of him,
in olive green, the soldier waits
to dress the limbs &

untamed temper of
his father's labouring days,
the soldier who'll complete
the village's betrayal
by his industrial king.
Not long ago wasn't it? that
a boy might work beside his father
all his life, and understand
his knuckles and his purpose
in the curling of his hands.
I'm drawing Superman
over and over,
trying to get that beautiful linear
face just right, like it is
in the comics – a few lines
that could bless
with an uncle's smile for a nephew,
and then go grim to reap
what a villain sows.
I want it all back.
Here's a picture of my father
at 28 at his brother's
wedding. Look at that face –
see the anatomical plan of his cheek,
clean and without a sign of
anything but future in
the gorgeous symmetry of his smile.
I am not yet born.
The war is over, the home planet
is dust. I cannot get it right.
They say what needs to be done
is clear out the fridge
so Dad can't overeat,
feeding a need that nothing will.
What an image it is –
my dad opening and re-opening

> the Arctic door of his insatiable want:
> it befits a curse from Greek myth.
> I cannot explain it to him;
> his body has wrested
> the mind's knowledge of the body
> from the mind – and it has taken
> even his power to understand that, too:
> He rages at an empty box –
> an unfillable thought consuming him.
> This is my father.
> This is my Superman.
>
> (CV2, April 2007)

The Stanley Cup and Superman. Each is a hybrid with a Canadian root. The Cup, the Governor General's gift to Canadian youth to develop their character through play and their ambitions through victory in the form of a winter sport his own children played. Superman, a Canadian youth's gift to popular culture in the shape of an Olympian figure filled with a new generation's need to fix things – fast. Each has three names: "Superman" and "Stanley Cup" to the press; "Clark Kent" and "Lord Stanley's Mug" to those who think of them as a reporter for a major metropolitan newspaper and a bowl a child could hold; and "Kal-El, son of Jor-El," and "Hockey's Holy Grail" for those who think, without irony, that the truths of their faith can still be found in a people's secular world. Both are represented by American interests. Each marks the passing of time with their regular appearance. Both have been locked away from their familiar place when a Doomsday came that couldn't be beaten by fists or negotiation – only to be returned from such a "death" the following year. Both are remnants – Krypton and the Empire long gone. In their best pictures, both are aloft.

They have lived with us during sweeping changes of thought and power – from pre-modernism to modernism to post-modernism in architecture, art, philosophy and writing; from nationalism to internationalism to tribal-nationalism in politics; from World War to Cold War to Terrorist War in conflict. But each has continued to be meaningful, each has continued to represent something admirable and worth striving for.

Which is not to say that they remained unchanged even as they remained constant. I would argue, in fact, that it is only through their changes that they have been able to keep their place. As Sandra LaLonde, director of Red Sky Performance – which brings aboriginal dancers from around the world to dance together in ways that blend traditional and modern forms – says, "tradition evolves … it move[s], just like the contemporary" (Little, 58). So set their histories side by side. In terms of the periods familiar to comic fans and refined by Peter Coogan in his chronology, Superman and the Stanley Cup have each gone through distinct and roughly parallel stages from their origin to the present. A Golden Age of invention in comics (up to and including the era of the Original Six in hockey), a Silver Age of widening variety and popularity (the First Expansion years), a Bronze Age of talent too thinly spread (the NHL vs. the World Hockey Association), an Iron Age of collapse (over-expansion to decline) and a Renaissance. And through these ages, the narrative, the meaning and possibly the future of each can be seen by considering both the Stanley Cup and Superman through the symbol they share: The letter "S."

In its original appearances (1938–1949), Superman's chest logo was the English letter "S," the first letter of the name he took when he accepted the responsibility of his powers under the guidance of his decent Midwest American parents, who were not just the adoptive parents he was lucky enough to have found, but also the only parents he ever knew he had. The name made sense; so did the symbol, the "S" like a brand, or, perhaps more accurately, like the logo on a hockey sweater, a sign that means something personal to the wearer, in part because it represents a team. As far as he knew, Clark Kent was a super man, a gifted child who could jump higher, lift more and see further than anyone else. The readers understood why: in fact, he was the survivor of a planet whose people were what we might be given several thousand more years of civilization. But in his own mind, even though the champion of the little guy was a man above all others, above all else, he was still one of us. He rose to power by his natural gifts, hard work, perseverance and a dedication to the good.

In its original form, Stanley (1893), was an Englishman's challenge cup, open to any team its guardians, trustees acting in the spirit of Lord Stanley himself, deemed worthy. With the exception of a Seattle team named, foretellingly perhaps, after Superman's adult home, Metropolis, all of these teams were Canadian. And they mixed established and sponsored clubs from the big city with everyman teams like those from Kenora, Ontario, or the Yukon.

Though some challenges were single-game matches – which thus favoured the stronger team – most were decided over a series of games, a tradition the Cup carries to this day. In a 1999 article in *The American Statistician*, Jess Boronico explains that when a playoff is decided by a single series of games between two teams, the odds still favour the team with the better record during the regular season, and this advantage actually increases the more games there are in the series. However, when a championship is decided through a system of playoff rounds, with each round having two teams play each other in a series of games for the right to advance to the next round, there is less advantage to being the regular season's stronger team. The more playoff rounds there are, the less being the regular season's stronger team affects the outcome. In this way a multi-round playoff format makes the quest for a championship more competitively exciting by balancing regular season power with in-the-playoffs readiness and good fortune.

Looking at the same events not statistically, but in moral terms (not so far from the British tradition of sport as a shaper of character), the team that wins the Cup is the one that has endured the most, worked best with its gifts, been most dedicated to its goal, and may have caught the flash of battlefield luck that we think of as being blessed by the gods of the game. Having, by and large, the longest and most grueling playoff system in North America, the Stanley Cup represents the values of a people for whom the idea of enduring a lengthy winter is an integral part of the national identity. As much as it is possible, then, the first letter in Stanley Cup is a people's letter, the capital of a trophy competed for by the people themselves according to their most cherished values.

In 1949, his powers magnified to match the real-world presence of the atomic bomb, Superman discovers that, in fact, he is not the best of his kind, humanity, but the last of an alien race. Since, instead of leaping prodigiously, he can now fly (sometimes faster than the speed of light, which leads to time-travel and the discovery of his past), breathe in space, and push Planet Earth out of harm's way if such harm should threaten it, this discovery should come as no surprise. But the magnitude of the destruction at his origin fascinates and changes both the character and his writers forever. Superman's story from the early 1950s to the 1978 release of *Superman: The Movie* is the story of Superman's understanding of himself as the alien presence, alone but not alone in the world. Over that time, the meaning of his symbol changes from an English letter to a Kryptonian family crest whose yin-yang resemblance to a stylized "S" inspires Lois Lane to name him "Superman" in the press. In this change, the symbol and the name become not only a claim made by its wearer, but also a sign of the hopes of those who see him. In many ways, this period, and the one that follows it, becomes one in which the narrative of Superman is about a man not at the height of his powers, but at their limit. A man who is not clear, but is often confused about his actions and their effects.

From the fifties to the seventies, the Stanley Cup was a trophy to be competed for only by those within the NHL family. Hockey, too, has increased its power levels – the slapshot, created in anger by one player, is perfected by a smiling Olympian whose team was one of the few exceptions to the all-Canadian championship group that takes home the Cup year after year. Until 1972, the League perceived itself as the home of the world's best hockey; in 1972, it learned otherwise. Just as Superman's time travel to the planet of his birth reveals to him not only a race of people that he has never known, but a startling alternate history to the one he grew up with, The Canada/USSR Summit Series shocks the NHL, and Canada, with players of a higher quality and an approach to the game different from anything they'd expected. Though Team Canada (or, as Phil Esposito points out in his autobiography, "Team NHL" parading as "Team Canada") eventually wins the series, the period of NHL isolation is over. From now on European teams and European-stocked WHA teams challenge the worldview that places the Stanley Cup, confined to NHL teams, as hockey's crown. The NHL, aware that it is not alone, still needs to understand and accommodate its new place in the world.

Comics went into decline in the eighties and nineties. In this Iron Age, titles were expanded beyond the market's ability to sustain them. Parent companies relied on gimmick books – changing covers to drum up sales – and the niche and collectibles markets to sustain economic growth. Those markets collapsed due to over-pricing and dilution of the product. The audience complained that creativity had given way to commodity as the driving force of the business, and the very veterans who'd made such wealth possible were treated with disrespect and disdain.

Sound familiar?

Since then, Marvel, one of the two giants of the comic business, has gone bankrupt. Canada lost the Jets to Phoenix, and the Nordiques to Denver. Proportionally, Canadian players have shared the ice with more and more players from Europe and the United States. And since 1993, close as they have sometimes come, no Canadian-based team has won the Stanley Cup. The NHL has been locked out twice and lost a season and a half of play. Hockey is among the least popular televised sports in the United States. And Superman died – needing to be reborn.

In his graphic novel, *Superman: Birthright*, Mark Waid revises the Super-Symbol. Following the lead of the film version, Clark Kent discovers his identity and heritage as a youth, but the dramatic "S" that adorns the fabric he was sent to earth with isn't a member of our alphabet, nor is it a family crest, it's the Kryptonian flag itself. Superman becomes Clark Kent's conscious choice to represent his people where their best values coincide with those of the human beings who raised him even as he is unique among those he most deeply loves. In a sense, too, the modern Superman is an attempt to make up for the failings of his origin planet, the chief of these always having been the failure to listen. The scene that has consistently haunted the Superman myth is that of Kal-El's father, Jor-El, pleading with the ruling Scientist-Kings of his planet to pay attention to the signs that their world is heading for destruction. Not only do they deny his conclusion, they mock him, and they do so in ways that mirror far too closely for comfort the specious arguments used to ridicule and attack the almost Kryptonianly-named Al Gore whose message is almost the same. I say this, though as I write, popular opinion and political opposition is shifting around us to acknowledge the reality of man-made climate change and both the possibility and necessity of its alteration through changes in our own behaviour.

Where is hockey in this? And the Stanley Cup? With the exception of the North and Northeastern seaboard states, hockey in the United States will never be more than a gate-driven sport, a boutique entertainment in a land where sports live and die not in terms of the qualities of the teams, but in terms of the spectacles they create. This is not an anti-American position. (Who can love Superman as much as I do, or acknowledge him as, as Rob MacDougall rightly says, "an avatar of the American nation," and be anti-American?) But neither is it a necessarily pro-Canadian one. If the Superman myth had to grow from one of personal choice to family heritage to planetary legacy, then the meaning of hockey in its mythic sense can equally be seen to need to grow from local significance to national sport to something beyond either the nation or the two-nation National Hockey League. The meaning of hockey lies in what we are now being asked to protect: the North. Winter.

What the 1972 Series began to alert us to was not that there was another country with a claim to hockey supremacy, but that Canada and Russia – and the Northern United States and the Czech Republic; and Slovakia, Sweden, and Finland, and many more – are all provinces of a culture of winter. A culture that sees the ice as a way to dance on death and make beauty out of a season known for being unforgiving. In our new and planetary consciousness, we know that the seasons of ice and snow are essential for life on earth.

Regardless of the outcome, the present has changed. Hockey has been a way that Canadians have loved ourselves and made meaning out of winter. In the new world coming, it can be a way that we, a people for whom hockey was never *not* front-page news, can treasure winter itself. If so, it will represent a shift in our culture towards the central article of faith that I, as a Canadian, have associated most closely with an aboriginal way of life – that the highest moments of a civilization are the ones that connect a people most with the sacredness of nature. Emerging at first out of fear inspired by scientific knowledge, but I hope in the end out of love, I see Lord Stanley's Mug being played for as the ultimate challenge cup in the League of Hockey Nations (LHN).

Could the NHL ever see itself – and its own best interests – as part of the LHN?

Who knows? The letters are there. But whether it's a dream or a fantasy, imagine two hockey seasons among teams from cities where hockey is truly profitable – and if my argument is right, this means cities where the money reflects the love of the game – culminating in two three-round playoffs to decide North American Conference and European Conference finalists. Imagine them playing a best-of-seven championship to determine the best club team in the world. Wouldn't it be as exciting as the Stanley Cup is now? If not more so? And wouldn't it be among the many things we are looking for to represent something bigger than mere national interest?

Would Canadians still desire such a trophy?

In his 2003 graphic novel, *Red Son*, Mark Miller contemplated a world where the infant Superman landed in the Ukraine during Stalin's rule of the Soviet Union. Despite the world-on-its-head story that emerged, the Man of Steel still became a figure of triumph of good country-folk morality over earthly politics. Would the Cup mean the same to me if it were carried home by Moscow Dynamo? I'm from Toronto. For forty years I've seen the Cup go to teams playing out of more than a dozen other cities – and counting. And as far as I can see the people of the town of my birth long for it more than ever, the way we long for the hero we never forget. Exactly the way we need one.

Works Cited

Boronico, Jess S. "Multi-tiered playoffs and their Impact on Professional Baseball." *The American Statistician* 53, no. 1 (February 1999): 56–61.

Coogan, Peter. *Superhero: The Secret Origin of a Genre*. Austin: MonkeyBrain Books, 2006.

Esposito, Phil, and Peter Golenbock. *Thunder and Lightning: A No B.S. Hockey Memoir*. Toronto: McClelland and Stewart, 2003.

Harrison, Richard. "Stanley Cup." In *Hero of the Play*. Toronto: Wolsak and Wynn, 1994, 40.

Harrison, Richard. "Superman." *Contemporary Verse 2*, 29, no. 4 (Spring 2007): 38–9.

Little, Melanie. "The Nature of a Warrior." *Fast Forward Weekly (FFWD)*, 11, no. 31 (July 2006): 58.

MacDougall, Rob. "Superman Returns." *Old is the New New*, June 22, 2006. http://www.robmacdougall.org/archives/2006/06/superman_returns_1.php (accessed July 20, 2009).

Millar, Mark. *Superman: Red Son*. New York: DC Comics, 2003.

Puzo, Mario. *Superman: The Movie*. Directed by Richard Donner. Burbank, CA: Warner Bros., 1978.

Waid, Mark. *Superman: Birthright*. New York: DC Comics, 2004.

David McNeil

The Story of Hockey Photography in the Early 1950s

Sports photography enjoyed a boom in the decade after WWII as improvements in film quality found their way into mainstream journalism, and hockey was covered as one of the "big time" team sports in Canada and the northern United States. The camera favored by the press of this time was the large-format "Speed Graphic," whose 5 x 4 negative surface was capable of capturing lush detail and a rich depth of field when used with a flash. The Turofsky brothers (Nat and Lou) of Toronto and Scotty Kilpatrick in Detroit rigged powerful strobe flashbulbs on the top of the protective glass at Maple Leaf Gardens or wire-mesh at the Olympia, which were simultaneously linked to their shutters. Being powerful, the flashbulbs took about twelve seconds to recharge, so photographers had only one chance to capture key action shots. (The exploding sound of these flashes is often exaggerated in contemporary movies.) These factors, among others, are responsible for the fact that pictures from the 1940–50s era have a very different feel than those taken with 35 mm cameras and zoom lens in the 1960s. This essay tells a story about two such pictures: one very well known, and another hardly known at all.

    The well known one is the Turofsky shot of Bill Barilko scoring his famous overtime goal in Game Five of the 1951 Finals at Maple Leaf Gardens which won the Stanley Cup for the Leafs (see fig. 1). It was first published in the *Globe and Mail* the Monday after the game

(April 23, 1951), and there is nothing special about its presentation. The shot is trimmed, which has the effect of emphasizing the Barilko/McNeil duel, and the players are all labelled, as is the puck (with an arrow). Another picture by Michael Burns is actually featured at the top of the page with a large title, "It's the Goal That Paid Off on Another World Hockey Title for Toronto." There is nothing here that hints at the notoriety that would eventually attach itself to the Turofsky picture in the decades ahead – nothing to explain why this would be a shot that launched a thousand comments.

Barilko's tragic disappearance on a fishing trip that summer and the mystique that followed are widely known. The plane wreckage was not discovered until 1962, the next year that the Maple Leafs won the Stanley Cup, and these events are chronicled in the Tragically Hip song, "Fifty Mission Cap." A large copy of Turofsky's picture hung prominently for years in the middle of the west-end lobby of Maple Leaf Gardens. Andrew Podnieks correctly draws our attention to what makes it so memorable as a sports photo – that it captures the exact split second after the puck has entered the net yet before the goal has registered on the faces in the crowd (Podnieks, *Portraits of the Game*, 62). This precise timing cannot be attributed to another famous picture of a defenceman scoring a Stanley Cup overtime goal. I'm referring, of course, to Ray Lussier's image of Bobby Orr airborne in 1970 against St. Louis, and the subject of another book by Andrew Podnieks (*The Goal*). Selected for inclusion in *Sports Illustrated*'s "The Pictures: 50 Years of SI Photography" special issue (April 26, 2004), Lussier's shot is probably better known among Americans than Turofsky's. It is worth noting that the puck is still suspended in the mesh in Turofsky's picture, while in Lussier's it has already come back out of the net and lies in the crease. Orr's airborne position is celebratory – i.e., the fact that he has scored has already clearly registered. In fact, it is worth noting that Lussier himself didn't think the photo would be printed because the puck had already exited the net (Berger).

One element I have always been struck by about Turofsky's picture and many others of this era is how a wide chunk of the playing surface and bank of spectators are all in focus. Another noteworthy detail is that one can count four Leaf skaters in the frame (Barilko, Watson, Meeker and Gardner) and only three Canadiens (Johnson, Bouchard and Richard). Had the Habs gained control of the puck, they would have outnumbered the Leafs two to one going the other way. Barilko was taking a real gamble and could have ended up the goat instead of the hero. Still photography freezes the moment but tells us nothing about what transpired just before, or just after. Growing up and seeing the picture, I often wondered to myself – what happened exactly? How did my father end up on his ass in the net?

There have been several narrative descriptions of the goal – one of the most detailed, and I believe accurate, is by Paul Patskou reproduced in Kevin Shea's biography of Barilko.[1] Meeker, now behind the net and being checked by Tom Johnson, had attempted a wrap-around on McNeil's right; McNeil went down to stop Meeker and the puck came out to Harry Watson to McNeil's left (right side of photo), Watson shot it back towards the net where McNeil, still on the ice, moved to block it. At this point the puck then mysteriously appeared back on the goalie's right where Barilko had pinched in. He appeared to shovel it on his backhand. We're now at the point when Turofsky pressed the shutter. McNeil tries to get back over to the right, but the puck sails over his arm into the net. The one aspect of the sequence that remains a mystery is how Watson's shot ended up bouncing to the right of the Canadiens' goal. Patskou agrees with Duplacey and Wilkins who suggest that the puck hit Bouchard's skate, but there is no way to be certain about this detail. My father confirmed that the shot never hit him or got to the net; so it would appear that Duplacey and Wilkins are right. I once asked my father what he thought of confirming this idea with Butch Bouchard, and I can recall vividly how he and my mother just laughed.

"Sure, I can ask Butch, and he would probably respond with something like, 'What, half a century later, you're trying to blame me for the goal?!'" It was simply a moment in the careers of several players, a moment determined by innumerable circumstances too mundane to be of any interest but to those fascinated by Turofsky's picture. Reviewing the footage of the goal, which I have done now countless times, does give one a general sense of what happened.[2]

The Leafs simply stormed the Montreal end and pressed successfully for the winning goal. That is all we know, and all we need to know. Forget the fact that hundreds of details could be cited from regulation time that determined any of the previous four goals or that thwarted all kinds of close chances for an earlier winning goal. History follows a very narrow and precise path, and in our retrospective glance, that path does not change.

Over the years my father was asked to autograph copies of Turofsky's picture for countless fans. At one such event in Toronto, he was billed as "The Goalie in the Barilko Picture," and a good number of these signed photos have been bought and sold on eBay. I think that this notoriety bothered him a little, as well it should. All reports of the '51 Finals make mention of McNeil's superlative play, which of course is not conveyed at all by Turofsky's photo. However, my father would still take the opportunity to remind people that he did win the Stanley Cup in '53, posting two shutouts, one being the clinching game that also went into overtime. He would also talk about the two marathon overtime games in the '51 Semi-Finals against Detroit, which included a two hundred and eighteen-minute shutout streak – the longest in the modern day playoffs until Ilya Bryzgalov went two hundred and twenty-nine minutes without allowing a goal a couple of years ago.[3] Of the 1951 Finals my father would say, "you don't always win when you play your best."

The cultural significance of Turofsky's picture is reflected in the fact that it was selected for inclusion in Kingwell and Moore's compilation of twentieth century photographs entitled *Canada: Our Century* (276); it would be one of nine hockey pictures in the collection.[4] With an exception or two, the other eight photos form a virtual who's who of hockey culture in Canada: 1) Foster Hewitt doing a radio broadcast in 1923; 2) Lester Patrick, the manager of the New York Rangers, replacing his injured goalie in 1928; 3) Jimmy Orlando bloodied after a fight on November 7, 1942; 4) Maurice Richard on the occasion of the riot in March 1955 – although it must be said that the photo is not related to the riot; 5) Bobby Hull pitching hay on the family farm; 6) Gordie Howe on a poster after scoring his 1,092 point in 1960; 7) Paul Henderson scoring the winning goal against the Soviets in 1972 and finally 8) Wayne Gretzky raising his first Stanley Cup in 1984. Podnieks remarks that the picture of Barilko scoring his famous goal is "[q]uite likely the most reproduced Turofsky image at the Hockey Hall of Fame" (*Portraits of the Game*, 62), which has over nineteen thousand items in its collection. Its popularity from the 1960s onwards is due to Barilko's tragic story, the fact that the Leafs have not won a Stanley Cup since '67, the large Leaf-fan base around the Hockey Hall of Fame and, of course, the picture itself. Similar to how Bobby Thompson's pennant-winning home-run (also in 1951) has been called "the shot that was heard around the world" due to its overseas radio broadcast (i.e., "the Giants win the pennant, the Giants win the pennant"), so Barilko's feat manifest in Turofsky's image is ubiquitous in pictorial histories of hockey.

The second picture is virtually unknown. It shows my father kicking out a shot by Gordie Howe (see fig. 2). I have yet to identify the precise game or moment the picture was taken despite going through reel upon reel of *Detroit News* microfilms. The imaged is as seared into my memory as the Turofsky one because my father made sure to hang it in the den or rec-room of the family home. The image lurked in the background of my childhood. Many times as a youngster, and then even later when I was older, I paused to inspect the expressions it featured. On the left is my father with his familiar panicky expression, foreboding some disaster. That look I knew so well whenever he noticed that I, and years later my children, had left a glass of milk too close to the table's edge. "That's going to get knocked over. I can see it coming." (My father sometimes spoke as if he had some kind of extrasensory power, especially when it came to household disasters. In any case, the ability to "see it coming" is not a bad thing for somebody whose major life-occupation was goaltending.) On the right is Gordie Howe staring ahead in sheer awe at the goalie thwarting his effort. Howe also looks so incredibly young; my father not so much young as frazzled. In the background between the two adversaries, one can see the expressions of a number of fans. There is a woman who appears behind my father; she looks as though she could be a little bored with what's going on in front of her, either that or she just can't follow the speed of the action. Another man sits in the middle of the principal adversaries; he leans forward, enthralled by the play. The photo had to have been taken near the beginning of a period because the surface is still quite shiny. This condition is responsible for another special feature, which is the reflection of the end red line painted on the boards; it just happens to run across the ice dividing the space between the shooter and the goalie (the actual red line painted under the ice is there on the left *but not visible*); this division lends the scene a mano-a-mano quality. The puck is in clear view in the centre, having just been kicked out by my father's right pad. A definite point of aesthetic distinction about the sports photo is the importance of having the puck or ball in the frame. It gives meaning to the bodies in motion, a clue as to what has just happened or is about to happen.[5]

So much nostalgic history may be read in the sticks alone. Howe's, from which the shot obviously originated, reveals a perfectly straight blade emblematic of a simpler era when equipment was less sophisticated and team allegiance more pronounced. It cuts diagonally across his half of the picture from the middle right to the lower left and is offset by the goalie's stick on which one can tease out the words, "Raymond Hardware" (the main supplier of sticks in Quebec), which crosses the left half of the picture, centre to bottom right (Dowbiggin). So the game was played by our ancestors – the sticks as bygone as almost everything else in the frame.

None of these details are composed by the photographer, of course, who was James "Scotty" Kilpatrick of the *The Detroit News*. Kilpatrick had made a name for himself when, in May 1937, he managed to get some shots of a fight between striking auto-workers and management-hired security guards. The incident, known as the "Battle of the Overpass," ranks as a significant event in the labour history of the United States, and, on the basis of Kilpatrick's photos, the Pulitzer Prize Committee decided to institute an award for photography (Nolan). The only thing one can say about Kilpatrick's hockey photos is that he knew where to position himself and he got results.

Cultural context means everything in how a photo is deemed significant. The best known mano-a-mano (or defeat/victory) image is, of course, Neil Leifer's shot of Ali standing over a prone Sonny Liston and taunting the older fighter to get back up. *Sports Illustrated* voted it the sports photo of the century (July 26, 1999), and Leifer himself, who personally thinks that his shot of Ali/Williams is technically better, understands why. He points to the fact that the photo didn't make the cover of *Sports Illustrated* at the time, only when it was selected in 1999; instead the magazine chose a shot that featured both fighters still on their feet (June 7, 1965).[6] The Ali/Liston photo has grown with time to represent an iconographic moment not just in Ali's career or the history of sports, but in the history of the civil rights movement in the United States (Berman and Maher). Leifer is well aware that luck has to cooperate for composition elements to come together in an aesthetically pleasing fashion – all the photographer does is make the most of fortuitous opportunities. Perfectly visible between Ali's legs is the face of the other *Sports Illustrated* photographer, Herbie Scharfman, helplessly positioned to see little else but Ali's back. (But even this sense of achievement/failure was more just a part of the overall successful *Sports Illustrated* strategy to ensure that Leifer and Scharfman were on opposite sides to maximize the chance of getting a good shot.)

Kilpatrick's photo of my father kicking out a shot by Howe is devoid of any cultural significance beyond familial history, but that it was my father's favorite picture and the one that always hung somewhere in the house does hint at why a particular image has particular meaning. My father had some great games at the Olympia, and after his amazing performance in the Semi-Finals of '51 when he helped eliminate the heavily favored Red Wings, the Detroit press dubbed him "the Magician." At the end of the '53 season, Howe was on the verge of matching and perhaps breaking Richard's record of a fifty-goal season. The last game of the regular schedule was against the Habs at the Olympia. Howe had five shots on net, including a clear break with ten minutes left. My father stopped him every time. In the dressing room afterwards he apparently went over to Richard and said, "Well, Rock, he's got to start at one again" (Irvin, 94). Howe would never again get as close to the fifty-goal mark. I have fantasized about this picture being that final shot, but the original is undated and I have never found it in any publication.

Kilpatrick was in the exact same location for the picture he got of McNeil and Howe as he was when he captured Terry Sawchuk going down to smother the puck, an image that *Life* magazine used in its profile of the Red Wing goalie ("Greatest Hockey Goalie Ever"). How my father came to possess his Kilpatrick photos remains a mystery (he couldn't recall), but Kilpatrick may well have done what a number of photographers did at the time – i.e., given prints of his photos to the people captured in them. What makes his prints special is their size. The McNeil/Howe shot is one of two 12 x 9.5 glossies; another goalmouth shot featuring Butch Bouchard as well as my father measures 14 x 11. (Believe it or not this photo was folded in half and shoved into a barrel of junk in my father's basement where it remained for over twenty-five years!) Most press prints that I have seen from the 1940s and '50s are 8 x 10 or smaller. Kilpatrick used special film techniques to enlarge his photos. Retired photographer Dick Van Nostrand, who remembers talking with Kilpatrick in the 1960s, writes that he "rigged Olympia Stadium with some of the first strobe lights and had them controlled by switches so he could change lighting effects. He also experimented with developer/film combinations so he could enlarge small sections of the negative shot with Hasselblad and Rollei cameras and make nearly grain-free enlargements. As a teenager I fought my dad for the paper so that I could see his photos" (Van Nostrand). It may well be that the photos were done for an issue of *The Hockey News* (December 23, 1950). Although the five column photograph that was used on the front page appears without a photo credit, it depicts another shot on McNeil by the Red Wings at the Olympia, and one of my father's glossies had "5 col cut The Hockey News" scribbled on the back. Another possibility is that it was one of a group that was taken for a special feature on my father that appeared in *The Standard's* weekly magazine.[7]

Turning back to the McNeil/Howe shot, we have noted the clarity of some of the faces in the crowd, and I am forever amazed at being able to see both the hinges in the door along the boards and the knit in my father's socks. While Kilpatrick was definitely using a large-format camera (the 5 x 4 negative containing approximately thirteen times the detail of 35 mm), it may well have been a Hasselblad or Rollei rather than a Speed Graphic.[8] You can spot one of his strobes on the top of the mesh in other photos. With the subsequent widespread use of 35 mm and the telephoto lens, we still have sharp action shots but the backgrounds – that is other players, the fans – tend to be blurry. Sports photography of the 1940s and 1950s includes the crowd as a subject in a way that was subsequently lost for decades, or at least restricted to a few special shots in *Sports Illustrated*. Technological advances have now brought detail and depth of field back; the megapixel levels and options on digital cameras provide rich creative capabilities, but not exclusively so, for now twenty thousand spectators each click away with their own cellphone cameras. As for the moving images, here too we now have High Definition (HD) detail and sharpness, more possible angles with net- and cable-cams and wide angles.

Two other factors make hockey photos of Turofsky's time distinctive: one is technical, the other historical. First, the grey-scale composition imparts an imaginary nostalgia, an otherworldliness that we associate with the mid-twentieth century. Looking at collections of pre-1950 photos, one can easily forget that previous generations did live in a world of colour. Free of any noise from the colour palette, grey-scale emphasizes all non-colour aspects: line, texture, depth. Woodward reminds us of how journalism retained a snobbishness about black and white film, how colour film wasn't deemed trustworthy (he notes how even Lussier's 1970 image of an airborne Orr was originally shot in black and white). The second aspect is purely historical: the lack of face masks or helmets gives greater access to the facial expressiveness of the individuals depicted. We easily read and feel Howe's sense of awe, McNeil's desperation. Similarly, recent proponents of High Definition (HD) television point to the new wonder of being able to read the faces of football players through the mask.[9]

One reason we value the photos from this era is that they are the best visual record of the events depicted. Film footage from the '40s and '50s does exist, such as the highlight reels done by Briston, but the angles are so poor, the perspectives so distant and fuzzy that it tells us very little about the game. As the home goalie in the first television broadcast – that being the '52 Saturday night opener at the Forum between Detroit and Montreal – which aired on the French CBC, October 11, 1952, my father may well have been the first NHL player to ever be seen on Canadian television.[10] Goalies then, as is still the custom, led their teams onto the ice. I have watched a few of these early broadcasts (although the CBC archives have no recordings of them, some copies are held by the Hockey Hall of Fame). Their quality, restored by Paul Patskou, is remarkably good, but as moving images they are not nearly as well known as the photography. Most hockey fans would recognize Roger St. Jean's famous picture of Rocket Richard and Elmer Lach in their airborne embrace seconds after the latter scored in overtime to win the Cup in '53. René Lecavalier's play-by-play of the same goal is not nearly so familiar. Over the years as television improved and permeated our lives to the extent it did (and still does), this preference would change. There are all kinds of visual representations of Henderson's famous goal in '72, but most remember it by the television clip with Foster Hewitt's call. Sports photography still has its moments, but it has never held the privileged position it did before television.

Every picture has a story to tell, which is another difference between the still and moving images. Roger St. Jean only got his famous shot because he missed shooting the goal itself. His view of the action was blocked (he didn't even have a seat) and so he never saw the puck go into the net. However, as people rose to start cheering a clear view suddenly opened before him and, with his flash still charged, he was able to capture the celebration (Derosiers). Even when there are no pictures, the storytellers will entertain us. Nobody, to my knowledge, got a photo of my father while Lach and Richard were in their embrace. Wayne Johnston, however, has fictionalized such a picture in his novel *The Divine Ryans*. Blending fiction with fact, Johnston has a character in the novel at the final game who claims to have grabbed a puck kicked into the crowd by the Montreal goalie. The puck, identified as one that was "Deflected into the stands by Canadiens goalie Gerry McNeil" (Johnston, 152) serves as a family heirloom, and the son searches a photograph (in one of the many illustrated histories of hockey) of McNeil apparently taken just after Lach scores to see if he can find his father's face in the crowd. The textual description of this photograph, which follows a couple of pages later (Johnston, 155), might be likened to what is known as an *ekphrasis* in classical rhetoric – the verbal representation of the pictorial. While only a "few faces" were unobstructed or in clear focus, the depth of field required to see "the Montreal zone" with my father and *any* individuals in the crowd behind him would obviously have owed itself to a Speed Graphic (with flash). Johnston, who seems fond of playing with history (see also *The Colony of Unrequited Dreams*), maintains that the photograph on which he based this scene actually exists. Perhaps, but I have failed to find it, despite being on a search similar to that of Johnston's narrator.[11] In fact, I have scoured scrapbooks, microfilmed newspapers and used bookstores without turning up Johnston's photo. I suspect that Johnston simply conflated the so-called facts of that game with another picture of another goalie to serve the purpose of his novel. My father didn't remember throwing his stick, which is what he is apparently doing in the photograph, but the television footage and photos that do exist of the on-ice celebration show him without a stick.[12] So we don't really know. The same footage also indicates that the puck did go over the boards during the first minute of overtime, but this was near the Canadiens' bench. The father in the novel records the exact game time when McNeil apparently deflected the puck over – 1:03 of overtime, or "[n]ineteen seconds" before Lach fired home the winner (Johnston, 152). According to the scoresheet that appeared in *The Gazette*, Lach's goal did come at 1:22, or nineteen seconds later, so Johnston is accurate in that respect. In any case, my father certainly enjoyed how Johnston had fictionalized what was one of the happiest moments in his life, and Johnston himself appreciated the fittingness of how my interest in my father's career resembled the protagonist's search for his father in the apparent photo. That his novel created a warm moment for a father and son was completely fortuitous. As in fiction that draws on historical fact, so in photography – so much depends on chance.

There are all kinds of stories surrounding the hockey photos taken during the decade after the Second World War. The photos first served journalism as the only visual representation that most hockey fans could feast their eyes on. Even though televised games began in 1952, it would still be years before the majority of fans moved from radio broadcasts to the new medium (Young, 74). A few photos would find broader audiences in pictorial magazines like *Life*. Later, in the case of Turofsky at least, the photos would become part of the Hockey Hall of Fame collection and be used in countless popular histories of the sport. For some sport aficionados these pre-television photos have a romantic or nostalgic appeal – for some (like myself) they become fetishized, wall art. It might be argued that the 1940s and '50s constituted the golden age of sports photography at least as far as infiltrating the popular media was concerned. The success of *Sport* magazine was largely attributable to its rich pictorial layouts – the same emphasis on the visual image that was responsible for the popularity of *Life* only scaled down from the large 14 x 10.5 size to what would become the magazine industry standard of 11 x 8.5. McNeil's portrait (see fig. 3) appeared in the February 1951 issue of *Sport*, with the caption "exclusively by International." It resembles the famous one of Maurice Richard insofar as the subject is depicted from the chest up, with arms crossed and eyes looking to the right. When *Sports Illustrated* began as a rival magazine in 1954, not only did Henry Luce imitate the pictorial layout, he actually tried to buy the name "Sport" from MacFadden Publications for $200,000 (Hoffer, 28, 35). The simultaneous rise of *Sports Illustrated* and television in the half century that followed suggests that the still action photo can co-exist with the moving image. However, there remains something truly unique and wonderful about the wide vistas and detail in sports photography before we began to gorge ourselves on the moving image and the convenience of the 35 mm zoom lens.

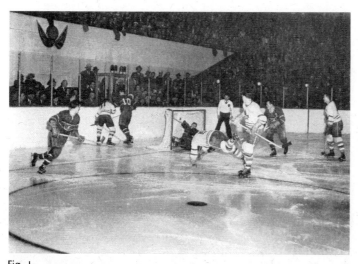

Fig. 1
Credit: Nat Turofsky.
Maple Leaf Gardens, 21 April 1951.
Globe and Mail, 23 April 1951: 20.
Permission: Hockey Hall of Fame & Imperial Oil

Fig. 2
Credit: James "Scotty" Kilpatrick.
Detroit Olympia, early 1950s.
Copyright: unknown

Fig. 3
Credit: "Exclusive color portrait for *Sport* by International."
Appears in *Sport* 10, no. 2 (February 1951): 19.
Illustration for an article titled, "The Dirtiest Job on Ice."
Copyright: Macfadden Publications Inc., 205 East 42 Street, New York 17, NY [defunct]

1   Patskou quoted by Shea, 153–55. Patskou basically repeats the description in James Duplacey and Charles Wilkins, 114.

2   Andrew Hunter's installation exhibit "Up North: A Northern Ontario Tragedy" included a five minute loop of footage from Game Five that included the end of regulation time and the overtime. I watched it repeatedly in 1998 at the Kamloops gallery, and the experience did not clarify anything with respect to the Barilko goal. My father and I subsequently received a tape from the Hockey Hall of Fame with the same footage. My father and I used to joke that there would soon be a musical based on the Barilko story.

3   Bryzgalov's shutout streak was stopped at 249:15, which puts the Russian goalie second on the list. McNeil drops from fourth to fifth.

4   Page 276. The other eight pictures are on pages 145, 155, 235, 289, 320, 321, 379 and 431. It should be noted that the Turofsky shot of a bloodied Tony Orlando was taken November 7, 1942 (not 1944).

5   I cannot find any evidence of the photo having been published in the early 1950s although I am still looking. It has, however, been published twice in recent years to accompany two articles that Dave Stubbs did on my father.

6   Ali lands a blow to Liston's head, but both fighters are on their feet. The caption reads, "The Fight You Didn't See."

7   O'Brien. Although the main photo in the feature resembles a Kilpatrick (i.e., same angle at the Olympia), it does not carry a photo credit.

8   Q.-Tuan Luong. For more technical detail, see Leigh Klotz.

9   Gordon Tubbs, assistant director of marketing for the broadcast division of Canon, comments: "In the old days, the cameras could barely penetrate the shadows under the helmets, so the players all looked like Darth Vader. Now because of HD, you not only can see the sweat on their faces when watching at home, you see their state of being, which brings a whole new emotional level to viewing the game." In Ken Freed, "ABC Sports Prepares for HD Super Bowl XL."

10 The French-language production with René Lecavalier doing the play-by-play only began at the beginning of the third period. "Habs to Televise Only 3rd Periods of NHL Contests." Two sources erroneously claim the first French broadcast to have been on opening night (October 9, 1952) the previous Thursday. Pincus, 90; and Irvin, "Writing and Broadcasting," 117. Recordings of three of René Lacavalier's broadcasts are held by the Hockey Hall of Fame (Boston vs. Montreal, November 15, 1952; Detroit vs. Montreal, February 6, 1953; and Boston vs. Montreal, April 16, 1953). I have not been able to find any archival recordings of any English CBC broadcasts from 1953 or 1954.

Danny Gallivan was the first English-language announcer at the Forum, and English broadcasts began later that season.

11 I had the opportunity to ask Wayne Johnston if the picture really existed after a reading he gave at Frog Hollow Books in Halifax (September 22, 1999). He claimed that it did, but I have never seen it.

12 Broadcast of Game Five of the 1953 Stanley Cup Finals, French CBC TV, April 16, 1953.

John Soares

Boycotts, Brotherhood and More

International Hockey From Moscow to Colorado Springs via Squaw Valley (1957–1962)

Avery Brundage, International Olympic Committee (IOC) president from 1952 to 1972, often expressed his hope that the Olympics and international sport could be free of the political contention that marred so many international organizations during the Cold War. Although a citizen of the US, he tried to steer the IOC into neutrality between Communism and the "Free World." He hoped that sport might be a way of moderating political clashes and that the Olympics could provide "a conspicuous example that when fair play and good sportsmanship prevail, men can agree, regardless of race, religion or political convictions" (quoted in Lechenperg, 5).

However appealing Brundage's vision was, on both sides of the Iron Curtain sport often appeared as a venue for Cold War rivalry. The Soviets explicitly considered their hockey players "at the leading edge of ideological struggle ... in the role of ideological warriors" (quoted in Baumann, 163). Even Canada's Lester B. Pearson, a diplomat and future Nobel Peace laureate, noted that "International sport is the means of attaining triumphs over another nation" (quoted. in Macintosh and Greenhorn, 98). Hockey, with its violent possibilities, was well-suited to be an arena of Cold War conflict. This came through in events such as Canadian Bobby Clarke's slash on Soviet star Valery Kharlamov's ankle during the 1972 Summit Series and the particularly physical games the Soviet Central Army played against the Boston Bruins and Philadelphia Flyers in January 1976. Even the NHL All-Stars' devastating loss to the Soviets in the 1979 Challenge Cup and the importance of the Canada Cup tournaments all showed hockey's potential as a venue of Cold War confrontation.

But there was more to the story. Not only was political rivalry played out on the ice, but the boycotts of the 1957 and 1962 world championships demonstrated that politics could even prevent the games altogether. In such circumstances, the games could not serve as an outlet for confrontation or promote the sort of friendship-building that occurred in between those tournaments at the Squaw Valley Olympics. Those Games saw both surprising friendship among American and Soviet players, and surprising violence – for Olympic hockey – in games involving Canada and Sweden, and Russia and the West Germans. In order to consider the possibilities and limitations of sport in building friendly transnational connections, the world and Olympic hockey tournaments of 1957, 1960 and 1962 need to be placed in their correct political and diplomatic context.

Moscow, 1957

With no prior record of competition in international ice hockey, the USSR burst onto the scene by winning the championship at its first world tournament in 1954. Two years later, the Soviets won gold in their Olympic debut at Cortina.[1] At the time, the International Ice Hockey Federation (IIHF) recognized the Olympic gold medalist as the world champion, so the USSR was the defending champion when Moscow hosted the world tournament in 1957. Hopes for a grand show including Soviet wins over Canada and the US, though, began falling apart soon after the USSR invaded Hungary in response to Hungarian leader Imre Nagy's announcement that he intended to withdraw his nation from the Warsaw Pact and pursue a neutral foreign policy.[2] Within days of the invasion, the Canadian Amateur Hockey Association (CAHA) announced that Canada would not participate in the tournament. Its general manager explained that the

CAHA leaders believed that because of the Hungarian invasion "Canada should not consider competing in Russia" (quoted in "Canada Out of Tourney: Will Not Send Squad to World Hockey at Moscow in '57"). On December 28, the Swiss Ice Hockey Federation announced that neutral Switzerland, too, would boycott the Moscow tournament ("Swiss Boycott Reds"). Other nations would join the Canadians and the Swiss.

For the US, though, the situation was complicated. The Amateur Hockey Association of the United States (AHAUS) hoped to build on its silver medal performance at Cortina. It assembled a team boasting a number of veterans of Olympic and international play and hired former NHL coach "Wild Bill" Stewart to coach the team. In his lone full season as head coach of the Chicago Blackhawks (1937–38), Stewart's club won the Stanley Cup (Nichols). Significant for his new position with the AHAUS, American players made up most of the winning team, an unimaginable feat in an era when the NHL was so dominated by Canadians that even the rare player from the US was remarkable ("Chicago Blackhawks").

So with a strong, veteran team led by a coach boasting a record of unprecedented success with players from the US, the AHAUS did not immediately announce plans to join the boycott. Rather, it hoped that the IIHF would be able to convince the Soviets to permit the removal of the tournament to Stockholm. As a neutral nation, Sweden could serve as an uncontroversial host, and most of the nations planning to boycott the Moscow tournament would compete in Stockholm, although the Canadians reportedly would not have competed in any event (Nichols). In early February, the US team travelled to Europe for a pre-tournament tour, AHAUS hoping that the team might yet get to compete at the world tournament.

In the end, the Soviets refused to permit a change of venue for the tournament, and the US did not participate. The reasons leading to the US's final decision to boycott still remain obscure. On February first, the *New York Times* reported that "the State Department has withdrawn permission for the [hockey team] to go behind the Iron Curtain" (Nichols). Two weeks later, after the effort to move the tournament failed and the US officially withdrew from the tournament, the *Times* reported that AHAUS president Walter Brown claimed "the State Department would not allow the team to travel to the Soviet Union" ("Russians Voice Surprise at Decision of U.S. Hockey Team to Cancel Visit; U.S. Denies Imposing Barrier"). At the same time, though, the Associated Press reported that:

> State Department officials said today that there was no passport barrier on travel to the Soviet Union and that no bar had been raised against the United States players' trip there. However, the department said, the players were told that the feeling among European hockey players was against going to the championships and that the question was one of making it appear that the United States was more friendly to the Soviet Union than to its European allies. ("Russians Voice Surprise at Decision of U.S. Hockey Team to Cancel Visit; U.S. Denies Imposing Barrier")

How this concern about undercutting allies translated into the official decision to withdraw from the tournament was not made clear. For their part, the Soviets expressed disappointment with the US's decision. The head of the Soviet hockey association said, "Our boys had a very good impression of the American players at the last Olympics. They would have liked very much to meet them again. We remember with pleasure their sportsmanship and friendship" ("Russians Voice Surprise at Decision of U.S. Hockey Team to Cancel Visit; U.S. Denies Imposing Barrier").

Without the boycotters, the tournament field included the Soviet Union, Czechoslovakia, East Germany, Poland, Sweden, Finland, Austria and Japan. The Soviets and Swedes were the stars of the tournament, marching undefeated through the round-robin competition until they met in the last game. But the Soviets had suffered a tie at the hands of Czechoslovakia, so the Swedes had a one-point edge in the standings. Their contest took place in a snowstorm at Lenin Stadium, an outdoor venue. It set a world record for attendance at a hockey game with as many as fifty-five thousand spectators.[3] Sweden overcame a four to two third period deficit to tie the Soviets, four to four, and clinch the world championship. The Soviet

Union finished second: although undefeated in the tournament, their two ties left them with a lower place in the standings. Czechoslovakia, meanwhile, took third ("Sweden Captures 2 Hockey Crowns").

Just a few years before they would dominate international hockey, the Soviets had hosted the signature amateur event and went undefeated in the tournament. The last game between Sweden and the USSR not only decided the world championship but also set a world record for attendance at a hockey game that would stand until 2001. Despite these positives, international politics had prevented the participation of teams from Canada and the US. Fallout from what contemporaries called "the tragedy of Hungary" (Nichols) thwarted Soviet hopes for a tournament promoting "sportsmanship and friendship" (Nichols) across international political lines.

Squaw Valley, 1960

The Squaw Valley Winter Olympic Games were spared any boycotting by hockey powers, and the US, USSR, Canada, Czechoslovakia and Sweden were represented. Also present was a team from West Germany, which represented "Germany." In 1960, the IOC insisted that Germany was one geographic area which accordingly should have only one Olympic team. The US, the USSR and the Bonn and East Berlin regimes all claimed that there was only one legitimate German government. After some delicate negotiations, athletes from the democratic West and communist East appeared as part of one unified team ("Germans to Compete Under One Olympic Flag" and Gruson). In hockey, the West German national team defeated the East German team in a two-game series to win the honor of representing "Germany" at Squaw Valley ("U.S. Hockey Team Picked; Werner Injured, To Miss Olympics "). Events at Squaw Valley lent credibility to fond Soviet recollections of the "sportsmanship and friendship" of the US at Cortina, although this tournament was not without conflict.

In the late 1950s, Canada and Sweden were beginning to assemble a history of mutual hostility in the realm of hockey: many Swedes found the physical Canadian style of play barbaric, while Canadians in turn found Swedes too fearful of being hit, foreshadowing the future Canadian denigration of "chicken Swedes."[4] When their teams met in the preliminary round at Squaw Valley, the game was notably violent. It included one fistfight and fourteen penalties; two Swedes suffered injuries, although one injury came from a puck to the head ("US Gets 4 Goals in 3rd Period To Beat Czechs, 7–5, in Hockey"). The Swedish public reacted so sharply that the Canadian ambassador in Stockholm wrote Ottawa, warning that this game had brought an "ignominious and abrupt end" to "the placid surface of Swedish-Canadian relations" (quoted in Macintosh and Greenhorn, 99).

The day after the Sweden-Canada showdown, the Soviet Union trounced the team from West Germany by a lopsided eight to zero margin. However, one Soviet player "was carried off [the ice] unconscious" and two "suffered head gashes," and there were "two all-out fist-fights" late in the third period. Sounding surprisingly jovial for a player whose team was on the short end of an eight-goal rout, one of the West German players said, "It was a good game even though we lost. Those Russians put up a good fight" ("German Six Loses But Isn't Beaten").

Interestingly, the players from the US and the USSR not only avoided such violence in their own match-up, they got along very well off the ice. The Soviet captain even gave the Americans some assistance on the final morning of the tournament that may have helped to pull off the first-ever hockey gold medal for the United States. But these Russian-American friendships are even more surprising given the political backdrop to the tournament. Those in the US tend to conflate "the Fifties" into one uniform time period, often characterized as the "Happy Days." This is especially true for those who continued to live through the international developments of the 1970s, with the rise of pro-Soviet regimes, an escalating arms race and the pronouncement of the "Carter Doctrine" under which the United States would use force to prevent domination of Middle Eastern oil reserves by a hostile power. Overall, they lived through the overarching threat of impending nuclear doom.

From this perspective, 1960 looks like a period of comparative quiet in the Cold War. But if the mid-1950s were a peaceful time with Cold War diplomacy characterized by the optimistic "Spirit of Geneva," the late 1950s saw considerable Cold War tension. There was the Soviet invasion of Hungary, the Suez Crisis and Khrushchev's nuclear saber-rattling, Castro's rise to power in Cuba, growing American support for the Saigon government that eventually would consume the United States in the Vietnam War, looming turmoil in the Belgian Congo, and a festering crisis over Berlin.

Despite tension between their governments, players from the US and the USSR "hung out together like frat brothers" during the Olympic Games at Squaw Valley (Powers). A number of the American players, as well as their Soviet counterparts, were veterans of the '56 Games at Cortina.[5] The US players befriended the Soviet captain, Nikolai Sologubov, and gave him the nickname "Solly." US team captain Jack Kirrane recalled his Soviet counterpart as "a great guy" (Kirrane interview). US scoring star Bob Cleary said of the Soviets, "They're real friends. They don't talk about Communism. Like us, they talk about hockey – and girls" (quoted in Wallace). Cleary claimed to have taught Soviet star Veniamin Aleksandrov how to swear, with comical consequences: in a later game Alexandrov was given a minor penalty; in frustration he used the word his new American friends had taught him, and was hit with an additional misconduct penalty (Powers).

The US and the Soviet Union met on the ice during the round-robin play in the tournament's six-team medal round. Two days after the US beat Canada, a crowd of ten thousand packed into the eight thousand and five hundred-seat Blythe Arena to see the US battle the USSR. ("US Olympic Icers Beat Russians, 3–2") So many spectators jammed in that the US's trainer had to evict squatters from the team's bench, with the California governor reportedly among them (Crumpacker).

The game was intense and passionately played, but without the fighting of the USSR-Germany and Canada-Sweden games. The Associated Press called it "a hard-checking, viciously played game on both sides, but with no untoward incidents" ("US Olympic Icers Beat

Russians, 3–2"). The *Times* of London described the Russians as playing with "smooth competence" while the Americans countered by playing with "a kind of wild abandon ... looking faintly surprised but grimly determined whenever the puck came into their possession." The only "untoward incident" the English paper reported occurred when a cheering reporter kicked a hole in the press box ("US Successes to Round Off Olympics"). The Soviets opened a two to one lead, but the US rallied behind Bill Christian, who scored the tying goal in the second period and notched the game-winner in the third.

The next morning the US played its final game. The organizers had expected the contest between the USSR and Canada to decide the gold medal, and they had scheduled that match-up for the afternoon so that it could be shown on television in the Eastern United States. As a result, after such an emotional win over the heavily favoured Soviets, the US took to the ice to face Czechoslovakia with the chance to clinch a gold medal in a game that started at the unseemly hour of eight o'clock a.m. local time. Before the morning was over, the US would have its first gold medal in hockey, and proponents of US-USSR friendship would have a story to tell for years.

After two periods, the US trailed Czechoslovakia, four to three. Then Solly appeared in the American locker room. Despite his limited knowledge of English, he was able to communicate an idea to his American friends: that they use oxygen, which was not against Olympic rules. Squaw Valley was one mile above sea level, and using oxygen would help the Americans overcome the effects of the altitude and play with greater energy in the third period. Reports on how many Americans took the oxygen vary widely – from only two players to everyone on the team except Roger Christian – but what is not in dispute is the American rally. Roger Christian, Bill's older brother, scored three times in the final stanza to lead the US to six unanswered goals and a nine to four win.

After the game, the press made much of Sologubov's "sportsmanship" in helping the underdog Americans against the perennially powerful Czechoslovaks. What generated less attention in the US was Sologubov's ulterior motive: a loss for Czechoslovakia to the US meant that the European title would go to the Soviets. The European championships were determined by final standings at the Olympics, including even games against North Americans. This event became even more important that afternoon when the Canadian team thumped the Soviets, eight to five. Had the Czechoslovaks held on against the US, that victory would have given Czechoslovakia the European crown.

While there was surprising violence in some of the Olympic hockey games at Squaw Valley, the American and Soviet teams had a very different experience. Despite the backdrop of Cold War hostility, players from the US and the USSR had demonstrated the "sportsmanship and friendship" Soviet sports authorities had hoped to see in their 1957 world tournament. This friendship among hockey players from the US and USSR served as a vindication of those who placed faith in the peacemaking possibilities of sport, living up to IOC President Avery Brundage's hope that the Olympics would promote fair play, good sportsmanship and good relations across political barriers.

Colorado Springs and Denver, 1962

Hockey helped build friendships among American and Russian Olympians at Squaw Valley, but it would not have the same effect when the United States again hosted the highest level of world hockey in 1962. The backstory to this world championship tournament began in Germany in 1961, when the IIHF abandoned the claim that there was only one Germany, enabling both East and West Germany to send teams to the '61 world championships. Because it was the custom for the losing team in each match to salute the victor's flag, the West Germans forfeited their game against East Germany rather than risk the possibility of saluting the symbol of German Communism. This gesture had real impact in the standings, as West Germany ended up in last place, one point behind both the United States and Finland and two behind East Germany. Had the West Germans played and defeated East Germany, West Germany would have finished fifth and the East Germans last ("Canadians Win World Hockey Title" and Daley). There was subsequent speculation that the West Germans might refuse to participate in the 1962 world tournament if the East Germans also competed, and rumors that the IIHF would expel the West Germans if they skipped the tournament. But in December 1961, the West Germans announced that they were coming whether the East Germans competed or not ("West Germans to Play").

By that time, though, events had already begun that ultimately would keep the East Germans out of the tournament. For several years before August 1961, the East German government had to deal with an exodus of many of its brightest, most educated and most ambitious people who took advantage of the ease of transit within Berlin to get into West Berlin and flee from there to the West. Soviet leader Nikita Khrushchev initially rejected East German head Walter Ulbricht's demand to seal off West Berlin and cut off the flow of émigrés. Finally, lacking any better alternative, in August 1961, Khrushchev authorized the construction of what became known as the Berlin Wall.[6]

In retaliation, the Western allies adopted policies designed to prevent visits to the West from those the East German government wished to send. No Western government recognized the Communist regime in East Germany, so East German passports were not valid for travel to the West. Any East German planning to travel to the West had to obtain necessary documents from the Allied Travel Office in West Berlin. In January 1962, the American, British and French governments, which ran the Allied Travel Office, announced that they would refuse to issue the necessary travel documents in all but a limited number of cases justified by "compelling personal reasons." Sports teams coming to the West to try to promote and glorify East Germany would not be among those compelling cases (Frankel).

This had ramifications in sport beyond the world hockey championships. The world alpine skiing championships were scheduled for Chamonix, France, in March 1962. Because the East Germans could not travel to France, the *Fédération Internationale de Ski* decertified the tournament, so that it was no longer a world championship event ("Chamonix Skiing Meet Loses Its World Championship Designation"). Also affected were the world weightlifting championships, scheduled for

Hershey, Pennsylvania, but moved to Budapest, Hungary ("Tourney Goes Abroad" and "Weight Lifters Latest Affected In War of Visas"). The hockey championships were a source of concern because they would be hosted by Colorado Springs and Denver in the US. Echoes of 1957 could be heard as the Soviets and Czechoslovaks called for the IIHF to move the championships; unlike American calls in 1957 for a shift to a neutral site, though, the Soviets and Czechoslovaks wanted to serve as the alternate site ("Czechs Offer to Hold World Hockey Event" and "Russians Bid to Take Over World Hockey Event"). The IIHF declined to move the tournament, and refused on procedural grounds to even consider the Soviet request to decertify the tournament ("Motion Refused on Technicality").

Under the circumstances, the Soviets refused to compete ("Russians Withdraw From World Hockey in Colorado Next Month"). They were joined in their boycott by the teams from Czechoslovakia, Romania and Yugoslavia, some of which had planned to participate in the B Pool ("Revised Hockey Draw Will Omit Five Nations" and "Yugoslavs Withdraw"). The US and Canada were joined in the tournament by Sweden, Norway, Finland, West Germany, Switzerland and Great Britain. In another echo of 1957, the Swedes emerged from the depleted field with the championship, their first since that Moscow event. The '62 Swedes went through the tournament field undefeated and untied, winning close games against both the US and Canada.

Perhaps there is a lesson about the virtues of neutrality in Sweden's success in tournaments other hockey powers boycotted. For the clashing Cold War powers, hockey served as a political pawn to little effect. Just as the Western boycott of the '57 world championships did not force the Soviets to withdraw from Hungary, the Western allies were not about to back down from their retaliation for the Berlin Wall because of Communist absence from a hockey tournament.

Between 1956 and 1962, four different nations won the world championship in hockey: Canada, Sweden, the US and the USSR. In 1963 though, the Soviets began to dominate the sport, claiming the first of nine straight championships that transformed the world tournament from a highly competitive event into a predetermined affair.

In most years, the only nation that appeared capable of challenging Russian dominance was Czechoslovakia. Even though after 1962 political issues remained, no controversies compared to the USSR hosting the world tournament after invading Hungary or the US's refusal to admit the East German team onto their ice.

Still, hockey during the Cold War offered some useful lessons. Squaw Valley taught about the possibility for sport to promote friendly relations even among rivals in a tough, combative game at a time of pronounced hostility between their governments. But the boycotts surrounding the world tournaments in Moscow and Colorado proved that politics could place limitations on sport, regardless of the goodwill built among players and coaches. Hockey could be a surprising avenue of friendship-building during the Cold War – when tournaments were not disrupted by politics.

1. For more on the origins of Soviet hockey, see Baumann, Tarasov, Jokisipilä, Cantleton and Stark.
2. For a quick introduction to the Hungarian Revolution and the Soviet response, see Granville and Litván.
3. The Associated Press account of the game put attendance at fifty thousand. ("Sweden Captures 2," 49). When the record was broken in October 2001 by an intercollegiate game in Michigan, reporting identified the record set in Moscow at fifty-five thousand; for example, see McCabe, C22.
4. This denigration of Swedes became so pervasive that a Lexis-Nexis Academic Universe search of News, All (English, Full Text) found two hundred and sixty-two articles containing the term "chicken Swede" (search conducted August 25, 2008).
5. Five US players were on both the '56 and '60 teams: Bill Cleary, John Mayasich, Richard Meredith, Weldon Olson and Richard Rodenheiser. Because reports from the Squaw Valley Games sometimes use only surnames, it is more difficult to confirm the Soviets in attendance at both games, but it appears that four played in both: Alfred Kuchevski, Nikolai Puchkov, Genrikh Sidorenkov and Nikolai Sologubov. (Brown, 682 and "Ice Hockey Competition," 124–34).
6. For more on East German pressure and the Soviet decision to build the Wall, see Harrison.

Works Cited

Baumann, Robert F. "The Central Army Sports Club (TsSKA): Forging a Military Tradition in Soviet Ice Hockey." *Journal of Sport History* 15.1 (1988): 151–66.

Brown, Walter A. and J. F. Ahearne. "Ice Hockey." In *VII Olympic Winter Games: Official Report*, 678–88. Cortina d'Ampezzo: Comitato Olimpico Nazionale Italiano. http://la84foundation.org/6oic/OfficialReports/1956/orw1956.pdf.

"Canada Out of Tourney: Will Not Send Squad to World Hockey at Moscow in '57." *New York Times*, November 15, 1956. http://www.proquest.com/.

"Canadians Win World Hockey Title." *Washington Post*, March 13, 1961. http://www.proquest.com/.

Cantleton, Hart. "Revisiting the Introduction of Ice Hockey into the Former Soviet Union." In *Putting it on Ice*. Vol. 2, *Internalizing "Canada's Game,"* edited by Colin Howell, 29–38. Halifax: Gorsebrook Research Institute, 2003.

"Chamonix Skiing Meet Loses Its World Championship Designation." *New York Times*, February 6, 1962. http://www.proquest.com/.

"Chicago Blackhawks." *Total Hockey: The Official Encyclopedia of the National Hockey League*. 2nd ed. Edited by Dan Diamond, 213–7. New York: Total Sports, 2000.

Crumpacker, John. "As Cold War Raged, U. S. Hockey Team Made History." *San Francisco Chronicle*, January 15, 2002. http://www.lexisnexis.com/.

"Czechs Offer to Hold World Hockey Event." *Washington Post*, February 2, 1962. http://www.proquest.com/.

Daley, Robert. "Canada Trounces Soviet Union and Captures World Amateur Hockey Crown." *New York Times*, March 13, 1961. http://www.proquest.com/.

Frankel, Max. "West Bars East Germans In Retaliation for the Wall." *New York Times*, January 27, 1962.

"German Six Loses But Isn't Beaten." *New York Times*, February 21, 1960, sec. 5.

"Germans to Compete Under One Olympic Flag." *New York Times*, November 20, 1959.

Granville, Johanna C. *In The Line of Fire: The Soviet Crackdown on Hungary, 1956–1958*. The Carl Beck Papers in Russian and East European Studies. Pittsburgh: Center for Russian and East European Studies, University of Pittsburgh, 1998.

Gruson, Sydney. "A German Flag Set for Olympics." *New York Times*, December 7, 1959.

Harrison, Hope M. *Driving the Soviets up the Wall: Soviet-East German Relations, 1953–1961*. Princeton: Princeton University Press, 2003.

Howell, Colin D., ed. *Putting it on Ice*. Vol. 2, *Internationalizing "Canada's Game."* Halifax: Gorsebrook Research Institute, 2003.

"Ice Hockey Competition." In *VIII Olympic Winter Games 1960, Squaw Valley, California: Final Report*, edited by Robert Rubin, 123–35. Irvine, CA: California Olympic Commission. http://www.la84foundation.org/6oic/OfficialReports/1960/1960w.pdf.

Jokisipilä, Markku. "Maple Leaf, Hammer, and Sickle: International Ice Hockey During the Cold War." *Sport History Review* 37, no.1 (2006): 36–53.

Kirrane, Jack. Telephone interview with John Soares, February 4, 2004.

Lechenperg, Harald, ed. *Olympic Games 1960: Squaw Valley, Rome*. New York: A. S. Barnes & Company, 1960.

Litván, György. *The Hungarian Revolution of 1956: Reform, Revolt and Repression, 1953–1963*. Translated by János M. Bak and Lyman H. Legters. London: Longman Publishing, 1996.

Macintosh, Donald and Donna Greenhorn. "Hockey Diplomacy and Canadian Foreign Policy." *Journal of Canadian Studies* 28, no. 2 (1993): 96–112.

McCabe, Jim. "Pond Hockey on Center Stage Spartan Stadium Site of Showdown." *Boston Globe*, October 7, 2001. http://www.lexisnexis.com/.

"Motion Refused on Technicality." *New York Times*, March 8, 1962.

Nichols, Joseph C. "Wild Bill Stewart's U.S. Sextet Hopes to Tame Its Rivals." *New York Times*, February 1, 1957.

Powers, John. "The Little Site That Could The 1960 Winter Games Were A Major Success For a Miniature Ski Resort Called Squaw Valley." *Boston Globe*, January 20, 2002. http://www.lexisnexis.com/.

"Revised Hockey Draw Will Omit Five Nations." *New York Times*, February 20, 1962.

"Russians Bid to Take Over World Hockey Event." *Washington Post*, February 10, 1962. http://www.proquest.com/.

"Russians Voice Surprise at Decision of U.S. Hockey Team to Cancel Visit; U.S. Denies Imposing Barrier." *New York Times*, February 17, 1957.

"Russians Withdraw From World Hockey in Colorado Next Month." *New York Times*, February 16,1962.

Stark, Tobias. "The Pioneer, The Pal and the Poet: Masculinities and National Identities in Canadian, Swedish & Soviet Hockey During the Cold War." In *Putting it on Ice*. Vol. 2, *Internalizing "Canada's Game,"* edited by Colin Howell, 39–43. Halifax: Gorsebrook Research Institute, 2003.

"Sweden Captures 2 Hockey Crowns." *New York Times*, March 6, 1957.

"Swiss Boycott Reds." *Los Angeles Times*, December 29, 1956. http://www.proquest.com/.

Tarasov, Anatoly. *Road to Olympus*. Toronto: Pocket Books, 1972.

"Tourney Goes Abroad." *New York Times*, March 8, 1962.

"U.S. Gets 4 Goals in 3rd Period To Beat Czechs, 7–5, in Hockey." *New York Times*, February 20, 1960.

"U.S. Hockey Team Picked; Werner Injured, To Miss Olympics." *New York Times*, December 13, 1959, sec. 5.

"U.S. Olympic Icers Beat Russians, 3–2." *Cincinnati Enquirer*, February 28, 1960.

"U.S. Successes to Round Off Olympics." *The Times* (London), February 29, 1960.

Wallace, Bill. "First Olympic Hockey 'Miracle' Men Are Worth Remembering." *Bridge News*, February 29, 2000. http://www.lexisnexis.com/.

"Weight Lifters Latest Affected In War of Visas." *Washington Post*, March 9, 1962. http://www.proquest.com/.

"West Germans to Play." *New York Times*, December 22, 1961. http://www.proquest.com/.

"Yugoslavs Withdraw." *New York Times*, February 21, 1962.

Sam McKegney

The Aboriginal Art of Wake-Swimming

or The Media Mythologization of Jonathan Cheechoo

Long before they became teammates for the San Jose Sharks, the NHL's deadliest scoring duo and the winners of the Hart and Rocket Richard trophies, Joe Thornton and Jonathan Cheechoo met at the waterfront home of Sharks' netminder Seamus Kotyk. Regarding this "chance summertime" engagement, Thornton recalls, "I got him out water-skiing behind my boat," adding, "It's funny when you look back on it" (Cruickshank). The anecdote is funny, I suppose, because of the perhaps unintentional analogy it supplies, suggesting that when Cree sniper Cheechoo catapulted to the top of the NHL scoring race in the latter half of the 2005–2006 season he was actually being propelled by Thornton, who had been acquired by the Sharks on November 30, 2005. In fact, during Cheechoo's rise to scoring supremacy that season, various commentators described Cheechoo in words similar to those of Scott Cruickshank: as "coasting in the big man's wake, ... being pulled along by Thornton, ... riding the Joe-created wave" (Cruickshank). While Cruickshank is quick to dismiss his own interpretation as "too easy. Vaguely insulting. And, in fact, wrong," the wake-swimming analogy aptly captures dominant media constructions of the Thornton-Cheechoo relationship throughout and following the 2005–2006 NHL season. *The Halifax Daily News*, for instance, argues that Thornton's arrival in San Jose "*transformed*

Cheechoo from a solid third-line forward ... into an elite winger," a sentiment echoed by CanWest reporter Joanne Ireland who claims Cheechoo was, again, "*transformed* [by the trade] into the league's most dangerous goal scorer." Greg Davis of *The Timmins Daily Press* contends that "Cheechoo's scoring surge can be *attributed* to the arrival of Thornton"; while Darren Eliot suggests that "Cheechoo went from average winger to super sniper with Thornton feeding him the pucks"; *Sports Illustrated*'s Allan Muir argues most pointedly that Thornton "*turned* Jonathan Cheechoo into the league's most deadly sniper. Let that sink in for a moment," he adds condescendingly, "*Jonathan Cheechoo.*" Muir actually places the name in italics to suggest his, and presumably the reader's, disbelief.

Media renderings of the Thornton/Cheechoo duo consistently afford subject status to the former while withholding it from the latter; the character of Joe Thornton is constructed as active agent, as "hero" and as star of the Sharks' 2006 season, while the character of Cheechoo is constructed as a once-dormant entity activated by the hero, a sidekick, a member of the supporting cast. Consider, for example, the Mike Brophy headline – "Riding Shotgun" – which positions Cheechoo as a passenger along for the ride while placing Thornton in the proverbial driver's seat. Yet surprisingly, with the possible exception of Muir, none of these commentators is expressly derisive towards Cheechoo. In fact, virtually all of the dozens of articles from 2006 celebrate the *story* of Jonathan Cheechoo (even if they don't construct the winger as the protagonist in his own tale). *Edmonton Journal* columnist John MacKinnon characterizes Cheechoo's journey from the Cree community of Moose Factory to Sharks sniper as a "feel-good story" that "doesn't get old." Pierre LeBrun calls Cheechoo's 2006 season "one of the game's great stories". And Bob Duff calls Cheechoo's "torrid" scoring pace, "combined with [his] native heritage and the circuitous route he took to the NHL ... among the most romantic and compelling" stories in recent NHL history.

Let's wrestle with this paradox: why is Cheechoo's story one that hockey reporters, and Canadians more generally, love to tell and retell, yet they feel the need to place Cheechoo in a subordinate role in that tale. In general, Canadians love Cheechoo, not as scorer, but as scorer-by-proxy. The source of the paradox is anxiety about the Canadian self-image, anxiety the sport of hockey has historically been wielded to relieve. The media-constructed story of Jonathan Cheechoo reacts to the psychic needs of a nation threatened by the loss of 'its sport.' Cheechoo's often romanticized upbringing in the "True North" of Moose Factory northern Ontario, where he learned to play the game on outdoor rinks, situates the nation's sport in the Canadian landscape as firmly as any narrative. His Cree heritage further serves to indigenize the game, accentuating the perception that it is *Native* to Canada. Thus when the Cree sniper takes the American city of San Jose by storm, he is not demonstrating the game's departure from Canada but rather the retention of Canadianness on foreign soil, because by virtue of his indigeneity Cheechoo's attachment to a Canadian landscape remains unquestioned in the Canadian national imaginary. However, by virtue of this same indigeneity, Cheechoo alone cannot provide the mirror in which mainstream Canada can validate its self-image; the Native remains "Other" or "not self" to many Canadians. Enter Joe Thornton, a big, strapping Canadian lad from London, Ontario, whose mercurial hands are matched only by his hawk-like vision. If Cheechoo, as romantic embodiment of "Canada the hockey nation," *requires* the influence of the non-Native Thornton to be successful, then the Canadian national image is doubly protected. Indigeneity, which is required to support the belief that hockey is Canada's game, is celebrated through Cheechoo's success, but that success is not generated solely by an Indigenous figure with whom mainstream Canada will never wholly identify. By making Cheechoo the sidekick in what is essentially a western hero myth, members of the Canadian hockey media incorporate the indigeneity of hockey without arresting Euro-Canadian dominance or complicating mainstream Canadians' sense of belonging within the Canadian nation.

The idyllic image of hockey as national sport arising naturally from the Canadian landscape is currently besieged by two forces, southern expansionism and commercialization, the first of which threatens the game's connection to place, the second of which threatens its integrity, or perhaps authenticity. In the face of such toxins,

Cheechoo's story offers, if not an antidote, then certainly a form of life-support that comforts Canadians against the idyllic image's (perhaps inevitable) demise. Cheechoo's hockey story resists the siren pull of commercialization by emerging in response to the landscape itself. Growing up in a community way up north on James Bay with no arenas or leagues and only outdoor ice on which to play, Cheechoo learned to love the game through what many commentators have referred to as its purest expression: shinny. In fact, Cheechoo didn't play what could be referred to as organized hockey until he was fourteen. The idea of shinny not as *supplement* to hockey development but as *source* suggests the material and symbolic importance of a northern landscape, where ice is a natural process rather than a synthetic product. In the face of the diaspora of Canadian NHL players to US cities (not to mention former Canadian teams), the recognition that the Canadian north is still one of the few places on earth where one can become a hockey player without institutional interventions is immensely important to the Canadian self-image. Furthermore, the idea of hockey as a cohesive force for community formation, as opposed to the dispersing force for expansion in an American or colonial model, cements the symbolic attraction of Cheechoo's story. The close-knit community of Moose Factory has rallied around him to foster his growth as a hockey player, raising more than $10, 000 over the years to send him to hockey schools and different lessons. The community came out in droves to support Cheechoo at the OHL draft, and at his NHL draft, "about one hundred twenty family members and friends from Moose Factory" were in attendance (Laskaris). Hockey, in this depiction, becomes a source of community cohesion that brings people together, a vehicle for mutual identification and the creation of communal meaning.

Northrop Frye argues that:

> [a]t the heart of all social mythology lies what may be called ... a pastoral myth, the vision of a social ideal. The pastoral myth in its most common form is associated with childhood, or with some earlier social condition – pioneer life, the small town, the habitant rooted to his land – that can be identified

> with childhood. The nostalgia for a world of peace and protection, with a spontaneous response to the nature around it, with a leisure and composure not to be found today, is particularly strong in Canada. (362)

Cheechoo's symbiotic relationship to his nurturing community, as constructed in media depictions of his youth and childhood, provides a "vision of [the] social ideal" often configured through the language of "pastoral myth." The exotic distance to Moose Factory, and its miniscule population of two thousand seven hundred, offers an image readily aligned with "pioneer life" – or perhaps traditional Indigenous existence – where one can choose, as Cheechoo is described in one article as choosing, between being a hunter/trapper and being a hockey player. "The land beckoned," writes Michael Farber, "but so did a net designed to trap nothing but pucks." Motivated by what Frye might describe as the nostalgia of disillusioned hockey reporters writing in Canadian and American cities, the world created in narratives of Cheechoo's youth is indeed one "of peace and protection" and one in which hockey emerges as "a spontaneous response to … nature."

Given the omnipresence of references to Cheechoo's Cree heritage in media depictions of his development, this nostalgia seems complicated, to some degree, by race. And if the goal of rehearsing Cheechoo's upbringing through media representations is to soothe Canadian anxiety about the loss of Canada's sport, then the question of what is at stake for mainstream Canadians in depicting Cheechoo's cultural background must arise. First, the flipside of mobilizing Cheechoo's indigeneity in the symbolic project of keeping hockey Canadian is the admission of non-Native Canadians' lack of indigeneity; if hockey truly springs from the Canadian landscape, then it is not technically "ours," the settler Canadian must confess. Second, the image of the Native is burdened by the weight of colonial history. When non-Native Canadians, who are the beneficiaries of land theft, governmental duplicity and attempted cultural genocide, confront the image of the Native, they must simultaneously confront their complicity. Thus in order to render the image of the Native capable of consolidating the mainstream Canadian self-image (which most desire to view as benevolent and just rather than corrupt and racist), commentators are inclined to employ narrative strategies of manipulation; they are encouraged to construct stories that facilitate feelings of vicarious indigeneity for non-Native Canadians, but ones that do not force them to face the reality of Canadian treatment of Natives which would tarnish the national image thus created.

In *Fear and Temptation: Images of the Indigene in Canadian, Australian, and New Zealand Literatures,* Terry Goldie argues that "Canadians have, and long have had, a clear agenda to erase [the] separation of belonging" that impacts their relationship to the Canadian landscape. Goldie explains the condition as follows: "The white Canadian looks at the Indian. The Indian is Other and therefore alien. But the Indian is indigenous and therefore cannot be alien. So the Canadian must be alien. But how can the Canadian be alien within Canada?" (12). The national neurosis thus produced generates a need for what Goldie calls "indigenization" or "the impossible necessity of becoming indigenous" (13). By controlling images of indigeneity through literature, media and art, non-Natives pressure "the indigene as not-self [to] become self" (223); they incorporate the image of the Native into the national self-image, but by maintaining non-Native control over that image, they avoid troubling the power dynamics of white privilege in Canada or addressing the misery of the colonial past. This is how the media constructions of the Thornton/Cheechoo duo from 2006 function; this is their ideological baggage; these are the anxieties they endeavour to soothe.

At the opening of the 2006 Stanley Cup playoffs, *Sports Illustrated* columnist Darren Eliot (who is from Milton, Ontario, by the way) wrote: "In San Jose, [Joe Thornton] is authoring a West Coast thriller – one in which he asserts himself as the hero." Eliot's literary metaphor is apt, given the way sports media narratives colour Canadian perceptions of characters like Thornton or Cheechoo and the way narrative provides the link between sporting action and national mythology. The positioning of Thornton as both author and hero is similarly telling. As author/hero, Thornton is multidimensional whereas Cheechoo is one-dimensional, a stock character and, according to Jim Matheson, "Jumbo Joe's sidekick." As Thornton characterizes Cheechoo in an interview: "He just scores – that's what he does" (Cruickshank). The stereotypical sidekick image of the monolithic Native defined by a single characteristic – here scoring ability – suggests the limits imposed on Native identity by the Canadian national imaginary. By misrepresenting the complexity of lived experience and the multi-faceted nature of individual existence, one-dimensionality betrays a dehumanizing impulse. Also, as author, Thornton is afforded the luxury of self-creation. To extend the literary metaphor, Thornton writes himself into being, charting his own course and mapping out his own actions, while Cheechoo remains constructed from without, his actions circumscribed by a dominant and dominating discourse.

By depicting Joe Thornton as the hero in stories celebrating the rise of Jonathan Cheechoo from pond skater to Rocket Richard winner, non-Native commentators (however subconsciously) seek to naturalize hockey to the Canadian landscape while simultaneously erasing what Goldie calls their own "separation of belonging." Because, according to this mythic storyline, the Native *requires* the non-Native in order to actualize his potential, the indigenization of hockey can ultimately be shared by non-Native Canadian writers and readers, by the "imagined community" of the Canadian hockey state. Yes, the Cree character of Cheechoo embodies for these scribes the idyllic image of pure Canadian hockey that initially appears impenetrably indigenous, but because the professional consummation of the character can only occur through the heroism of the non-Native character of Thornton, the non-Native discursive body can create for itself a vicarious indigeneity. In Goldie's words, they can indigenize. Moreover, they can exult in the Indigenous while maintaining a colonial power structure that privileges the non-Native. As far back as *The Jesuit Relations* from the seventeenth century, European commentators have been recognizing the *natural* gifts of Native peoples while arguing for European intervention to bring those gifts to fruition. Father Paul Le Jeune wrote in 1634 that the Natives he encountered in Quebec "have good figures, their bodies are well made, their limbs very well proportioned, and they ... are fairly intelligent" (*The Jesuit

Relations and Allied Documents, 18). Yet, he maintained that they lack the necessary "education and instruction" that could be acquired, in Le Jeune's mind, solely through Europeans; hence his unwavering promotion of the missionary endeavour. Le Jeune's views in this regard characterize what James (Sákéj) Youngblood Henderson has defined as "Eurocentric diffusionism": the belief that "the normal and natural way that the non-European world progresses – or changes for the better ... – is by the [spread] of innovative, progressive ideas from Europe, which flow into it as air flows into a vacuum" (61). Although they may appear antiquated, Le Jeune's ideas explicitly underpinned Canadian federal policies of assimilation until very recently, and we find in the media-constructed story of Thornton and Cheechoo their contemporary echo: Cheechoo is "honest" and "hard-working," an imposing presence with a knack around the net, yet what Sharks' coach Ron Wilson has characterized as Thornton's outstanding "vision" is lacking. The Euro-Canadian is *required* to harness the potential of the Indigenous. Joe Thornton is needed, again quoting Muir, to "[turn] Jonathan Cheechoo into the league's most deadly sniper" (Muir). The story thus validates the colonial myths upon which Canada has been built, painting in broad strokes over historical legacies of dispossession and injustice.

It has been my goal to neither debunk Cheechoo's naysayers, nor to recoup his *actual* performance in the 2005–2006 season. That is largely beside the point. (Although I do find it surprising that anyone with even a passing knowledge of high-level hockey could imply, as many commentators do, that a mediocre player could rack up fifty-six goals simply by being placed with a superstar, particularly when that player scored twenty-eight goals in his sophomore campaign skating on the third-line.) According to Wilson again, "that's not the way it works in the NHL. You have to have the ability to score. [And Cheechoo] has that knack" (Brownlee). Rather, my purpose has been to demonstrate how something like sports writing that is often perceived as politically benign can be racially inflected and how the stories we tell about our sports stars often invoke the images they do, not because of the stories' truth but because of our own anxieties and desires. With the Canadian self-image threatened by the ongoing loss of "Canada's game," stories that highlight hockey's natural connection to the northern Canadian landscape, while simultaneously imbuing with national significance the southern success of quintessentially Canadian heroic duos, are likely to continue to be embraced by both mainstream Canadian readers and the sports writers who address them. Thus, like most narratives readily absorbed into the national imaginary, Cheechoo's story tells us more about popular Canadian desires than it does about the characters upon whom national mythologies are built and rebuilt. It tells us about the racialist nature of the Canadian self-image, about Canadian anxieties and desires and about relationships to Canadian history. The story of Jonathan Cheechoo, as it is articulated in sports pages and barrooms and basements, is a story about what Canadians *want* to believe about Canada, its game and its national identity.

Works Cited

Brophy, Mike. "Riding Shotgun." *Western Star*, February 13, 2006.

Brownlee, Robin. "Jonathan Cheechoo hits scoring stride for Sharks." *North Bay Nugget*, January 28, 2006.

"Cheechoo's amazing season pays off." *Halifax Daily News*, April 20, 2006.

"Cheechoo sets a fine example." *Timmins Daily Press*, February 9, 2006.

Cruickshank, Scott. "Cheechoo can light the lamp – Joe or no." *Calgary Herald*, February 7, 2006.

Davis, Greg. "Cheechoo hits 40 goals." *Timmins Daily Press*, March 15, 2006.

Duff, Bob. "Pride of Moose Factory lighting up NHL scoreboards." *Windsor Star*, March 24, 2006.

Eliot, Darren. "Rising to the occasion: Brodeur and Thornton answer questions at key time." *Sports Illustrated*, April 20, 2006. http://sportsillustrated.cnn.com/2006/writers/darren_eliot/04/10/brodeur.thornton/index.html.

Farber, Michael. "Do you know the names in San Jose?" *Sports Illustrated*, April 26, 2004.

Frye, Northrop. *Northrop Frye on Canada* V. 12. Eds. Jean O'Grady and David Staines. Toronto: University of Toronto Press, 2003.

Goldie, Terry. *Fear and Temptation: The Image of the Indigene in Canadian, Australian, and New Zealand Literatures*. Montreal: McGill-Queen's University Press, 1989.

Henderson, James (Sákéj) Youngblood. "Postcolonial Ghost Dancing: Diagnosing European Colonialism." In *Reclaiming Indigenous Voice and Vision*, edited by Marie Battiste, 57–76. Vancouver: UBC Press, 2000.

Ireland, Joanne. "Thornton-Samsonov: Once Bruin teammates now foes." *CanWest News*, May 7, 2006.

Laskaris, Sam. "Cree youth tabbed as future NHL star." *Windspeaker*, July 1997.

LeBrun, Pierre. "Cheechoo." *StarPhoenix*, March 18, 2006.

MacKinnon, John. "Cheechoo giving his fans a thrill." *Edmonton Journal*, May 6, 2006.

Matheson, Jim. "Cheech and Chong make great pair." *Edmonton Journal*, March 4, 2006.

Mealing, S. R., ed. *The Jesuit Relations and Allied Documents: A Selection*. Translated by Reuben Gold Thwaites. Ottawa: Carleton University Press, 1963.

Muir, Allan. "Something to prove: MVP candidate Thornton needs to shine in playoffs." *Sports Illustrated*, May 8, 2006. http://sportsillustrated.cnn.com/2006/writers/allan_muir/05/05/thornton.mvp/index.html.

Anne Hartman

"Here for a Little Pickup?"

Notes on Women's Shinny Hockey in Toronto Public Parks

Shinny, outdoor ice hockey played with a minimum of equipment and few formal rules, is often considered the "heart and soul" of hockey, a sport itself saturated with mythologies of Canadian identity. Shinny is used to symbolize Canadian democracy, "fair play," closeness to nature and innocence, all with a tint of nostalgic longing; an image of children playing shinny appears on our five-dollar bill. Although the professional and international levels of the game take up a lot of energy in the discussion of hockey's place in Canada, these versions of hockey, which are enthusiastically used to represent us to each other and to the world, are played by a select few under the gaze of millions on the sidelines. Shinny, on the other hand, is supposed to be, as the title of a National Film Board documentary puts it, "the hockey in all of us." In shinny, we are all invited to join the game. Yet upon examination, it is abundantly clear that even when it comes to shinny, "all of us" are not the same in hockey culture, nor, by extension, in current narratives of the nation. It is from a somewhat marginal position that I do research on hockey culture in Canada, as someone who is part of the richly textured, vibrant and yet undocumented phenomenon of women's shinny in Toronto parks.

I am a social anthropologist, a discipline that most people associate with a search for the "exotic" practices of people in cultures radically different from our own. This may have been more accurate at one time, before post-colonial critique forced the discipline to address its own locations, although historians of anthropology (Darnell, Di Leonardo) argue that anthropologists have always worked in ways that critiqued and contextualized their own cultural backgrounds. In many cases, anthropologists' work far afield reflected their own cultures back to them and revealed different possibilities for ways of being in the world. So people are often curious about what a Canadian anthropologist might make of shinny hockey – perhaps especially an anthropologist who passes as an "unhyphenated Canadian" studying the dynamics of such a potent symbol of Canada. Many expect me to make pronouncements about how shinny is "Canadian culture," which of course it is, but that can be said of anything that happens here. Shinny is fascinating because it is so clearly and emotionally marked as being quintessentially Canadian that it has become a lightning rod for sentiment about the nation. Also, because it is by definition unbounded by rules, it can also exist both inside and outside the dominant discourse in unpredictable ways, and it is this complicated relationship that makes it interesting to me as an anthropologist.

My research on shinny comes to life in a very literal way. I get cold, tired, exhilarated, annoyed, thrilled; I get caught up in the game and sometimes in the tensions and struggles over access to space or between competing visions of what shinny is or ought to be. Because of the sprawling, urban character of Toronto, I spend a lot of time on public transit and have conversations with fellow passengers and drivers who see me coming and going with my gear. One of the tricky things about doing fieldwork on shinny is that it is an inherently *disorganized* sport. Shinny players are by definition not bounded by any organization and usually resist attempts to formalize anything, including rules. Finding them and hearing their stories requires the researcher to break a sweat.

Rather than aiming to celebrate shinny uncritically, my research is at least partly motivated by a longstanding interest in questions of "belonging," and in what Ann Stoler calls the "politics of affect" in a multicultural settler society that casts itself, paradoxically, as postcolonial. Canada was founded as and remains a settler society, and is thus always "unsettled" in another sense, unsure about its rootedness and self-conscious in its declarations of identity. Because shinny is so thoroughly entangled in Canadian nationalism, it cannot be understood as just a game. For some, shinny hockey feels like a birthright, and for others, it is not an easy fit: it must be negotiated at every turn. And yet shinny is compelling. Despite the barriers that many of us face, it is an awful lot of *fun*. Women who come out to play in Toronto often express degrees of ambivalence towards mainstream hockey culture, noting its sexism, homophobia and culture of whiteness, and yet they are passionate about the game itself. Many relish the speed, danger and good-natured aggression, as well as the emphasis on equity and the do-it-yourself aspects of shinny.

What happens to hockey when it is played by those sidelined by the dominant narratives of Canada? Can shinny-playing be understood as a potentially resistant practice, or the shinny rink as a sort of queer space? These games are at once examples of creative collective endeavour and fraught with narratives that have never easily fit gendered, racialized or queer bodies and experiences. For example, although shinny is usually defined by its lack of set rules, as part of hockey culture in Canada it is still full of unwritten norms that make it a potentially uncomfortable experience for those who don't fit the standard image of the hockey player.

Having spent the last several years conducting ethnographic fieldwork on women's shinny in Toronto, I find I can neither argue that women's shinny games are attempts to fit in to dominant notions of Canadianness – an example of the "opening up" of hockey culture – nor that they are wholly oppositional. They are deeply ambivalent, shaped by struggles over access and resources, full of mixed feelings and degrees of complicity and resistance; such games occupy what ethnographer Kathleen Stewart calls "a space on the side of the road," a location which everyone thinks they know because it is already defined by the dominant culture, but which can also be understood as a space where Other things can happen.

Gender, ambivalence and shinny hockey

Like most of the female players that I have met on the ice, I did not grow up playing hockey. Although as a kid I was quick to point out that I wasn't wearing *boys' skates*, but *hockey skates*, playing hockey was not really on the radar until I was a graduate student in Peterborough, when some friends dragged me away from my stacks of books, and out to the frozen canal. A scholar of post-colonial and post-structuralist theory and critical Canadian studies, I was surprised, even somewhat embarrassed, at my immediate love of shinny hockey. With our breath fogging as we careened crazily around the ice in the moonlight, snow falling on the pines, I felt like I had landed in a doughnut commercial. How could I possibly square this newfound love of the game with hockey culture as I knew it – that anxiously hetero Old Boys' Club, that overstated nationalist icon? I wasn't sure, but I went out the next day and bought myself a stick.

During the early phase of my PhD in Toronto, I spent a lot of time worrying about what my doctoral research project would be. The pressures of research and writing papers and teaching made this a stressful time, and after hearing about a city-run hockey skills program at a nearby park, I relieved the tension by playing every chance I got. Unlike league play, it was very inexpensive, didn't require much more than skates and a stick, and I could get there on the streetcar. As I played improvised but intense games with an ever-changing assortment of strangers, friends and acquaintances, I was struck by what seemed more and more to be an amazingly vibrant subculture that "someone should write about." It was later, during the winters of 2007 and 2008, that I undertook ethnographic fieldwork on women's shinny; playing, talking, interviewing and engaging in a lot of what anthropologist Clifford Geertz called "deep hanging out" in rink clubhouses, penalty boxes, bars and greasy spoons. These other shinny fanatics, who came out all winter long, often traversing the city with hockey sticks in tow several times a week, ranged from university students to women in their sixties, moms with their kids, constellations of queer and straight, a whole range of personalities. They were a critical and creative bunch of documentary filmmakers, microbiologists, social justice activists, teachers, performance artists, lawyers, musicians, professors and writers. I was also surprised to learn that I was far from the oldest beginner when I started in my late twenties; many took up the game in their forties and fifties. Although many of us were first- or second-generation Canadians, the vast majority were "white" (small-town Euro-Canadian, Jewish, Northern European), with only a smattering of players of Japanese, Chinese and Afro-Caribbean heritage. A number of interviewees pointed out this rather glaring absence as disconcerting, given Toronto's diversity, noting that whiteness has long been part of the image – if not the reality – of hockey culture. While we all came to shinny from different directions, it seemed that most had ambivalent feelings about hockey culture and our uneasy places within it. This all suggested alternate ways of thinking about shinny, about other types of hockey not reflected in stories of "hockey's heart."

The City of Toronto operates several dozen artificially-cooled outdoor ice rinks in the heart of downtown, and assists in the maintenance of some unofficial natural rinks as well. Toronto also has its share of "illegal" games on Grenadier Pond in High Park and at the rink at City Hall at night when the pleasure-skaters have gone home. My research focused most closely on the rinks at which women's shinny has taken hold. At these rinks I played with, met and spoke to many of the women I would later interview about their experiences playing shinny. These conversations often touched on childhood and the degree of access to hockey, the appeal of shinny as free play, and included oral histories of local women's shinny. The recent history of women's shinny at Dufferin Grove, for example, officially only goes back about five years, although someone has taped a newspaper clipping documenting a women's game in the park in 1938 on the clubhouse wall. Trinity Bellwoods Park has had women's shinny on Monday nights for at least a dozen years. One experienced player, Susan,[1] recalled that there have been women's games at Greenwood Park since the 1980s, which were apparently started by some players from the Women's Hockey Club of Toronto (known colloquially as "the dyke league" or "the Moss Park league"). To this day the Saturday morning games at Greenwood are a popular pre-brunch activity for east-end dykes, while players at other rinks are more mixed.

At Dufferin Grove, now a popular site for women's games and free skills classes, women's shinny began at the urging of players like tournament organizer Deirdre Norman. Norman found that the "open shinny" times were a barrier to women's participation; rinks dominated by men could be intensely uncomfortable and even downright hostile to female players. At present some rinks have developed popular weekly games for women, while at others, such as Rosedale, the women's game is more subject to attendance and often gets pushed aside in favour of the fast-paced young men's games the rink is known for. And attendance itself can be difficult to gauge. There have been nights where I have shown up to check out a new rink, seen a group of guys in the middle of a game and decided that it was not worth my time and effort to take a stand about women's shinny. I have heard many stories of other women "lurking" by the shinny pad, waiting to see if other women showed up before deciding whether to play. Much depends on the willingness of staff – mostly young men on a first-name basis with the players – to step in when necessary to uphold the schedule.

Although the climate differs from rink to rink, male resistance to women's shinny is something players have to deal with regularly. Almost everyone has stories of occasional harassment, which sometimes takes the form of a heated rinkside debate over policy, or in some cases by male players refusing to stop interfering with a women's game by taking up space on the ice. In these situations, the guys often argue that a policy of women-only shinny is sexist, because "open shinny" is meant to include everyone. Thus, the argument goes, in having specific times set aside, women have "special rights" over and above those of male players. In these situations, the difficulty often lies in communicating to the men what's at stake in having "women's shinny," namely equity. While open shinny is an example of "equality" insofar as everyone has equal access to the rink regardless of gender, "equity" recognizes that equal rights on paper do not mean equality in practice, and thus there ought to be attempts made to achieve a better balance in terms of access to these public resources. Usually, the game goes on as planned after this is explained. However the women-only status is open to debate. For example, on a slow night, if there are only five or six women on the ice and more bodies are needed for a game, and *if* all the women agree, then guys hanging out in the penalty box might be told that it's alright if they want to join the game on condition that there's no "hot-dogging." If any of the women object to having men play, on principle, that is the deciding vote; consensus must be reached before bending that particular rule.

It is not the case that most of the women who play are separatists, or tar all men with the same brush, as the men often assume, but rather that they value the opportunity to play with other women because it is a more comfortable environment. It is somewhat ironic, but women's games are the times players often feel free to stop thinking constantly about their gender and how it influences their treatment by other players, whether hostile, friendly or patronizing. While some of my interviewees did claim that women play with a different philosophy than men do, and gave this as a reason for preferring women's shinny, most of the women I spoke with about shinny believe that differences between the "open" game and the women's games are the product of socialization rather than some inherent difference. Most female shinny players that I spoke with came to hockey as adults, due to the lack of access to hockey they experienced as children. But some players noted that it is not necessarily easier for male beginners, especially those marked by race, sexuality or class, to enter into hockey culture as adults.

Shinny is a game that is usually defined by its lack of formalized rules, but regular players have very clear ideas about what *is* and what is *not* shinny in terms of game play, aesthetics and philosophy, and these ideas are open to debate. Beginnings and endings are fuzzy; at the beginning of the game, players circle the rink, chatting and practicing their moves until someone throws her stick down in the centre, prompting others to do the same. Eyes closed, someone divides the sticks into two piles, creating the teams. Nobody keeps score, except to note when the teams seem unbalanced; if one team dominates, players will be reshuffled, which makes for some confusion – after such a realignment, I'll end up on the same team as Yellow Sweater and Sue from the game before, but The Girl in the Blue Helmet, who was on the other team ten minutes ago is now my trusted winger waiting for my pass. The game is over when the lights go off, the number of players peters out or the falling snow gets too deep to allow the puck to move. Equity is central to this version of shinny; most of the skilled players make sure that novices get to touch the puck, while also gently pushing them to skate faster. Players who hog the puck or raise it too high are restrained with a few well-chosen mutterings, as are attempts to impose too much order on the game. More than once I've heard it said of players who got angry or frustrated that "she has no sense of irony." Being "hard core" is respected – coming out to play on the coldest or wettest nights, or not wearing a helmet – but for us (a bunch of lefties, queer women and middle-aged moms) playing shinny is something that requires a sense of humour.

Roughly half of the women I interviewed were also members of organized hockey leagues; those who were not were adamant that shinny and hockey were different games. When asked about the appeal of shinny in particular, Nan, a self-described "adrenaline junkie" in her early sixties, laughs and says she loves having an outlet for her aggression. Diane, another player, talks about how we, counter to the widespread assumption that play is for children, never outgrow the love of "running in packs." Esther mentions that as a mother, it is not always easy to take time out for oneself rather than the kids or work, and shinny means fresh air and exercise minus the team-scheduled commitment and expense of league hockey. Although the women playing shinny in Toronto were overwhelmingly middle class, the principle of shinny is that it ought to be free of expenses for such things as helmets or fancy equipment. The aesthetic preference is for things well-worn and retro: you see more running jackets, handknitted curling sweaters and toques than official NHL jerseys.

Women's shinny is all the more intense because the time is limited; there are women's games almost every night of the week in different parts of town, but the season is at its peak for about three months, from December to February, and much hinges on the weather. One never knows whether an early thaw will mean a week's break or the end of the shinny season altogether. The hard core players talk of trying to cram in as much shinny as the season will allow, making sure that word gets out about sparsely-attended women's shinny timeslots lest they disappear from the schedule. Despite this intensity, when asked whether they know their fellow players outside shinny, most said no, that their fellow players were "hockey friends" – people seen around town occasionally in the off-season, but not part of their social circles. So while shinny players might talk of having a sense of community, shinny does not seem to create the same kind of hockey culture that is evident within the leagues, where you're either in the club or you're not. Players seem to like shinny that way: intense but not organized, with a degree of anonymity that city-dwellers find comfortable.

"Field" notes

The approach I am taking in my research comes from the anthropology of sport, which has its own history and context that set it apart from approaches in other fields. Social anthropologists have moved beyond the concept of "culture" as a distinct thing, defined against and separated from other cultures by solid boundaries of language, or religion, or geography. Culture is much "fuzzier" than that, and social anthropologists now assume that it is impossible to say where one culture begins and another ends. In keeping with this approach, where culture is a moving target, social anthropologists who study sport understand it as part of an assemblage of interrelated things that also includes performance, ritual and play. We have tended to be interested in the everyday cultural dynamics of sport and play, rather than, for example, their representation in mass media, which only gives us part of the picture. The grounded, grassroots practice of ethnography allows us to access everyday things that are undocumented in popular culture or in other academic disciplines, but which offer complex insights into local life.

Shinny fits well into such ethnographic sensibilities. Ritual and performance have long been of interest to anthropologists. From at least the 1960s, some were attempting to formulate critical approaches to collective activities that were, as Clifford Geertz wrote of Balinese villagers' obsession with cockfighting, "not vertebrate enough to be called a group and not structureless enough to be called a crowd" (424). In his classic essay, Geertz comments:

> Such gatherings meet and disperse; the participants in them fluctuate; the activity that focuses them is discrete – a particulate process that reoccurs rather than a continuous one that endures. They take their form from the situation that evokes them, the floor on which they are placed … but it is a form, and an articulate one, nonetheless. (424)

More recent anthropologists of sport such as Dyck and Archetti have continued to focus on the improvisational aspects of play and sport, especially in terms of performance theory. This provides useful ways to link official storylines with everyday practices and, of course, with events that are marked with extraordinary significance, like a cockfight in Bali or a game of shinny in Toronto. Feminist and post-colonial sport scholars have shown how ideas of gender, sexuality, race and citizenship have been expressed through organized forms of sport. They have also considered how the production of ideal bodies, through sport, has figured into nation-building efforts and into the social control of threatening Others (e.g., Vertinsky and McKay, Cole). Sports and recreation were considered important parts of efforts to socialize "proper" citizens, through education systems and community organizations, teaching values such as a strong work ethic, hygiene and self-discipline, and celebrating the strong, young body as a symbol of the nation. This 'ideal' body was usually male and invariably pictured as white. French social theorist and historian Michel Foucault's work is very useful for understanding how this set of ideas about 'ideal' and undesirable bodies worked in practice. In his writing on the development of the middle class, respectable citizen of the nineteenth and twentieth centuries, Foucault wrote about the importance of what he called "technologies of the self," or all of those forms of self-discipline that proper citizens were to undertake to maintain their health (and by extension, the "health" of the nation).

Other scholars studying the development of nationalisms have also paid attention to the growth of organized sports. For example, following Eric Hobsbawm's work on sports as "invented traditions," we may argue that constructions of history and memory are not about inert pasts, but are very much about relations of power in the present. Colonialism did not produce carbon copies of imperial games, as Appadurai shows in his work on cricket in contemporary India, but national sports are certainly shaped by popular ideas about history. If hockey itself is a mere hundred and fifty years old at the outset, how and why does it maintain such a symbolic hold on the national imagination as a symbol of national character, over other games that have a comparable history here, like lacrosse, for example, or curling?

In the Canadian context, hockey produces raced, gendered and classed citizens in some rather curious ways. Popular histories of hockey, such as CBC's *Canada: People's History*, are usually illustrated with grainy photographs of white boys on frozen lakes, but this imagery is selective. Popular debates over the origins of hockey consider First Nations, British and American beginnings (Kidd), and as sports in general were not standardized until the late nineteenth century, it seems likely that the sport we know as hockey is a sort of cultural amalgam. Historians of the game, such as George Fosty and Anne Hall, have shown that the nineteenth-century game was not, in fact, the exclusive terrain of white men, but also of significant numbers of women, as well as black players who organized leagues along the Eastern seaboard (Harris, Pitter). Historians of women's sport in Canada (e.g., Hall) show that women have played hockey for as long as men (early enthusiasts included Lord Stanley's daughter Isobel), although the women's game has never been as thoroughly documented or treated as seriously by producers of popular media. Still, there is ample evidence for women's university teams, as well as semi-professional teams and industrial leagues before World War Two in the US, Canada and Britain (Lenskyj, Hall).

A number of the women who came out to play shinny in Toronto told me stories about joining the neighbourhood boys in informal games from time to time, with differing degrees of acceptance, or being taught to skate by their mothers who had played hockey *before* local regulations made it difficult for females to play (Tillotson). In light of these and other examples, hockey's hybrid histories appear to have been continually whitewashed, with female and non-white players perpetually cast as anomalous newcomers, marked as different from the presumed core of white, male fans and players. This sport continues to be gendered and racialized in ways that mark some citizens as more "truly Canadian" than others, a fact that has made efforts to gain equal access highly charged.

While hockey culture highlights the uneven playing fields of citizenship in Canada, shinny figures into discourses of the nation in particularly complex ways. Organized forms of sport may be clearly tied to citizenship through systems of achievement and discipline, perhaps most obviously in terms of Olympic training. But practices of play, or quasi-sports like shinny, can also be deployed in ways that both mask and reinforce inequity. Just as Canada embraces multiculturalism in official terms, as Ghassan Hage has argued, the language of "tolerance" implies an unspoken audience of those who may choose (or not) to bestow it on the tolerated. In other words, even in self-conscious celebration of diversity and tolerance there may remain an unspoken assumption that there are 'regular' Canadians whose ethnicity is not remarked upon. In shinny, despite the ideal of the 'open' game we are all invited to join, many of us are still marked as Other.

This is more than just an academic matter of semantics, and what is going on with hockey in Canada is about more than representation. In his work on nations as "imagined communities," Anderson suggests that we must push beyond critiquing representations of countries as having a collective essence, an abstract set of things that mean "Canadianness" to many, like Mounties, politeness or public health care. Anderson suggested that we must get beyond the superficial aspects of nationalism to find ways to theorize the emotional pull of belonging to such a "public." He writes of nations as "imagined communities" not in the sense that they are not *real*, but to underscore that members of the nation must imagine themselves as part of a broader community of fellow citizens in order for the nation to make any sense. Someone from Flin Flon and someone from Halifax, from very different landscapes and without ever having met, might then recognize themselves as part of a collective whole that is an intimate part of their personal identity, not just their citizenship.

Recent anthropologists such as Ann Stoler have focused closely on the realm of emotional investment in concepts of the nation. In Canada, hockey, and especially shinny, is a powerful conduit for romantic and confining stories of the national past (Hughes-Fuller). Citing Eva Mackey's work on the construction of the unmarked "ordinary Canadian" and Gamal Abdel-Shehid's critical work on race and gender in Canadian sport, Mary Louise Adams writes that

> Nostalgia is a powerful means of keeping us from imagining how Canada might be different: it is part of the process of marginalizing women and people of colour, of limiting the stories we can tell about ourselves. At this particular historical moment, nostalgia for shinny is not about the complicated fabric of an evolving urban society. (82)

Perhaps in this sense, shinny *is* a tidy metaphor for Canada. In theory, the shinny rink, like the nation, is open to anyone who wants to play, and everyone will be welcomed on their own terms. However, in practice the hockey climate has indeed been "chilly." Most of my interviewees have been denied access to hockey at some time during their lives. Often such denial was effected by parents who feared that their daughters would become too masculine, but it also came from inhospitable social climates or lack of access to hockey teams. This was not always a matter of steady progress from one decade to another; in Phoebe's case, she might have come to hockey earlier had it not been for a town council in Labrador that explicitly barred women and girls from hockey in the 1970s, shutting down what had previously been a popular local pastime for her mother and aunts.

Cultural anxieties over non-normative gender and sexuality in women's sport have certainly coloured historic efforts to delimit access to hockey. Ringette was developed as an appropriately feminine alternative sport in the 1950s, although it is unclear what was supposed to be 'safer' about playing a hockey-like game in figure skates and the lightest of protective gear. While ringette continues to be played and defended by those who love that game in its own right, girls' and women's organized hockey has eclipsed the sport in recent years. Those interviewees who spoke about ringette tended to see it as an outdated and condescending form of "fake hockey."

Despite the passion for hockey that women's shinny players express, I never came across much discussion of professional men's hockey at the rinks I frequented. Instead, women who play shinny tend to be ambivalent about mainstream hockey culture of the kind reflected by *Hockey Night in Canada*. The feeling is mutual. While women's elite hockey garners some coverage every four years at the Olympics, commentators never seem to quite know what to do with it. Despite a string of gold medals (or in some arguments *because* of them), the women's Olympic hockey team is never granted the privilege of representing the nation on its own; it is treated as a Ladies' Auxiliary to the men's team, whose defeat or victory is more important. Admired but treated as slightly suspect, their femininity seems in need of continual shoring up. They no longer wear the Barbie-pink uniforms issued the first Olympic team, but upon the winning goal in the gold medal game during the last Olympics, a CBC announcer immediately commented that *every* player had the support of "husbands and boyfriends."

Indeed, spectres of queerness seem to haunt coverage of women's hockey. And here we find a significant irony: hockey, one of the central symbols of Canadian heterosexual masculinity, also has a long history and ongoing importance in queer women's communities. As Lenskyj and Cahn suggest, whether or not these were "communities" in the sense of being based upon shared membership in an identity category, women's sports have historically provided players with opportunities to socialize with each other in a context where traditionally-feminine behaviour was not required.

In a coffee shop in Toronto's gay village, Lisa told me a story about joining a women's hockey club as a young girl in rural Southern Ontario in the 1970s. In retrospect, she recognized that some of the older women had relationships with each other, and she wondered about these rural lives, far from the visible centres of queer life in the cities. As theorists of queer women's histories have often argued, fragmentary evidence is often all we have to go on (Cvetkovich, Rubin,

Kennedy and Davis). Hockey is full of potential for alternative readings, as suggested by the title of the Toronto Gay Hockey Association newsletter, *The Stickhandler,* or the evocative image of ten-year-old Abby Hoffman in her hockey uniform, hair cut short to go undercover on a boys' team in the mid-1950s. Carol, a filmmaker and avid shinny player who began a hockey skills class in her fifties, noted that she was not worried about how she would fit in because she knew it would be "our turf," and suggested that lesbians had a long history of opening up avenues for straight women to follow. Other shinny players spoke about the significance of joining the Women's Hockey Club of Toronto, a "lesbian and lesbian-friendly" league, in their own experiences of local queer community, even if they no longer enjoyed playing organized hockey. Asking someone whether she plays at Moss Park, the host arena, is a local equivalent of asking someone whether they are a "friend of Dorothy."

It is interesting that sport cultures have been almost completely absent from queer theory, although they have long been sites for performance, ritual and resistance that are arguably more central to everyday queer lives than are things like theatre or drag that have tended to capture the spotlight. Part of the problem may be definitions of activism that lump sports in with conservatism, discounting them as avenues for social change. However, it is possible to think of the shinny rink as a queer space on a couple of levels. I am not suggesting that all players are queer-identified; they are, of course, a diverse group of people. But all women who play hockey or shinny must to some degree negotiate the same discourses of sexuality and gender, however they identify. As one player – who also plays with her husband in a mixed league – said, "there's no room for homophobes in women's hockey. I mean, look around. You'd be in the wrong sport."

Women's shinny is not only a site for performance of non-normative gender and sexuality, a space that may be read as "queer." It is also queer as in "funny," in its nomadic, trickster stance, its playful refusal to set boundaries and rules. It is a transient space of ambivalent desire that raids the mainstream for its own purposes. The same rugged grace that a skilled male hockey player exhibits when executing a perfect tight turn or an accurate wrist shot, takes on a whole other set of meanings when performed by a girl. In other words, although hockey is overstuffed with meaning, these alternative spaces, or "counterpublics" (Warner), may still be brought into being. They are alternatives that hide in plain sight, seemingly blending into nationalist discourse that presents hockey as a bastion of heterosexual masculinity, and shinny as a neat metaphor for Canada. In other words, it depends on how you "read the game."

In recent years, the city of Toronto has begun to include times set aside for women's shinny. In reserving some space for those who otherwise might not have access to it, there is an effort to make shinny hockey live up to its reputation as a game open to all. But these timeslots and the frozen surfaces they govern remain precarious, a situation that continues to be a source of tension for many women who play. At some rinks, where women's shinny has been established for a number of years, games go on without incident. At others, male players often contest the idea of "women's shinny" on the grounds that the rink is a public space and should not be set aside for specific groups. Women's shinny players talk of the need for a "critical mass" of women to at least temporarily claim the space as their own, or else it will revert to the assumed norm: space for and about men. These tensions are coloured by the context of mainstream hockey culture, where women's hockey occupies an ambivalent position somewhere between nationalistic praise for its achievements and a certain unease. With shinny hockey, there may be a denial of prejudice, and even the language of openness, but subtle dynamics of exclusion still come into play where, to paraphrase George Orwell in *Animal Farm*, all players are equal, but some are more equal than others. If shinny is "open," but certain kinds of people dominate the rink, the lack of participation of other groups is rendered invisible and inarticulate. Given this cultural context, and my fellow players' acute awareness of it, it is especially interesting that these adult women, who are remarkably creative and critical individuals, have all decided to take up hockey in their own ways. Hockey's associations with power are a significant part of the terrain of my fieldwork. But it is also clear that passion for shinny is not limited to the cultural mainstream or the right of the political spectrum. Environmental activists at the Montreal Conference on Climate Change held a mock funeral for pond hockey, complete with a coffin draped in a Canadian flag, after the practice of state funerals (Deen and Markvart). A friend who attends a lot of demonstrations has mentioned the use of road hockey games as moving picket lines, with the added advantage of being able to take slapshots at tear-gas canisters, getting them out of harm's way. Toronto artist Liz Pead renders tongue-in-cheek reworkings of Group of Seven landscapes done in old hockey equipment. Shinny is a major element of neighbourhood efforts to build healthy communities at parks like Dufferin Grove. There players take part in free lessons, and photographs that document women's hockey and public skating over the last century are displayed in an effort to unearth little-known local histories and foster a strong sense of place. Historians of sport and recreation in Toronto, such as Tillotson and Kidd, have shown that union movements and the concept of citizens' rights to leisure had a major hand in shaping local recreation systems before the mid-twentieth century. The idea of shinny as a friendly game for players of all skill levels also resonates rather nicely with second-wave feminist efforts to foster equity in and through sport.

In her study of rural life in the eviscerated hills of West Virginia, gutted by strip mining and the effects of generations of poverty, ethnographer Kathleen Stewart uses the metaphor of the "space on the side of the road" to describe the ways in which local people, stereotyped as hillbillies in popular culture, take up aspects of that discourse in ways that actually do provide them with some degree of independence, a quietly oppositional way of life. I'd like to suggest that on women's shinny nights, the rink becomes such a "space on the side of the road," in this case a small rink outside the walls of the well-groomed indoor arenas of hockey culture in Canada. Shinny encompasses many disorganized versions of hockey that may challenge or resist accepted ideas of the sport which symbolizes the nation, but may also be thoroughly entangled in nationalist discourses of belonging. In some ways my research is an example of anthropology "at home," but as critical theorists of diaspora, race and sexuality remind us, "home" is neither necessarily a safe space nor an innocent one. Shinny can be understood as a "node" or, as Gilles Deleuze and Félix Guattari would have it, a "plateau" where a number of trajectories meet and disperse, a sort of collective improvisation where everyone knows the tune, but it always comes out differently. Shinny is homemade, borrowed, do-it-yourself. Yet in its playful dismissal of some of the more serious stories of the nation, it may provide some of the clearest insights into them.

1   All names of interviewees recorded here are pseudonyms.

Works Cited

Abdel-Shehid, Gamal. "Who da'Man: Black Masculinities and Sport in Canada." PhD diss., York University, 2001.

Adams, Mary Louise. "The Game of Whose Lives? Gender, Race, and Entitlement in Canada's 'National' Game." In *Artificial Ice: Hockey, Culture, and Commerce*, edited by David Whitson and Richard Gruneau, 71–84. Peterborough, ON: Broadview Press, 2006.

Anderson, Benedict. *Imagined Communities: Reflections on the Origin and Spread of Nationalism*. New York: Verso, 1991.

Appadurai, Arjun. "Playing with Modernity: the Decolonization of the Indian Cricket." In *Consuming Modernity: Public Culture in a South Asian World*, edited by Carol Breckenridge, 23–48. Minneapolis: University of Minnesota Press, 1995.

Shinny: The Hockey in All of Us. Directed by David Battistella. Toronto: National Film Board of Canada, 2001.

Brownell, Susan. *Training the Body for China: Sports in the Moral Order of the People's Republic*. Chicago: University of Chicago Press, 1995.

Cahn, Susan K. *Coming on Strong: Gender and Sexuality in Twentieth-Century Women's Sport*. Toronto: Maxwell Macmillan Canada, 1995.

Cole, Cheryl L. "Resisting the Canon: Feminist Cultural Studies, Sport, and Technologies of the Body." In *Women, Sport, and Culture*, edited by Susan Birrell and Cheryl L. Cole, 5–30. Champaign, IL: Human Kinetics, 1994.

Cvetkovich, Ann. *An Archive of Feelings: Trauma, Sexuality, and Lesbian Public Cultures*. Durham, NC: Duke University Press, 2003.

Darnell, Regna. *Invisible Genealogies: A History of Americanist Anthropology*. Critical Studies in the History of Anthropology Series. Lincoln, NB: University of Nebraska Press, 2001.

Di Leonardo, Micaela. *Exotics at Home: Anthropologists, Others, and American Modernity*. Women in Culture and Society Series. Chicago: University of Chicago Press, 1998.

Deen, Meribeth, and Tanya Markvart. "Hockey Activists Lace Up." *Alternatives* 32, no. 1 (2006): 6.

Deleuze, Gilles, and Félix Guattari. *A Thousand Plateaus: Capitalism and Schizophrenia*. Translated by Brian Massumi. Minneapolis: University of Minnesota Press, 1987.

Dyck, Noel. "Getting into the Game: Anthropological Perspectives on Sport." *Anthropologica* 46, no. 1 (2004): 3–8.

Dyck, Noel, and Eduardo P. Archetti, eds. *Sport, Dance and Embodied Identities*. Oxford: Berg, 2003.

Fosty, George Robert, and Darril Fosty. *Black Ice: The Lost History of the Colored Hockey League of the Maritimes, 1895–1925*. New York: Stryker-Indigo, 2004.

Foucault, Michel, Luther H. Martin, Huck Gutman and Patrick H. Hutton, eds. *Technologies of the Self: a Seminar with Michel Foucault*. Amherst: University of Massachusetts Press, 1988.

Geertz, Clifford. *The interpretation of cultures: selected essays*. New York: Basic Books, 1973.

Gruneau, Richard, and David Whitson. *Hockey Night in Canada: Sport, Identities, and Cultural Politics*. Toronto: Garamond Press, 1993.

Hage, Ghassan. *White Nation: Fantasies of White Supremacy in a Multicultural Society*. Sydney: Pluto Press, 2000.

Hall, M. Ann. *The Girl and the Game: A History of Women's Sport in Canada*. Peterborough, ON: Broadview Press, 2002.

Harris, Cecil. *Breaking the Ice: The Black Experience in Professional Hockey*. Toronto: Insomniac Press, 2003.

Hobsbawm, Eric. "Mass-Producing Traditions: Europe, 1870–1914." In *The Invention of Tradition*, edited by Eric Hobsbawm and Terence Ranger, 263–307. New York: Cambridge University Press, 1983.

Hughes-Fuller, Patricia. "The Good Old Game: Hockey, Nostalgia, Identity." PhD diss, University of Alberta, 2002.

Joseph, Miranda. *Against the Romance of Community*. Minneapolis: University of Minnesota Press, 2002.

Kennedy, Elizabeth Lapovsky, and Madeline D. Davis. *Boots of Leather, Slippers of Gold: The History of a Lesbian Community*. New York: Routledge, 1994.

Kidd, Bruce. *The Struggle for Canadian Sport*. Toronto: University of Toronto Press, 1996.

Lenskyj, Helen Jefferson. *Out on the Field: Gender, Sport and Sexualities*. Toronto: Women's Press, 2003.

Mackey, Eva. *The House of Difference: Cultural Politics and National Identity in Canada*. Anthropological Horizons. Toronto: University of Toronto Press, 2002.

Moore, Philip. "Practical Nostalgia and the Critique of Commodification: On the 'Death of Hockey' and the National Hockey League." *The Australian Journal of Anthropology* 13, no. 3 (2002): 309–322.

Pitter, Robert. "Racialization and Hockey in Canada: From Personal Troubles to a Canadian Challenge." In *Artificial Ice: Hockey, Culture, and Commerce*, edited by David Whitson and Richard Gruneau, 123–139. Peterborough, ON: Broadview Press, 2006.

Razack, Sherene H. "When Place Becomes Race." In *Race, Space, and the Law: Unmapping a White Settler Society*, edited by Sherene Razack, 1–20. Toronto: Between the Lines, 2002.

Rubin, Gayle. "Studying Sexual Subcultures: Excavating the Ethnography of Gay Communities in Urban North America." In *Out in Theory: The Emergence of Lesbian and Gay Anthropology*, edited by Ellen Lewin and William L. Leap, Chicago: University of Illinois Press, 2002.

Sandoval, Chela. "Dissident Globalizations, Emancipatory Methods, Social-Erotics." In *Queer Globalizations: Citizenship and the Afterlife of Colonialism*, edited by Arnaldo Cruz-Malavé and Martin F. Manalansan, 20–32. New York: New York University Press, 2002.

Stewart, Kathleen. *A Space on the Side of the Road: Cultural Poetics in an "Other" America*. Princeton: Princeton University Press, 1996.

Stoler, Ann Laura. "Affective States." In *A Companion to the Anthropology of Politics*. David Nugent and Joan Vincent, 4–20. Malden, MA: Blackwell Publishing, 2004.

Tillotson, Shirley. *The Public at Play: Gender and the Politics of Recreation in Post-War Ontario*. Studies in Gender and History. Toronto: University of Toronto Press, 2000.

Warner, Michael. *Publics and Counterpublics*. New York: Zone Books, 2005.

Wilson, Brian. "Selective Memory in a Global Culture: Reconsidering Links between Youth, Hockey, and Canadian Identity." In *Artificial Ice: Hockey, Culture, and Commerce*, edited by David Whitson and Richard Gruneau, 53–70. Peterborough, ON: Broadview Press, 2006.

Whitson, David, and Richard Gruneau, eds. *Artificial Ice: Hockey, Culture, and Commerce*. Peterborough, ON: Broadview Press, 2006.

E.W. (ED) MASON

Media Framing of the Other
Ice Hockey in the New Zealand Media

"Alright mums and dads, if you're looking for a safe sport for the kiddies to get into this may not be it. Welcome to ice hockey Kiwi style." Tony Veitch, Television New Zealand Sports Presenter, reporting on the October 2006 NZNHL Championship series.

Ice hockey in New Zealand faces a number of challenges not least of which is the application of traditional news values to a small sports organization. These values include an emphasis on conflict and the relentless search for something new. The sport is one of a large number of 'minor' sports seeking media attention in a ratings-driven news environment, which presents a further challenge especially in the search for players and sponsors. However, despite a negative or at least neutral sports news environment, media framing of New Zealand ice hockey points to a positive national and international future for the game.

New Zealand is a small country with a population of over four million people. The climate is temperate and with a population that is over 80% Anglo-Celt it is not surprising that the sports heritage is largely British. Rugby Union football, netball and soccer dominate the participation sports with each numbering well over one hundred thousand players. Rugby and cricket lead the sports pages and both major television bulletins. These two, along with the professional Rugby League and netball, dominate both free-to-air and subscriber channels' live game coverage. In addition, New Zealanders are used to their sports teams winning in the international sports field. The All Blacks rugby players, netball stars and especially Olympic heroes such as Peter Snell are celebrated and highly marketable.

By contrast, ice hockey, with approximately eighteen hundred registered players, is limited by the geographical reach and cost of rinks and public awareness. Ice rinks have always been a marginal business in New Zealand with many small rinks closing in the last decades of the twentieth century. Currently, there is not even a rink in Wellington, the national capital. However there are new larger arenas in Queenstown, Gore, Dunedin and Auckland, as well as a spectacular outdoor rink at Lake Tekapo in the Southern Alps.

The New Zealand Ice Hockey Federation is an active member of the International Ice Hockey Federation (IIHF) and plays in IIHF Division III, which the Ice Blacks recently won in April 2007. The senior men are usually ranked in the low thirties along with Greece, China, Australia, South Korea and Turkey.

The occasional win or lopsided loss attracts national media attention but otherwise the major media isn't very interested. Exceptions were the first ever victory by a New Zealand Under Twenty team over arch-rival Australia in January 2008 and the IIHF tournaments hosted in Auckland for the Asia-Pacific and Division III championships. A new five-team national league is a promising step in raising sponsorship and public awareness.

Despite the smaller place of ice hockey in the nation's sporting heritage there is a real tradition of the game in the South Island high country where the winters can be harsh enough to produce natural ice for two to three months at a time. There are news photos of people playing ice hockey on frozen ponds in the South Island in the 1920s but the official history of the sport starts with a game at Opawa in South Canterbury in 1937.

After the game, the New Zealand Ice Skating Association was formed and an annual outdoor tournament called the Erewhon Cup, named for Samuel Butler's nineteenth century utopian novel set in New Zealand, was established. The outdoor requirement combined with mild winters and wartime effectively prevented the games being held annually until the advent of artificial rinks in the 1960s.

In 1986, the New Zealand Ice Hockey Federation was established by the provinces of Auckland, Canterbury and Southern. Almost immediately the enthusiastic group formed a national team of mainly Kiwi teenagers and entered the Group D IIHF World Championships in Perth, Australia. The New Zealanders managed a win at the tournament but the biggest story was a fifty-something to one thrashing by an 'Australian' team made up of sixteen Canadians and Europeans and four Australians. This example of 'sportsmanship' led to the IIHF changing its eligibility rules but the score stayed in the *Guinness Book of Records* for nearly two decades, providing an easy source of mirthful dismissal for New Zealand sports media.

The IIHF and NHL connections helped improve the quality of New Zealand ice hockey. Former NHL goalie Dave Dryden spent six months in New Zealand on an educational exchange in the early 1990s and was an active coach on both islands. Patrice Tardif, who later played for the NHL's St. Louis Blues and Los Angeles Kings, spent the 1990 season playing in Auckland. In addition, NHL development money went into women's and youth goaltending equipment.

Tony Veitch's statement on the October 2006 NZNHL Championship series is an example of the wilful ignorance of New Zealand's sport's media in regards to ice hockey. In their defence, media, as a matter of daily professional practice, frame stories.

Storytelling techniques have helped the media sell their product to consumers since newspapers began in the seventeenth century. Conflict, selected visuals and a story catch and hold the audience's attention. The sports presenter quoted above actually said "the original point of the story ... a very dangerous sport," a clear example of editorializing without actually informing viewers of any other aspects of the game.

Griffin may just as well have had the TVNZ story in mind when he defined framing as follows: "the process of calling attention to some aspects of reality while obscuring others, which might lead to different reactions; according to agenda-setting theory, the selection of a restricted number of thematically related attributes for inclusion in the media agenda when a particular object is discussed."

Framing is influenced by professional news values such as perceived public interest, social and cultural prominence, famous people, newness, conflict and commercial value to advertisers (Tucker).

Ice hockey in the New Zealand sports media suffers as a result of ignorance and prejudice that the sport is somehow "foreign," therefore odd and not for us. Blackman and Walkerdine assert that "the media draws upon psychological knowledge in the ways it constructs the Other, producing a chain of associations through which we are invited to recognise their *deviant* (italics mine) nature, their difference from us" (10). The flip side of this Otherness is the inclusive alliance between the media and ordinary people. We don't understand but it doesn't matter anyway.

A good North American example is the use of the word "scrum," a technical rugby term used to describe a form of engagement of front row forwards when the ball is put into play. New Zealand rugby fans understand that a scrum is a mixture of art and science, a thing of technical beauty coordinating eight men against an opposing eight men. North American sports media uses the word "scrum" to describe a melee of players in any sport where discipline has broken down. They just don't get it so the audience doesn't get it either.

This is the essence of media framing. Street writes: "The media not only selects particular events, it also has to make sense of them. It has to make them matter to the readers and viewers, and this entails setting them within a narrative, a story of social change" (37). Our issue in the case of New Zealand ice hockey has much to do with the media's qualifications to "make sense" of the sport and its people, events, values and place in society.

Television in particular picks out hockey fights for special attention. This may have something to do with the contracted news feeds from US suppliers as part of the regular daily package but it is New Zealand producers and presenters who choose to use the material. Major print and electronic media often portray ice hockey's physical nature as its primary raison d'être.

Conflict is the news value most often applied to a contemporary event such as the New Zealand national ice hockey championships. A similarly "physical" sport, rugby union, is the national sport and is framed by the news bulletins as being of the greatest possible national interest. Relatively rare All Black losses are treated as a reason for national mourning and subjected to relentless and seemingly endless scrutiny by an impressive array of 'experts.' The difference in the framing of the two contact sports lies in ice hockey's apparently 'alien' place in the New Zealand sports landscape.

Just as many Canadians, including media figures such as Don Cherry, regard ice hockey fighting as a core value in the national game, New Zealanders have viewed "rucking" opposing players off the ball as a key part of the manly historical culture of their national sport. Rucking consists of one or more players using their cleats to roll an opposing player out of the way when they are on the ground and impeding progress to the ball. Both are examples of acts which would be regarded as a crime if it happened outside the context of a game. Media have tended to support the prevailing sports culture and to frame oppositional voices as alien or deviant. Both the NHL and the International Rugby Board have modernized their view to diminish violent tactics as core values while retaining the physical nature of their respective sports.

In December 2006, TV3 Sportsnight showed two NHL fights on its national network and several more in January and February 2007. The old cliché "I went to the fights and an ice hockey game broke out" was recently used on TV3 news in a mostly complimentary story about the Ice Blacks going to the IIHF World Championships in Newcastle, Australia. That quote seems to rule New Zealand editorial decision-making. Goals and great goalie play rarely feature so the audience gets no context for the fighting and little information about the game.

In their defence, the same channel also screened a positive feature in March 2007 about the New Zealand women's team going to Romania for the IIHF World Championships.

In early 2008, local media coverage was enthusiastic and extensive when the New Zealand Under Twenties beat Australia but most missed the story of the team being escorted by armed guards when the Serbian crowd turned ugly in an unexpected New Zealand win.

Collisions and "big hits" make effective television and ice hockey, whether local or overseas, provides plenty of both. The quote from Tony Veitch introduced a news report featuring a spectacular accidental collision which left one player dripping blood on the ice. The visual made the story. As in the Sunbelt states of the US, New Zealanders find the puck hard to see but the hits are easy to pick out. The cynical money-grubbing of the NHL and Hollywood, particularly in the 1970s and 1980s, have been major contributing factors in the fascination with on-ice violence.

The media coverage makes the game a hard sell to parents looking for a good game for their children to play. New Zealand media rarely if ever mentions that the New Zealand Ice Hockey Federation (NZIHF) is a member in good standing of the IIHF or that the game is an Olympic sport. Ice hockey is subject to international rules and values and the New Zealand Federation has always had an emphasis on skills and clean play. The Ice Blacks constantly win tournament Fair Play awards for fewest penalty minutes by any team.

This lack of context could be explained by the news working conditions. Reporters tend to be young and rushed off their feet so it is no surprise they know little about ice hockey. High staff turnover and low pay except for a few 'stars' means a lot of information will continue to be 'new' (Edwards, 1992).

New Zealand television channels are dependent on overseas suppliers such as the US, UK and Australia for news feeds of major news events. The supplier nations only regard ice hockey as a major sport during the Olympic Games. American sources often include an ice hockey "oddity" as part of the package. The impression of unrestricted violence is hard to shake when reporters have few balanced sources to use as visuals.

The corporate nature of even publicly-owned television in New Zealand ensures that amateur sport equates with small numbers and commercial irrelevance. New Zealand teams in Australian-based professional competitions are a growing part of what Mark Lowes has called "athletic entertainment." Currently rugby union, rugby league, netball, basketball and soccer teams are part of these leagues. All have national or international contracts for broadcast on free-to-air or pay television. Channels such as TVNZ, TV3 and Rupert Murdoch's Prime Channel and Sky Network have commercial interests in the major sports so it is no surprise that news bulletins exclude minor sports to make room for the favoured few.

Lowes asserts that "sports news is ideological precisely because it constitutes a discourse that serves the promotional interests of the major league sports industry's primary stakeholders. This means there is little room for news that doesn't promote the industry" (99). Losers in this equation tend to be local and amateur competitions.

The neo-liberal economic reforms of the 1990s emphasized the commercial orientation of news including the public broadcaster, which was required to return huge dividends to the government's general fund. This culture features presenter chit chat as critical to engaging an audience while reading the news. Reporters with no benefit of background knowledge or experience are expected to share their views with the audience and each other (Edwards, 1992, 2002; McGregor, 119–121). Smaller sports are marginalized by this culture of presenter and reporter celebrity.

Ice hockey is routinely framed and misrepresented as violent, unsporting and alien. During the 1990s there were a number of TVNZ reports which purported to report on local ice hockey but actually featured inserts of NHL collisions and the New Zealand reporter trying on skates and falling on his rear. The Otherness and alien nature of the sport was shown accompanied by the celebrity status of the reporter.

"Newness" as a news value relates in part to the previously mentioned inexperience of New Zealand sports reporters as well as its value in selling the story to the audience (Tucker). Ice hockey is often presented as new because it is new to the journalist. A *Weekend Herald* report of September 9, 2006, states "Ice hockey is a new sport here but we like a bit of rough and tumble so it's no wonder it's picking up in popularity." The sport is neither new nor popular in New Zealand.

Games reviewer Peter Griffin admitted, "I'm totally lost when it comes to ice hockey, something I associate with Canadians and horror movies" (*TimeOut*). His review of NHL 2K6 celebrated his ignorance and belittled the game and its electronic version.

Nationalism provides an interestingly complex dimension to reporting ice hockey and ice sports. New Zealand generally does badly at the Winter Olympics, with one silver medal in skiing and two fourth placings in speed skating in the 1990s. The New Zealand print media, especially the large-circulation, Auckland-based *New Zealand Herald,* conducts a campaign every four years asking the leading question "Why bother?" The sports media's obsession with winning is not exclusive to New Zealand but the tradition of winning in national sports has spoiled the country for a sense of perspective (Mason).

Sometimes the inattention of a sub-editor can benefit a small sport such as when the following headline appeared in Wellington's main newspaper. Patrice Tardif of Auckland's North Shore Vikings renown made it to the NHL with the St. Louis Blues and after was traded to the Los Angeles Kings for Wayne Gretzky. On March 19, 1997, Quebec-born Tardif scored a goal for the Kings against the Anaheim Mighty Ducks. *The Dominion Post* trumpeted this achievement with the timeless headline "Kiwi Stars on Ice." National pride rules no matter what the sport.

We may have to wait for a New Zealand born NHL player. The NZIHF is on the lookout for Canadians and others who may be entitled to a New Zealand passport. One son of Swiss parents was born in New Zealand but raised in Switzerland. He claimed New Zealand citizenship and played internationally for four years.

New Zealand ice hockey will continue to struggle to achieve a media profile. It will also have to continue advancing the case for the game as a sports alternative for young Kiwis. Sports reporters' misconceptions and ignorance will continue to be an important obstacle to understanding and accepting this important world and Olympic sport. The superficial framing of the game as a series of brawls must continue to be rejected and then replaced with support for a more balanced view.

The continued lack of a commercial side to the game ensures it will compete for very limited media exposure in the face of sports news' fascination with the major professional sports. New Zealand's recent international successes can help the sport gain traction with media representatives. However the IIHF has been so successful in supporting and developing minor nations' level of play that all have improved markedly. New Zealand is much stronger but its international ranking remains about the same as it was twenty years ago.

There are some genuine positives for New Zealand ice hockey. The willingness of the NZIHF teams to travel has endeared the country to the IIHF and there are generous travel subsidies as a result. The women's game has gained profile with recent television news reports and some international success. Maori Television's recent arrival means there is a new and adventurous outlet for minor sports. There is something very special in a Maori-English bilingual ice hockey broadcast.

Wellington City Council has thrown its support behind a city rink. The National League, which started as a four team circuit in 2005, added a Dunedin team in 2008 and continues to attract media interest (Kilgallon, 13). Local community television broadcasted a Dunedin game to a national audience in August 2008 over the Sky subscription television network.

The NZIHF needs to continue to positively manage its image in order to reverse or at least neutralise the negative framing it encounters. New Zealand sports media is still community-oriented enough to devote some resources to cover minor sports. The challenge is to be first in the queue for that coverage in a crowded sports market.

Works Cited

Blackman, Lisa, and Valerie Walkerdine. *Mass Hysteria: Critical Psychology and Media Studies*. Basingstoke: Palgrave Publishers, 2001.

Comrie, Margie, and Judy McGregor, eds. *What's news?: Reclaiming Journalism in New Zealand*. Palmerston North: Dunmore Press, 2002.

Edwards, Brian. "The Cootchie Coo News." In *Whose News?* edited by Margie Comrie and Judy McGregor. Palmerston North: Dunmore Press, 1992.

Edwards, Brian. "The Cootchie Coo News Revisited." In *What's news?: Reclaiming Journalism in New Zealand*, edited by Margie Comrie and Judy McGregor, 16–32. Palmerston North: Dunmore Press, 2002

Griffin, E. A. *A First Look at Communication* Theory. 3rd ed. Whitby: McGraw-Hill Ryerson, 1997.

Griffin, Peter. Time Out Games. *New Zealand Herald*, May 27, 2006.

Herman, Edward S., and Robert W. McChesney. *The Global Media: The New Missionaries of Global Capitalism*. London: Cassell, 1997.

Hope, Wayne. "Media, Politics and Sport". In *New Zealand Government and Politics*, 4th ed., edited by Raymond Miller, 499–511. South Melbourne: Oxford University Press, 2006.

Kilgallon, Steve. "Icebreakers are struggling to crack Kiwi consciousness." *Sunday Star-Times*, August 2005.

Lowes, Mark Douglas. *Inside the Sports Pages: Work Routines, Professional Ideologies and the Manufacture of Sports News*. Toronto: University of Toronto Press, 1999.

Mason, E.W. "Our Winter Olympians deserve respect." *New Zealand Herald*, March 4, 2006.

McCarroll, Jo. "TV news serves up a diet of trivia – study." *New Zealand Herald*, May 18, 2000.

McGregor, Judy. "Terrorism, War, Lions and Sex Symbols: Restating News Values." In *What's news? : Reclaiming Journalism in New Zealand*, edited by Margie Comrie and Judy McGregor, 111–125. Palmerston North: Dunmore Press, 2002.

McNair, Brian. *The Sociology of Journalism*. London: Arnold Publishers, 1998.

Norris, Paul. "News Through Alien Filters: The Impact of Imported News on a Small Nation." In *Global News: Perspectives on the Information Age*, 2nd ed., edited by Tony Silvia, 85–99. Ames: Iowa State University Press, 2001.

Street, John. *Mass Media, Politics and Democracy*. Basingstoke: Palgrave Publishers, 2001.

Time Out Sport. *New Zealand Herald*, September 9, 2006.

Tucker, Jim, ed. *Intro: A Beginner's Guide to Professional News Journalism*. Wellington: New Zealand Journalists Training Organisation, 1999.

BRIAN KENNEDY

"What Ever Happened to the Organ and the Portrait of Her Majesty?"

NHL Spectating as Imaginary Carnival

Hockey as we know it, the modern game with organized teams, was created when the game moved indoors, according to Michael McKinley in *Putting a Roof on Winter: Hockey's Rise from Sport to Spectacle*. The crucial element in this change was the presence of spectators, people who could count on being entertained in comfortable, familiar conditions night after night (19). From there, as any Canadian can tell you, the game acquired its accoutrements, including a portrait of the Queen standing at one end of the arena and organ music filling the breaks between plays.

However, in the past twenty years, hockey games have taken on a new dimension: the real rise of the sport as a spectacle, with ever-more-inventive ways to grab the attention of fans who might not otherwise be interested in spending their entertainment dollars on hockey. Many would argue that this was prompted by the game's move from Canada and the Northern USA into markets ill-prepared for it, such as California and Florida. Manifestations of this phenomenon include everything from players skating through giant sharks' heads at the beginning of games to members of the crowd participating in tricycle races between periods. At the same time, modern sound technology has made it possible for the arena to take on qualities similar to the atmosphere of a heavy metal concert.

Hockey as entertainment has gone from being a simple game which focused its fans' attention on the ice to something which resembles a circus, with the tricks growing increasingly spectacular in an effort to connect fans to the action. As such, it is tempting to apply the term "carnival" to the presentation of modern professional hockey. This word was applied by Mikhail Bakhtin to describe medieval life and literature, particularly the literature of Rabelais. Bakhtin defines carnival this way: "Carnival is not a spectacle seen by the people; they live in it, and everyone participates because its very idea embraces all the people. While carnival lasts, there is no other life outside it. During carnival time life is subject only to its laws, that is, the laws of its own freedom" (*Rabelais and His World*, 7).

In fact, much of what happens at an NHL game does resemble a medieval carnival, with its all-encompassing, ritualized behaviors of violence and excess and the inversion of hierarchies. As with medieval carnival, game-time carnival is carefully scripted. Everything that happens from the moment the lights go on to the announcer's "thank you for attending" takes place essentially the same way each game. However, unlike in Rabelaisian carnival, the ability to act out is strictly limited, primarily by concerns over spectator safety. Thus if there is a carnival element to watching hockey, it might best be labelled "imaginary," with each person exercising his or her emotions without inconveniencing the person in the next seat.

The presentation of hockey has evolved since the game was first invented around 1880. From this historical era to the "polite" era which started in the 1950s to what I call the "rock music and mascot" era that started around twenty years ago, you can trace the rise of this imaginary carnival as a feature of the modern game. However, I see the carnival as an inversion of, rather than a displacement of, traditional elements of hockey spectating, particularly since the two elements historically attached to hockey watching – violence and decorum – are not lost in the modern arena. These aspects instead are sublimated into forms which promise two things to spectators: a safe exercising of strong emotions and an experience which will be largely the same no matter what happens on the ice. This in turn yields what sports teams need in order to sell tickets: a product with remarkable consistency considering the unpredictable outcome of the live action.

1. Why Go?

Committed fans go to professional hockey games because they wish to cheer for their team, because they have a larger perspective on the meaning of a given game in the run of the season or because despite their hatred of the team visiting, they feel compelled to spend money to see the star of the opposing team. What fan wants to say that she or he lived through the Crosby era, for instance, and never saw him play?

Studies which attempt to determine both spectator motivation and satisfaction, however, rarely assume that the people answering surveys have intimate knowledge of the sport or attend purely for intrinsic reasons. Instead, they measure fan satisfaction with what researchers call the "sports event experience" (Kennett, Sneath and Henson, EP2). This method is preferred because, "In this maturing industry, competition for a share of consumers' leisure time is intensifying" (Kennett, Sneath and Henson, EP2).

The language used to code such research indicates that it is anything but what happens on the ice which might influence fan satisfaction. "Assessing consumers' perceptions of the service encounter … presents a special challenge to the sports organization," Kennett, Sneath and Henson say before asserting that "it is more difficult for consumers to evaluate the quality of the service experience than it is to evaluate the purchase of a good," which is why it is necessary to lean on tangible elements in measuring fan satisfaction (EP2). For this reason they weigh factors such as souvenir price and availability, parking cost and convenience and staff friendliness as predictors of whether paying customers feel satisfied with their ticket purchase and will therefore be likely to make a repeat buy.

This methodology leaves out one crucial aspect of the "service encounter": team performance on the ice, or spectator interest for reasons other than that the parking was cheap and the beer was cold. In fact, the outcome of the game is not considered a "controllable factor" (EP3) and so is relegated to the margins when deciding how to present the game. "Sports marketers must focus on and research the factors that are fully or partially controllable and accept the fact that certain things will be beyond their control," this research group says (EP3).

Other studies discuss the emotional satisfaction spectators gain from seeing their team play. For instance, Robert Madrigal says, "Meeting the need for enjoyment requires spectators to be favorably disposed toward one of the competing teams" (EP3). He argues that spectator identification with athletes, as a measurable quantity, can nudge teams in certain directions in terms of their advertising, for example, toward "creat[ing] messages aimed at specific target markets." This might be done by "plac[ing] greater emphasis on the personal characteristics of individual athletes than their athletic prowess when promoting aesthetic sports" such as gymnastics (EP12). These factors, however, are secondary to the fan satisfaction indices based on elements such as parking, souvenirs and customer service.

The attempt by the teams to polish their product presentation makes perfect sense, and it would be the rare person who would not take into account things like parking when evaluating his or her level of satisfaction with a game experience. However, modern sports franchises have not remained content to separate the controllable and non-controllable factors in game presentation. Instead they have devised a mechanized version of game-time which allows them to extend their control over fan satisfaction into the arena itself in an effort to manage what is otherwise unmanageable – the action on the ice.

2. Three Eras of Hockey Spectating

This attempt to control the game is a long way from the first era of hockey spectating, which started with modern hockey's invention around 1880 and ended sometime post-war, most likely when television became a factor. It was a time when, for instance, "Madison Square Garden ... offered one place where different social classes came together with relative ease" (Monk, 183). Images of this era live on mostly in black and white photographs, and with the passage of time, have left the impression of eager and well-behaved crowds.

The second era in hockey spectating began sometime in the 1950s and ended roughly twenty years ago. The "social imaginary," to use a term suggested by cultural historian Norman Klein, of hockey during this era is of a polite crowd, dressed in suits, who consumed the professional game with decorum similar to what they might have exhibited had they been watching the ballet instead of Rocket Richard or Teeder Kennedy. It is this image which I draw upon in my title, and the picture one gets is of people sitting politely in their seats, the ladies in hats and the men in suits, craning their necks to see the play and clapping at appropriate times in appreciation of the exploits of their hometown heroes. These images come from the grainy black and white game film which exists in archives and is dragged out for presentation on television in Canada even now and even in the USA on *ESPN Classic* and the *NHL Network*.

The third, and current, era of hockey spectating is, for lack of a more concise description, the "mascot and rock music" era. In this way of presenting the game, every excuse to "pump up the volume" is taken. Spectators are urged to "make some no-oise," and the scoreboard displays a supposed "noise-meter" to show them how they're doing. This is an invention of both possibility and necessity. Necessity, because it is believed that fans will buy more tickets if their experience is somehow rendered more exciting; possibility as a function of the availability of technology such as light boards and sound systems which were unheard of more than a couple of decades ago.[1]

Relying on quantifiable measurements of fan satisfaction has led sports organizations to focus increasingly on game staging. It is the one thing that an organization has power over regardless of how the team is playing or how strong or weak the visiting team might be. In this approach the game itself comes to matter less than the presentation of the game. This has led to the modern practice of staging sporting events almost as if they were concerts or plays.

Working from a "script" which controls everything from the greeting to the goodnight, event managers create the arena atmosphere, which combines music, lights, even lasers and smoke in an effort to enhance, if not replace, the product on the ice (Murray). What the single-game fan doesn't notice, however, is that in most arenas the sound and light show seldom varies from game to game. It makes little difference whether the home team is winning or losing, on the power play or shorthanded. When the segmented breaks in play occur (for instance, in NHL arenas at the first whistle after the five, ten and fifteen minutes of each period, for TV timeouts), the show is on. And if that show calls for the playing of a certain ad or spectator game at the five-minute break, then that's what's going to happen.

These days the game is staged like a production of *Hamlet* is staged in a theater: the same way at every performance. Going to *Hamlet* twice or three times a week for six months sounds like a boring exercise, but at least repeated viewings would teach one to expect each sound effect and light change. In theory, going to forty-one hockey games in the same arena should yield a noticeably different experience each time. But going to every home game an NHL team plays isn't that much different from seeing a stage play over and over. The only thing which changes is what happens between the drops of the puck. The rest of the experience is so tightly scripted that after a while, fans know what's coming next.

How different from the day when the only visual aid in a Canadian hockey arena was a large portrait of the Queen at one end, and the only sound effects were created by an organ, played by someone with a repertoire of songs and fillers that he or she could vary according to the situation. Fans would have been involved in an interactive experience which would have grown from their reactions, the game's events and the cues to cheer prompted by the organist.[2]

In contemporary arenas, fans no longer consume the game on their own terms, or really even consume the game at all. They now consume the *experience of* the game. Lawrence Scanlan says it perfectly in *Grace Under Fire:*

> I loathe the music they play in modern arenas, for it suggests a cynicism and lack of faith in the game itself. What is played up is hockey as entertainment – the spotlights roving the ice

surface for effect, the Jumbotron bullying us into making noise, the team mascot using a toy bazooka to launch souvenirs into the crowd.... How is one to focus on the play when the circus is not only there, but in your face? (216)

The fact is, one is not. The environment is primary, and the feeling is of barely controlled chaos – albeit carefully created chaos – in which fans can scream and get crazy, every night, regardless of whether their team is playing well or not. The music and effects play a role alongside the action in creating moments when fans can enact rituals of imaginary violence (yelling, standing on their feet, waving their arms), regardless of what is happening in the game itself.

However, in one respect the modern game still resembles the game of the past. Hockey has always fulfilled its spectators' need for catharsis. The difference is that in earlier days, fans purged their fury when violence on the ice bled over into the stands, which happened regularly. The modern presentation of the game, by contrast, marks two inversions: real violence has been replaced by imaginary violence, and fan involvement is spurred not by action on the ice, but by artificial stimuli orchestrated far from the action itself.

3. Why People Used to Go – the Real Story

In fact, the docile image of the first two eras of hockey spectating as I described them erases much of the violent history of playing and watching hockey. Despite common memories of the past, hockey wasn't always a safe sport to watch. There is abundant evidence that the violence on the ice often spilled over to interactions between players and fans as well as fans and fans. In the early twentieth century, for instance, "Ontario Hockey Association president John Ross Robertson would lament coal tossing by fans in Lindsay, bottle tossing in Peterborough, and 'the inadequacy of police protection in smaller towns,'" according to Scanlan (41–42). *The New Yorker* magazine coverage of the sport from the 1920s and '30s indicates that fans in Madison Square Garden were known to throw newspapers down from the balconies to show their dissatisfaction (Monk, 184) and reports instances of a fan who heckled the Montreal Maroons'

Archibald Wilcox so badly that he retaliated with a punch to the nose through the wire which surrounded the rink (Monk, 185).

At mid-century, after a fight during a Rangers-Canadiens game, Montreal player Ken Reardon headed to his dressing room for medical attention. As he passed the New York bench, the players there heckled him, with fans joining in. Reardon responded by swinging his stick at one fan. As events continued, both sides got involved, as Scanlan recounts: "Montreal players went after fans in the corridor [and] the Rangers entered the fray to defend their fans" (Scanlan, 199). This is not to mention the Richard Riot of 1955, nor the extremes to which players went during that time to vent their anger on one another. Richard said late in his life, "If you know nothing else about the time I played, know about how violent the game was" (quoted in Scanlan, 199). Michael McKinley explains, "Dick Irvin would goad the Rocket into violence by telling him that people would think he was a coward if he didn't bash his tormentors" (185). Fans responded both by buying more tickets, and sometimes engaging in punch-ups themselves.

Gradually, however, the violence of the game came to be contained. On the ice, fighting has been designated as the role of a few players. Off the ice, spectators have come to assume (not always rightly) that the feeling of excitement, perhaps even frenzy, that they feel in watching the game will not result in their physically experiencing danger. However, this does not mean that spectating at a hockey game has lost its violent qualities. It's just that the violence is now created by the arena environment, and is governed by two imperatives: that the fan exercise his or her emotions while not violating the space, safety or enjoyment of the person in the next seat; and that these emotions, now created more by the music in the air than by action on the ice, should come in equal measure no matter what. In other words, a violent, but paradoxically safe, spectating experience is offered to NHL fans *every* night, rather than as a result of a particularly exciting game. Hockey, in short, has become a product which has managed to package its outlaw element and deliver it reliably to whoever wants it, whenever he or she wants it.

4. The Staging of the Modern Game

There are nuances to game presentation in NHL arenas that are not evident at first glance. After attending approximately eighty LA Kings and Anaheim Ducks games as a hockey writer over two seasons (2005–2007) I concluded that there is neither a consistent American approach to the staging of games nor an easy way to pigeonhole fans in terms of their knowledge of the game or their ability to appreciate it.

Los Angeles has only recently started to use a mascot, and the team rarely uses physical props to sell the game to the stadium crowd. But the atmosphere in the building most nights is full of loud rock music which overrides fans' attempts to interact with the action on the ice even while seeming to heighten their engagement with the game.

And while there are many long-time hockey fans in LA, the fans often do not seem to be tuned in to the action on the ice. There is sometimes minimal reaction to goaltenders making big saves or to smart penalty killing. Instead, a lot of what the fans do at Staples Center is in reaction to the cues they are given during breaks in play.

In Anaheim, despite the recent erasure of the absurd Disney-inspired Mighty Duck motif, there is a mascot. Wild Wing rappels from the rafters onto the ice to begin each game. One might assume, then, that he would form an important part of the action during game breaks, and that the game for this audience would be sugared-up for consumption by an unaware crowd. In fact, the opposite is the case, with Wild Wing being largely invisible during the game.

The fans in Anaheim, though not dressed like a crowd in Montreal or Toronto in the 1950s, respond as such a crowd might have done. When their goaltender makes a good save, they clap. When their team kills a penalty, they applaud the end of the two minutes. Their reactions are in almost every case enthusiastic, spontaneous and offered in response to what has taken place on the ice.

Why the difference between these two American franchises? Partly, it might be put down to the history of sports spectating in Los Angeles, with its record of violent fan outbursts at Raiders football games. Anaheim, which lies "behind the Orange Curtain" in the popular turn of phrase, is culturally a world away. I learned through interviewing them that many of the fans here discovered hockey in LA, but moved to Orange County because it is safer, more middle-class, more suburban (Kennedy). It is likely that their perceptions of themselves and of where they live bleed over into their behavior at a public event like a hockey game.

The difference partially comes down to the choices that the teams make in their production of the games. Los Angeles chooses an approach which focuses on the experiential factors of music and spectacle, but they also have a much weaker product on the ice. Perhaps they feel that they must enhance the experience or risk losing casual fans. The Ducks, by contrast, allow the game to outshine the staging of it. Naturally, they use some loud music, and they do use the "noise-meter" previously mentioned, but they also use an organ during many breaks in play.

Which leaves us to wonder, does the fans' clear and obvious interest in the game create the team's willingness to let them experience it on their own terms, or does the fact that the game comes to fans in Anaheim in a less-mediated manner allow them to develop the level of appreciation for the game which they show on a night-by-night basis?

Ducks Director of Entertainment and Multimedia Rod Murray explained the team's approach. "It's a world of feel; there's no governing list of rules," he said in an interview. "We try to put the focus on the game – there's nothing more important than the game." He admitted that, as research into game presentation shows, the Ducks think of themselves as "a brand, a franchise," and he commented that, "In a way, the three hours the fans spend in our building is a three-hour infomercial for our brand." But he tempered this by saying, "We try to effectively integrate that into the flow of the game, so that the game is primary."

Murray explained that while they must work a certain amount of commercial announcement into the time fans sit in their seats, "We get that stuff done as early as possible. The third period is when fans are into the game and its flow, and fan energy takes over." Or it does in the way that Murray and his staff present the game.

The system for doing so includes a full-time staff of five as well as up to fifteen game-night personnel, including the Game Director. "He makes decisions about what is presented; he has to be into the game and its rhythm. We try not to make it feel pre-orchestrated, you don't want to default to a [metaphorical] button B-12 and off we go. The Game Director has to ask, 'What does the fan want to be hearing and feeling right now?'" Here, of course, Murray gives away his allegiance to the current school of game presentation. Why, for instance, is it not asked if the fan wants to hear nothing at all?

The goal is for the game to feel, in Murray's words, "Not overly delivered." When Disney owned the team, by contrast, "They tried to bring their show into our building. It didn't fit. Now we have a sport-first mentality that we adhere to." Murray calls himself a hockey traditionalist, which further explains the use of the organ.

While still acknowledging that "my job is an inevitable reality of what professional sports have become," and commenting, "You have to look at [hockey in California] as just one entertainment option out here," Murray says that the goal at a Ducks game is to reflect what's actually going on, on the ice, and to give the fans a sense that those staging the game understand that they as spectators are knowledgeable about the team. "Fans ask, 'Are you really being honest with me about what's going on?' I need to be honest with them," Murray summed up. For the most part, the arena experience in Anaheim bears this out, though the temptation to elevate the volume manifests itself at times, even when it would seem least needed, such as in the 2007 playoffs when the Ducks won the Stanley Cup.

5. *Imaginary Carnival Violence*

Despite Murray's insistence that his approach allows the game itself to be the focus, his job would not exist without the current practice of staging games the way theatre is staged. And he is not alone. Most arenas, even those in Toronto and Montreal, manage the fan experience, and do so with the soundtrack, which changes remarkably little from arena to arena and game to game.

Teams, according to Ketra L. Armstrong, often appeal to the self-image of fans, attempting to lure them to games in the understanding that "consumers tend to select products/events that correspond to their self-concept" (EP3). Apparently, "The more similar images of product categories and brands are to individuals' real or aspirational images of themselves, the more likely individuals are to consume them" (EP4).[3] Perhaps related here is Hans Ulrich Gumbrecht's claim that "the rules of ... North American sports that deal with a mass spectatorship, [sic] are constantly fine-tuned in order to improve and intensify the possibilities of spectator participation. We can therefore be assured that the link between the game shaped by these rules and the spectator fascination is as close as possible" (361). How, then, should hockey spectating be understood, given the ubiquity of stadium music and the constant invitations to fans to step outside the decorum of their lives?

Karen Bettez Halnon uses language which might be useful in understanding this process as she discusses heavy metal concert-going. She says, "[W]hat takes place inside heavy metal carnival challenges ... a society that is everywhere 'marked by alienation, totalitarian control, and passive spectacular consumption'" (46). In such spectator experience, loud music "breaks through the noise of commercial culture by raising the transgression ante to the extreme and challenging nearly every conceivable social rule governing taste, authority, morality, propriety, the sacred, and, some might say, civility itself" (34).

The hockey arena environment hardly reaches the extremes that modern metal concerts do, though players battering each other with bare fists, often leaving the ice bloodied and sometimes being rendered unconscious might border on such transgressive action. However, the violence of the game, and the contained violence incited in the emotions of hockey fans, might allow the same opportunity to "vent, release, hector, parody, and rebel" (36) which Halnon says the metal concert does.

Using the ideas of Bakhtin as he described medieval carnival, Halnon says, "It is a highly transgressive, playful retreat from, and inversion and debasement of, the totality of officialdom" (36). And while spectating at a game does not involve the ritual debasement and sharing of the grotesque body which Bakhtinian carnival and heavy metal concerts share, it might not be a stretch to describe the activity as "giving free reign to the uninhibited, spontaneous 'me'" (43) or, at least, having the illusion that this is what one is doing.

The fan, in becoming wrapped up in the music, in screaming on cue, in being urged to identify with the team by the wearing of a replica jersey, can enjoy the sort of purgative experience which Aristotle said was the purpose of mass entertainment (even though he was speaking of drama, not sports), and this way the game may fulfill the mandate that the crowd be given the chance to vent their spleen in a controlled environment as an alternative to releasing these emotions on unsuspecting members of society.

One might read modern game presentation as a kind of sanitized regression to the early era of hockey gamesmanship. It could be argued that the contemporary version of hockey staging combines decorum with violence, retaining the two elements which have always been part of watching hockey in an inverse form which cleans up, if you will, the watching experience. The result is a kind of ritualized carnival where each spectator can experience the violence of the game, which in earlier eras spilled out into the stands with regularity, but a fan can experience it from a safe and secure position, protected even from the person in the next seat, who is perhaps similarly engaged in the violence of the game.

Hockey carnival gives people the chance to express themselves and be other than what they are in "real" time within a world of game-time where all is secure and violence doesn't spill off the ice, nor (hopefully) from spectator to spectator. The violence remains contained in a safe cell of carnivalized behavior, ritualized because it happens the same way game after game and rendered into a product itself, because it is packaged and delivered reliably and consistently.

A sort of controlled chaos is created by the staging of professional hockey games. Its purpose, from the team's perspective, is to enhance the spectator experience and sell tickets while controlling for the seemingly uncontrollable element in sports marketing – team performance. Analysis shows that such staging does two things: in the negative, it flattens the game out, taking emphasis off the action on the ice and the spontaneous reactions of fans to that action by treating all games as equal. In the positive, it allows for the kind of controlled carnival which gives fans the chance to vent their emotions and to participate in the violence of the game without personal risk, and it does so consistently.

While it seems that hockey spectating differs now from what it was when the only enhancement to the on-ice action was the organ, one might argue that at some level, the game fulfills the same essential function for fans as it always has as a cathartic experience marked by violence. But because the game in certain non-hockey markets is consumed by people who don't necessarily know how to react to it, it is "necessary," at least in these markets, to package it in such a way that they may reliably consume its carnivalesque elements simply by following the cues offered to them in light and sound.

1. In my implied critique of this era, again characterized by the "whatever happened to" portion of my title, I draw upon two emotions, nostalgia and ethnocentrism – nostalgia for the days of the suit and tie crowd, and ethnocentrism, anti-Americanism actually, which tells me that the current style of marketing the game is clearly "their fault." That is, without the need to sell the game in places where people don't love it on its own merit, or because they played or play it themselves, it wouldn't be necessary to wrap it in the garments of fuzzy creatures who wander the aisles nor ear-splitting music designed to engage the audience in the action.
2. There is, of course, still some flexibility in what happens during game-time in many arenas. Most NHL teams, for instance, still use the organ at times. However, for most, the script varies little from night to night.
3. Her study does admit that many marketing surveys take into account elements like facility, concessions, etc. (EP6), but she's interested in the sport itself as product, and she discusses the team primarily in relation to that.

Works Cited

Armstrong, Ketra L. "Self and Product Image Congruency Among Male and Female Minor League Ice Hockey Spectators: Implications for Women's Consumption of Professional Men's Sports." *Women in Sport and Physical Activity Journal* 10, no. 2 (2001): EP 1–16.

Bakhtin, M. M. *The Dialogic Imagination: Four Essays*. Translated by Caryl Emerson and Michael Holquist. Austin: University of Texas Press, 1981.

—. *Rabelais and His World*. Translated by Helene Iswolsky. Bloomington: Indiana University Press, 1984.

Gumbrecht, Hans Ulrich. "Epiphany of Form: On the Beauty of Team Sports." *New Literary History* 30, no. 2 (1999): 351–72. EP1–16.

Halnon, Karen Bettez. "Heavy Metal Carnival and Dis-alienation: The Politics of Grotesque Realism." *Symbolic Interaction* 29, no. 1 (2006): 33–48.

Hodgetts, William E. and Richard Liu. "Can Hockey Playoffs Harm Your Hearing?" *Canadian Medical Association Journal* 175, no. 12 (December 5, 2006): EP 1–5.

Kennedy, Brian. "Cities Apart: The Battle for SoCal Hockey Supremacy." *Inside Hockey*, January 29, 2005. http://www.insidehockey.com.

Kennett, Pamela A., Julie Z. Sneath and Steve Henson. "Fan Satisfaction and Segmentation: A Case Study of Minor League Hockey Spectators." *Journal of Targeting, Measurement and Analysis for Marketing* 10, no. 2 (2001): 132+ EP 1–10.

Klein, Norman M. *The History of Forgetting: Los Angeles and the Erasure of Memory*. London: Verso, 1997.

Madrigal, Robert. "Measuring the Multidimensional Nature of Sporting Event Performance Consumption." *Journal of Leisure Research* 38, no. 3 (2006): 267+ EP 1–16.

McKinley, Michael. *Putting A Roof On Winter: Hockey's Rise from Sport to Spectacle*. Vancouver: Douglas & McIntyre, 2002.

Monk, Craig. "When Eustace Tilley Came to Madison Square Garden: Professional Hockey and the Editorial Policy of the New Yorker in the 1920s and 1930s." *American Periodicals: A Journal of History, Criticism, and Bibliography* 15, no. 2 (2005): 178–95 EP 1–19.

Murray, Rod. Anaheim Ducks. Telephone Interview. April 4, 2007.

Scanlan, Lawrence. *Grace Under Fire: The State of Our Sweet and Savage Game*. New York: Penguin, 2002.

Wilkinson, Todd, and Richard Pollard. "A Temporary Decline in Home Advantage When Moving to a New Stadium." *Journal of Sport Behavior* 29, no. 2 (2006): EP 1–6.

CRAIG G. HYATT, WILLIAM M. FOSTER AND MARK R. JULIEN

"But What about My Feelings?"

Examining Edmonton Oilers Fan Reaction to Chris Pronger's Trade Demand from a Gift-Giving Perspective

Just days after leading the NHL's Edmonton Oilers to game seven of the 2006 Stanley Cup Finals, Chris Pronger informed the team that he wanted to be traded, and explained only that it was for private family reasons. Pronger was no run-of-the-mill NHL blueliner; he was a former league MVP who had just completed the first year of a five-year, $31 million US deal he signed after being traded to Edmonton.

Things were supposed to be different in Edmonton after the new collective bargaining agreement (CBA) between owners and players ended the lockout that cancelled the NHL's 2004–2005 season. Oilers fans had gotten used to watching unsuccessful teams since their last Cup victory in 1990. After winning five Cups in seven years, the team slowly became one of the economic "have-nots" in a league dominated by teams in much bigger markets with seemingly endless revenues to buy the best talent. Oilers management traded star players before they became free agents, knowing they could not afford to pay full market value to keep them. And available free agents the team could afford shied away from Edmonton because the team was not very competitive, the town was less-than-world-class or the winter was too cold. All that was supposed to have changed with the "cost certainty" of the new CBA, which imposed a salary cap that was designed to even the playing field. The trade for and subsequent signing of Pronger in the summer of 2005 was proof that things were changing for the better. Here was a star who wanted to be in Edmonton, on a team poised to be a championship contender for years to come. His demand for a trade seemed to come out of nowhere.

One reason why Pronger's trade request became an especially hot issue is the timing of the request. Rumours that Pronger wanted to be traded started less than a week after the Oilers lost game seven of the Stanley Cup finals. Getting to within one victory of the Stanley Cup yet ultimately falling short was a bitter pill for Oilers fans to swallow. When combined with the unhappiness of the team's star player and his decision to leave, the fans' frustration and anger quickly grew.

Fan reaction to the news Pronger wanted out of Edmonton came fast and furious. Oilers fan message boards in late June and early July of 2006 were filled with postings from angry fans expressing their frustrations. Many of these postings expressed a common theme. These fans had given the defenceman their hearts and souls in a very public manner, and now felt as if he had failed to reciprocate by asking to be traded from their favourite team.

Sociologist Alvin Gouldner noted that when people give gratification, they expect it in return. He called this the norm of reciprocity, and explained its importance in the maintaining of stable social systems, which is reflected in the fan-player relationship. The venomous fan reaction to Pronger's actions can be explained in terms of his violating this norm of reciprocity.

Explaining the how and why of sport fan behaviour, thoughts and emotions has kept academics busy for a generation. One seminal study[1] examined American college students' attachment to their school's football team. It noted that students were more likely to wear clothing identifying their school on Mondays following a football victory, than on Mondays following a defeat. It also noted that students were more likely to refer to the team as "we" following a victory than following a loss. The authors suggested that fans tried to associate themselves with the successful football team in order to have others hold them in higher esteem, and labelled this behaviour basking in reflected glory (BIRG). A decade later, Snyder, Lassegard and Ford conducted research and found that people separate themselves from unsuccessful groups in order to cut off reflected failure (CORF) and protect their image in the eyes of others. Other researchers have discovered that a fan's tendency to BIRG or CORF is related to his or her level of identification with a team. Die-hard fans have their identity as a fan so intertwined with their personal identity that they internalize both the team's wins and losses, while fair-weather fans are much quicker to distance themselves from the team when they are unsuccessful.

But there is not just a relationship between fan and team; there is also a relationship between fan and athlete. Identifying with specific players on the team is a big part of identifying with the team itself (Gladden and Funk; James; Kahane and Shmanske; Wann, Tucker and Schrader). In his study of the development of fan loyalty, James (222) found support for the notion that children who become fans typically first become attached to a sport, then to a team, and finally to a specific player on that team. Kahane and Shmanske (429–30) found that a Major League Baseball team's home attendance will drop as a result of high levels of player turnover on the team's roster. In a study of highly identified fans of North American big league sport teams, Gladden and Funk asked fans to indicate the importance of sixteen different things associated with their favourite teams including nostalgia, logo design, success, venue, head coach and peer group acceptance. "Star player" received the highest score (64). Wann, Tucker and Schrader surveyed undergraduate students to figure out why they continue to follow their favourite sports teams. While the number one reason was the success of the team, an attachment to the players was the second-most common response of the forty-eight students listed (998). The results of these studies lend support to the notion that maybe comedian Jerry Seinfeld was a bit off when he said loyal team fans merely "root for laundry." It appears that it matters very much to fans what players wear their favourite team's uniform.

What is it that directs these strong, personal attachments by fans towards individual athletes? The work of Alvin Gouldner on the norm of reciprocity and the nature of gift-giving can help answer this question. Gouldner, in his classic 1960 study, "The Norm of Reciprocity," reflected on the nature of basic trading relationships between natives living in two separate villages that made up part of a primitive society. The inland villagers traded vegetables for fish with the coastal villagers, and both parties appeared to live by a code where they understood not only that they were obliged to give as they receive, but also that if they did not, there would be negative consequences. Gouldner claimed that the give and take between the two parties ran so smoothly because there was something more going on than merely the mutual dependency created by the division of labour. He claimed that, "the partners share the higher level *moral norm*: 'You *should* give benefits to those who give you benefits'" (170, italics original). In further explaining the universality of this norm, he stated:

> There are certain duties that people owe one another ... because of their prior actions. We owe others certain things because of what they have previously done for us, because of the history of previous interaction we have had with them. It is this kind of obligation which is entailed by the generalized norm of reciprocity. (170–171)

Sport sociologist Todd Crosset drew upon similar theories to explain how bad feelings can develop between fans and golfers on the Ladies Professional Golf Association tour. He noted that it is common for fans and commentators to describe highly skilled professional athletes as "gifted," and suggested that the breakdown in the relationship between fans and athletes can be explained in terms of violating the rules of gift-giving. According to Crosset, the awesome skill great athletes display through sport is a gift they give to the fans (152–154). Reciprocity dictates that the fans return the favour by giving a gift back to the athlete – an appreciation of the skill shown in the form of cheering and clapping (156). Upon receiving the fans' gift, the athlete then is bound to return the favour through more inspired play, and the fans are bound to reciprocate again – possibly by asking for and cherishing the player's autograph (154–157). In the particular case of giving the gift of the autograph, the athlete also gives the gift of status due to the fan's personal interaction with the athlete (157). The fan then gives the gift of praise to the athlete. This cycle continues indefinitely, or until one of the two parties perceives a lack of reciprocation from the other and breaks off the relationship.

Crosset gives examples of such lack of reciprocation causing strained fan-athlete relations that he witnessed while conducting field research on the LPGA tour (165–171). He noted that golfers viewed certain fan actions as inappropriate, such as cheering particular golf shots that looked impressive but really were not or not cherishing an autograph that the golfer signed for them. From the fans' perspective, the gift-giving chain could be broken by golfers refusing to give autographs or by golfers who were perceived as not giving it their all and failing to give the gift of inspired play. When the rules governing reciprocity are broken, there are consequences. As Crosset explains, "infractions of the rules of reciprocity, felt as insult or offense, disrupt the status order. Infractions often generate a response which involves the loss of social standing for the perpetrator. Punishments include shaming, degradation, loss of reputation, and expulsion" (153).

Evidence of all four of these responses can be seen by examining the postings that appeared on Oilers fan chat rooms after it was announced Chris Pronger was traded to the Anaheim Ducks.[2] Many of the fan postings were short, to the point and quite venomous. Posts similar to the following from hfboards.com's "FCP Get the Hell out of Edmonton" thread from July third were not uncommon:

> "Gretzky and Messier look upon him with SHAME! Pronger, you ignorant ape, enjoy Disneyland. I hope you fall off space mountain!"

> "... get the hell out of here you ungrateful sack of poo!"

> "I hope that he still has a press conference tomorrow and no-one from the Edmonton media gives a crap. We got what we got in the trade, I could care less if he tells the world that he eats puppies. Good riddance to a multi-million dollar talent with a $0.02 popcorn fart of a brain."

> "Good riddance ... I hope you blow a knee and your career ends in the preseason ... you never will nor had any class."

"This guy is the biggest piece of **** in the world."³

While none of the messages contained a mention of the norm of reciprocity, we can hardly expect hockey fans to analyze their own reactions using sociological theory. However, some more detailed and thoughtful messages mention that something is "owed" the fans, and in these, fans may be trying to articulate that they gave Pronger something and feel he broke off the relationship before he gave them that necessary "something" in return. The following exchange between "okgooil" and "rec28" exemplifies this:

> "okgooil": … if you are having issues with your family, you probably should let the people that those problems affect know. In Pronger's case, this is most of the city of Edmonton that have paid to see him play – every season ticket holder that bought tickets to see him next year. No he doesn't have to spill his guts and give us a tell-all account, but a formal explanation would be the thing to do … if you don't want people to be curious about things that affect the team, and this does, don't play in the NHL.

> "rec28": Sorry, you and others here are operating under the assumption that the fan-player relationship is a very personal, two-way affair. As fans (i.e., "fanatics"), we invest a lot of energy, effort and emotion into our favourite teams and players and we like to believe that those teams and players have every bit as much affection for us. Sorry – they don't. It's a business. We pay them money to watch them play hockey. That is as far as the relationship goes. Any emotional investments that we make that go beyond this are our own problems. That we have paid money to watch Pronger play does NOT also imply that we should have unfettered access into his personal/family life.

> "okgooil": I know, but you are missing the point. Again, I am not asking for a tell-all book. I am a musician and have had to cancel gigs before. I feel like I owe the people who bought a ticket at least a small explanation. Well, and to be honest, I

guess that is the thing – I owe them nothing. But I feel I should give them something because it is the decent thing to do. If you want to keep fans you should try and make them happy. Yeah, I guess he owes us nothing, but come on, coming out with a statement for the rough cause of it all isn't asking too much. It is just the nice, polite thing to do ... and if you choose a career in the public eye, then you will ask for some of this ... It is just the reality of the situation. It isn't so much that I think it is right or wrong, as I am stating that it is just the way it is.

Here we have two fans trying to make sense of what is going on between Pronger and the Oilers fans, and trying to reconcile the dual nature of being a spectator: it is both a business involving economic transactions, and a passion involving seemingly irrational emotions. Both fans acknowledge that there is a component of market transaction (buy a ticket and watch a game), but that there is something much more going on (energy, effort and emotion).

There is a lot of evidence that sport fans mix economic exchange and reciprocity together and that it is very hard in professional sports to "unmix" them. Crosset addressed the topic in 1995 when he drew on the work of sociologist Lewis Hyde, who, in turn, had attempted to explain the intersection of the art world and western capitalist society. Crosset claims that art is analogous to sporting performance and athletes are gifted like artists. Consequently, he notes that Hyde's understanding of the existence of the market in the art world is applicable to sport:

Athletes, like artists, often feel that they have been given a gift, and thus feel obliged to display their talent through sport. The spectators, in turn, receive the gift of sport. In the same way that art lovers are moved by good art, and feel as if they have received a gift, fans are moved by displays of athletic prowess. With only slight revisions, the following quotation from Hyde about art seems equally applicable to sport.

> The [game or match] that matters to us – which moves the heart, or revives the soul or delights the senses, or offers

> courage for living, however we choose to describe the experience – that [game] is received by us as a gift is received. Even if we have paid a fee at the door of the [stadium], when we are touched by [excellence in sport] something comes to us which has nothing to do with price. (152)

In other words, even if you are paying for a gift, it is still a gift. Even with economic exchange, the norm of reciprocity continues to apply.

One of the potential links in the reciprocity chain between fan and athlete that Crosset notes involves the asking for, receiving and cherishing of an autograph (157,166–67). On one of the message boards, a thread developed where the topic turned to the destroying of Pronger's autograph. In the following exchange, we can see that the emphasis clearly is personal, not economic:

> "Flame killer": I have Pronger's signature on my Oilers jersey. If he ends up leaving, I will want to take it off my jersey. Does anyone know any way to get permanent marker off clothing?

> "Tekneek": Put it on ebay. There may be some jackass out there that will give you decent cash for it. Make some money off of fools who want the autograph of punk ***** players.

> "bleed_oil": If Pronger signed my jersey, I would burn it. Now my most hated Oiler ever ahead of Danny Cleary and even Comrie.

A breakdown in market transactions does not explain what is going on here – if we presume that "Flame killer" did not buy the autograph. The sentiments expressed by the fans seem to support the notion that Pronger violated the norm of reciprocity. By asking for autographs, fans give their gift of adulation to Pronger. In exchange, he gave the gift of status by signing. The fans in turn gave the gift of public displays of cheering in continued appreciation of his talent. They expected more gifted play in return. In this case, "Flame killer" did not get it, so he denounces Pronger's gift – the autograph.

Further evidence of the breakdown in the norm of reciprocity can be found in a posting by "Wyntermute," who started a discussion thread he labelled "When Pronger returns" with the following:

I hope his coach puts him in the starting lineup, so he's standing at the blueline [sic] during the anthems. Everyone with a Pronger jersey, bring a 12" square piece of cardboard, wrap your jersey around it with the 44 or nameplate showing, and frisbee it at his feet during the anthem. If you've got a Pronger jersey and can't make it to the game, give it to someone who can return it for you. The next time he's back, return those life-size Pronger posters the Oilers gave out, to his feet, during the anthem. The next time, give him a collection of Pronger-cover Oilers game day programs. Rinse and repeat until traces of Pronger are gone from your fine city. I hope he gets booed every time he plays in a Canadian rink until he retires. Further, I hope if Gretz is still managing Team Canada, Pronger won't get a sniff for disrespecting a great Canadian hockey city. Plus, wouldn't it be ironic if Mrs. Pronger filed for divorce shortly after he was traded into oblivion, and then she married a homeless pet in St. Louis?

This example is not unlike a person buying a birthday gift for someone weeks before the big day only to find out just before the birthday that the special someone has no intention of reciprocating on the buyer's birthday. In such a case, the buyer would have every right to return that gift to the place of purchase for a refund. From the fans' perspective, the gift they had for Pronger was their adulation shown in the form of wearing a jersey with his name and number on it, displaying a poster of him in their home or buying a game program with him on the cover. While love may be an abstract concept that is difficult to "return," the concrete symbols of that love might conceivably be returned. With the case of a well-worn customized jersey or a year old game day program, the seller will certainly not give a refund. When it comes to the poster, it was given away free to those in attendance on a specific night, so there was no economic transaction to refund. This left the fans little choice but to "return" them to Pronger himself, in a manner that could conceivably shame and degrade him – two of the common responses to a person who has violated the norm of reciprocity (Crosset, 153).

Fan reaction to a player who they feel has betrayed them can come in many forms. Trying to understand their strong negative feelings can lead to multiple explanations. One interpretation is to use the norm of reciprocity and the rules of gift-giving. From their words, however, we can see evidence of other events at work. As alluded to by "okgooil" and "rec28," some fans touched on the economic reasons behind their anger. It was mentioned more than once that season ticket holders would receive less value for their money in the upcoming season because the team would certainly be less talented and less entertaining to watch.

An alternate explanation for the vehement fan reaction to Pronger's trade request is that the fans were trying to repair the damage that they thought was inflicted on the City of Edmonton. Many Oilers fans took Pronger's trade request as an insult to the reputation of the city. To repair this damage fans engaged in a process of organic boosterism. Similar to civic boosterism, where civic leaders, organizations and the business elite promote a city to encourage economic growth (Artibise, Voisey), organic boosterism is a process where average citizens engage in activities designed to repair the perceived damage done to the city.

While "Wyntermute" says, "Rinse and repeat until traces of Pronger are gone from your fine city," other fans went much further. To repair the perceived damage done by the "knockers" (Artibise) fans took two approaches: demonizing the city's detractors and valourizing the city's virtues (Lawrence and Suddaby). Many fans attacked other cities, Pronger and his family, and the media from eastern Canada. All were portrayed in less-than-flattering terms to minimize what they perceived was the damage Pronger and others had brought upon the city. The one person who bore the brunt of the attacks was Pronger's wife, Lauren. Many fans held her responsible for Pronger's trade request and the damage inflicted on the city. As "callighenfan" writes:

> Truth is, Edmonton isn't exactly geared toward someone used to the lifestyles of the rich and famous (yet). Not a lot of high-end restaurants. Our domestic servants are horribly sub-

par (I've heard it said that they occasionally use no-name brand window cleaner ... :amazed:). The Lamborghini dealership is so hard to find it might as well not be there. Worst of all, some people insist on wearing flannel shirts. It must be like the Mars colony in *Total Recall* for her..

The fans' needed to portray Lauren Pronger as a woman who was unwilling to adjust to living in a new city. Fans claimed that it was not the city that was lacking but the wife of the superstar who wanted to leave the city.

Another technique that the fans used to repair the damage to the city was to trumpet its virtues. The city's parks, health care system and low crime rate were touted as some of the many reasons why people want to live there. Moreover, Pronger's decision to leave the city was interpreted as an act of irrationality. As "Canadian26" writes:

It's all about the wives/family ... But I don't really understand that either ... I mean it's not like Edmonton is a bad city or anything, low crime rate, good education/healthcare [sic] ... I don't get it ...

Pronger's non-disclosure for his trade request had insulted the city and the fans felt the need to repair those hurts by focusing on the city's good points.

Another explanation for the hostile reaction from fans is gender role theory, which suggests that men and women have a different core role that is primary to this gender identity (Barnett and Baruch). These core roles are driven by society's expectations and pressures. Societal norms support the notion that the man is the good provider and breadwinner (Barnett and Baruch, Simon, Voydanoff). Society also supports the notion that the woman is the nurturer and caregiver of the family (Barnett and Baruch, Simon, Voydanoff). Fans who have internalized these norms expect a male professional athlete to put his job first and family concerns second, while expecting his wife to look after the domestic situation while letting her husband concentrate on athletic excellence that will help his team win a championship.

Pronger refused to disclose the exact reason for wanting out of Edmonton, beyond repeating that it was for private family reasons. With no further explanation, fans speculated that his wife Lauren was to blame for his trade demand. "Wyntermute's" hope that her life would undergo major upheaval once she returned to her hometown of St. Louis is typical of the frustration many Oilers fans directed to Mrs. Pronger. Some fans likened Lauren to Janet Gretzky, who many feel caused the breakup of the Oilers' 1980s dynasty, or to Yoko Ono, who music fans blame for breaking up The Beatles. This evidence suggests that the fans' anti-Pronger sentiment may also be explained in part by the couple's apparent refusal to conform to their respective gender roles.

Then there is the reoccurring issue of Canadian national pride. Scholars have long noted the place that hockey holds in the Canadian national psyche, and how strongly Canadians will defend their national institution from attacks from outsiders – often Americans (Gruneau and Whitson). Some fans saw the Canadian Pronger coming to Edmonton after playing in two American cities (Hartford and St. Louis), then demanding a trade out of that Canadian city after only a single season, as an affront to hockey as a Canadian institution. "Wyntermute" sees Pronger's actions as disrespecting a "great Canadian hockey city," and suggests that he be booed by fans in every Canadian city he ever plays in, and hopes that he never plays for Team Canada in international competition again.

Like boosterism and gender role socialization, Canadian nationalism seems to play a part in explaining Oilers fan reaction to Pronger's trade demand, beyond what can be explained by the norm of reciprocity or poor economic value. Future research with other fans of different sport teams who feel betrayed by a favourite player may provide further insight into how these, and other factors, interact and overlap in producing the thoughts, feelings and actions they do.

Studying sports fans is nothing new. The relationship between fan and team has been researched for decades, and the bonds between fan and player have recently received quite a lot of attention. However, most of the analysis has examined the positive bonds between fans and their favourite players, not the nature of how and why those bonds can break.

The Pronger situation gave a unique opportunity to gain insight into a complex array of fan reactions. Fans expressing frustration over a player's poor play, or his desire to leave as a free agent to pursue more money or play on a Cup contender, or his being part of bitter contract negotiations is not unusual. With Pronger, however, he willingly signed a long-term contract with a team that seemed to now be one of the league's elite. His trade demand resulted in fans struggling to make sense of a situation that made little sense.

Fans thought his actions took value away from ticket buyers, knocked the city of Edmonton, flew in the face of gender role socialization and threatened hockey's place in Canadian culture. Underlying all of these reactions, however, was the notion that Pronger violated a universal social norm. While difficult for them to put into words, fans reacted as if they had given Pronger the gift of appreciating his awesome talent and loving him as a result, while the player refused to return the gift of inspired play. As predicted, shaming, degradation, loss of reputation and expulsion resulted.

1. Cialdini, Borden, Thorne, Walker, Freeman and Sloan (1976).
2. This is based on examining the messages posted in both the chat room on oilfans.com and the chat room on the Edmonton Oilers' section of hfboards.com. Fan postings were collected from the different threads that were created during the period of study. All messages dealing with Chris Pronger from when the rumours of his impending departure began (June 23, 2006), until he addressed the public after his trade to Anaheim (July 3, 2006) were read. In total over fifty threads and thousands of posts were examined.
3. Using chat room postings as data has its limitations. Unlike face-to-face interviews, follow-up questions cannot be asked to clarify points raised by the fans. For example, in the exchange between "okgooil" and "rec28", it would have been helpful to learn the extent to which "rec28's" Oil fandom was simply an economic transaction versus an emotional passion. A one-on-one interview with him would have provided an opportunity to find out.

   Chat rooms also enable the fans to post anonymously, meaning they do not have to take personal responsibility for their thoughts and opinions. This could quite easily lead to fans exaggerating the intensity of their feelings, as a kind of mob mentality sweeps them away in a wave of hate. On the other hand, anonymity allows fans to express thoughts and feelings that the social norms of polite conversation would dictate they not express in a formal interview. As a result, it is not known if statements such as, "I hope you blow a knee and your career ends" are an exaggeration by a fan who wants to go along with the crowd, or a true feeling that a fan would be too ashamed to admit to an academic gathering field data.

Works Cited

Artibise, Alan F. J. "Boosterism and the Development of Prairie Cities, 1871–1913." In *Town and City: Aspects of Western Canadian Urban Development*, edited by Alan F. J. Artibise, 209–235. Regina: Canadian Plains Research Center, 1981.

Barnett, Rosalind C., and Grace K. Baruch. "Social Roles, Gender and Psychological Distress." In *Gender and Stress*, edited by Rosalind C. Barnett, Lois Biener, and Grace K. Baruch, 122–143. New York: The Free Press, 1987.

Cialdini, Robert B., Richard J. Borden, Avril Thorne, Marcus R. Walker, Stephen Freeman, and Lloyd R. Sloan. "Basking in Reflected Glory: Three (Football) Field Studies." *Journal of Personality and Social Psychology* 34 (1976): 366–375.

Crosset, Todd W. *Outsiders in the Clubhouse: The World of Women's Professional Golf*. Albany, NY: State University of New York Press, 1995.

Gladden, James. M., and Daniel C. Funk. "Developing an Understanding of Brand Associations in Team Sport: Empirical Evidence from Consumers of Professional Sport." *Journal of Sport Management* 16, no. 1 (2002): 54–81.

Gouldner, Alvin. W. "The Norm of Reciprocity: A Preliminary Statement." *American Sociological Review* 25, no. 2 (1960): 161–178.

Gruneau, Richard, and David Whitson. *Hockey Night in Canada: Sport, Identities and Cultural Politics*. Toronto: Garamond Press, 1993.

James, Jeffrey D. "Becoming a Sports Fan: Understanding Cognitive Development and Socialization in the Development of Fan Loyalty." PhD diss., Ohio State University, 1997.

Kahane, Leo, and Stephen Shmanske. "Team Roster Turnover and Attendance in Major League Baseball." *Applied Economics* 29, no. 4 (1997): 425–431.

Lawrence, Thomas B., and Roy Suddaby. "Institutions and Institutional Work." In *Handbook of Organization Studies*. 2nd ed., edited by Stewart R. Clegg, Cynthia Hardy, Tom Lawrence and Walter R. Nord, 215–254. London: Sage Books, 2006.

Robinson, Barrie W., and Edna D. Salamon. "Gender Role Socialization: A Review of the Literature." In *Gender Roles: Doing what Comes Naturally?*, edited by Edna D. Salamon and Barrie W. Robinson, 123–142. Toronto: Methuen Publications, 1987.

Simon, Robin. "Gender, Multiple Roles, Role Meaning and Mental Health." *Journal of Health and Social Behavior* 36, no. 2 (1995): 182–194.

Snyder, C. R., MaryAnne Lassegard, and Carol E. Ford. "Distancing After Group Success and Failure: Basking in Reflected Glory and Cutting off Reflected Failure." *Journal of Personality and Social Psychology* 51, no. 2 (1986): 382–388.

Staples, David, and John MacKinnon. "How the Prongers Broke our Hearts." *The Edmonton Journal*, April 6, 2007. http://www.canada.com/edmontonjournal/story.html?id=92fab5f6-a0e8-43fe-bcb2-43fad1a44471&k=87141 (accessed July 18, 2007).

Voisey, Paul L. *Vulcan: The Making of a Prairie Community*. Toronto: University of Toronto Press, 1988.

Voisey, Paul. L. *High River and the Times: An Alberta Community and its Weekly Newspaper, 1905–1966*. Edmonton: University of Alberta Press, 2004.

Voydanoff, Patricia. *Work and Family Life*. Thousand Oaks, CA: Sage Publications, 1987.

Wann, Daniel L., and Nyla R. Branscombe. "Die-hard and Fair-weather fans: Effects of Identification on BIRGing and CORFing Tendencies." *Journal of Sport and Social Issues* 14, no. 2 (1990): 103–117.

Wann, Daniel. L., Kathleen B. Tucker, and Michael P. Schrader. "An Exploratory Examination of the Factors Influencing the Origination, Continuation, and Cessation of Identification with Sports Teams." *Perceptual and Motor Skills* 82 (1996): 995–1001.

Kelly Hewson

"YOU SAID YOU DIDN'T GIVE A FUCK ABOUT HOCKEY"[1]

Popular Culture, the Fastest Game on Earth and the Imagined Canadian Nation

In October 2003, I didn't give a fuck about hockey.[2] But that changed on June 7, 2004, the day the Calgary Flames lost to the Tampa Bay Lightning in Game Seven of the Stanley Cup finals. I live in Calgary. The Flames, who weren't even expected to make the playoffs, had won their way to a berth in the final, and with each successive series victory, the city had become increasingly hockey-mad. Houses were festooned with "Go Flames Go" posters; one hundred seventy thousand cars had Flames' flags flying from their windows; and there were upwards of fifty thousand fans on an avenue dubbed the "Red Mile" for every Flames game along the way. Many of us who were ignorant of or indifferent to the game suddenly became citizens of the hockey nation.

"You said you didn't give a fuck about hockey" comes from a song by The Tragically Hip, a band characterized, among other things, as quintessentially Canadian. Revered here, they play to sold-out stadiums in major cities in Canada, but are barely acknowledged in the United States, where devoted Canadian fans can cross the border and see them play to a crowd of a mere two hundred – mostly fellow citizens judging by the flags unfurled in the venues. Part of the reason for The Tragically Hip's success here and perhaps its lack of cross-border appeal has to do with its songwriting focus on Canadian points of reference: from painter Tom Thomson to the Golden Rim Motor Inn; from the Quebec ice storm to David Milgaard's wrongful imprisonment. But most significantly, perhaps, to hockey – from Bill Barilko (the Leafs player who mysteriously disappeared on a fishing trip in the summer of 1951 after scoring an improbable Stanley Cup-winning goal against arch-rival Montreal the season before) to Paul Henderson's "goal that everyone remembers" that earned Canada's last-minute victory over the Soviet Union in 1972. The band's associative relationship with the sport is forged by the lore surrounding them: they show up at arenas in the towns in which they perform for some pre-concert hockey; a music video of theirs includes a cameo by Don Cherry, Canada's most infamous hockey commentator; "Fifty Mission Cap," the Bill Barilko song, opens the Leafs' games in the Air Canada Centre; and on one year's tour, their concert shirts were replicas of the Maple Leafs' jersey. As well, the majority in attendance at Hip shows, which I faithfully attend wherever and whenever I can, are young men and boys wearing those same hockey jerseys and drinking beer.

These musicians from Kingston, Ontario – Kingston being one of the claimants of the almost sacred title, Birthplace of Hockey – are captivating songwriters. They may seem like lads. They may love and play hockey, but they are also able to imagine there are others for whom the game simply doesn't register. I used to be one of those. And because I have never been one to strap on a jock, fork over for season's tickets or drive the kids to practice in a minivan, I want to enter the arena the way I know best – by analyzing its cultural surface. I want to examine how ice hockey builds and signifies our nation.

The Hip song "Fireworks" is written from the perspective of a young man looking back on the conflict he experienced within a particular relationship. He is a hockey nut and his girlfriend, who doesn't "give a fuck about hockey," something he has never heard anyone say before, is "loosening his grip on Bobby Orr." She is diluting the brotherhood, opening him up to other sensations, like the intensity of that first "me and you." Against the romantic pull of his love for her is that most deeply mythologized element of Canada's construction of its nationhood: Paul Henderson's iconic Summit Series winning goal.

Iconic, indeed. This is one of those moments that acts as a historical beacon – a landmark around which many Canadians can communicate their exact whereabouts. And for most of my generation, the memory has to do with the state-sanctioned cancelling of classes so that a 20" TV could be wheeled into a gymnasium for us to watch (as if following the puck on a big screen television isn't hard enough!) And if you weren't there, it doesn't matter because the magical moment of Paul Henderson scoring that winning goal is so often reproduced, played and replayed that Canadians born well after the fact can still experience that thrill of victory, that fundamental moment of national identity presumably never to be felt again.[3] Or at least never again with the same purity or intensity.

Team Canada's last-minute win over the Soviet Union's hockey elite was a narrative of nation. For many observers, if not the players themselves, the Series would represent the first exposure of the Soviets to the reality of Westerners and the West, the land of decadence, profit, greed and temptation. Soviet officials were concerned about defections, many, of course, which occurred in the years following the series. On the hockey side, they took a humbler line, saying they were playing to learn from the experience. We Canadians already knew that our side, hockey- and otherwise, was naturally superior; the point was to demonstrate it against the representatives of the dreaded Red Army. These hockey players were, after all, also the soldiers of Soviet Socialism. So there was a Cold War scenario being played out: not only would our 'triumph' be sporting, it would be political. And as always, there was a third character in the romance – the United States. In defeating the Russians, we could show up our mutual neighbours, who were fighting the still evenly matched battle of the Space Race with the Soviets. In September 1972, hockey was the nation. Team Canada won … barely … and that narrow victory has been enlarged to contain all that is good and great about the game and our country.

But there's a nasty underlying truth to this fiction. Ice hockey is our symbolic capital – something for which Canada has historically garnered an international reputation for excellence. In this instance, though, national pride was revealed as national hubris. It was a complete humiliation and shame both to Team Canada and Canadians to discover that the Russians could outskate, outplay and outscore us. We resorted to desperate tactics. Our play got chippy; fans booed the players, and Phil Esposito, captain of Team Canada, had to make a public appeal beseeching fans to stop demoralizing the players. Later, Esposito confessed that he would have killed to win the Series, a feeling no doubt shared by the entire team ... which perhaps explains the shockingly vicious and debilitating slash by Bobby Clarke to the ankle of Valery Kharlamov – a player arguably as good if not better than any in the NHL. For a nation that banks on a myth of politeness and – preceding our involvement in Afghanistan – peacekeeping, we certainly revealed a brutal aggressiveness that significantly complicates whatever nationally-unifying 'victory' was achieved.

And to further complicate the sentimental constructions of national unity in 1972, that imaginary unity was on the verge of collapse. True, five years earlier, Canada was busy in identity formation mode: we had come off our Centennial, the 100th anniversary of Confederation, with everybody singing together "Ca-Na-Da"; our image as a nation of peacekeepers had been forged by Lester Pearson's solution to the Suez Crisis; and to distinguish ourselves from Britain, in a declared effort to encourage national identity, Pearson launched the initiative which saw Canada ditching the Union Jack for the Maple Leaf flag.[4]

But the putative unity of Canada was under siege in 1972, with the late '60s and early '70s unleashing the political energies of separatism. The Parti Québécois emerged in 1968, its primary goal the political sovereignty of Quebec by democratic means. In 1970, members of the *Front de libération du Québec* (FLQ) kidnapped and murdered Quebec's minister of Labour, Pierre Laporte. Soon, French would be declared the official language of Quebec, and Bill 101, the French Language Charter, would be instituted. By 1976, the Parti Québécois would come to power in Quebec, with 1980's referendum to its populace on Quebec's succession from Canada on the horizon.

Hockey had always been able to contain Canada's national schisms within itself. Divisions in Canadian society that expressed themselves politically as the desire for separation actually fed the unity of the game by fuelling the desire to compete on ice, and to celebrate that competition along municipal, provincial and, most importantly, linguistic lines. The chance to play out French/English rivalries in the rink necessitated an overriding commitment to the game; and that overriding commitment to hockey was rewarded with packed arenas and passionate play fueled by French/English rivalries.

Yet in 1972, the purity of ice hockey was under pressure from the other organizational system at work in the game: corporate ownership. To thwart the emergence of a rival league, the NHL expanded – really, doubled – in 1967, but even that move was not enough to stop the early-1972 establishment of the World Hockey Association and its flashy, salary-raising, player-defecting rivalry with the NHL. This rivalry did not leave the Summit Series untouched, with several Team Canada-worthy players, most notably Bobby Hull, barred from the team because of their affiliation with the WHA. The Team Canada/Team Soviet on-ice battle was seen to represent the clash between capitalism and communism – with the victory of the capitalist side a victory for capitalism itself. But the composition of Team Canada can be seen to represent the way in which a capitalist conflict undermined the interests of both the game and the nation which capitalism was supposed to serve best. Canadians saw the problem, and tried to overcome it. Famously, Prime Minister Trudeau himself appealed to the warring sides to allow Hull to play. Trudeau was rebuffed because the NHL had the power to deny him. In hockey, then, all the elements that both pull Canada apart and keep it together are in play. From the Canadian side, the Summit Series manifested a national team shaped by an international corporate war in a game that was supposed to represent unity for a country itself split apart by fault lines that the game used to mend.

To deepen the exploration of how nation and hockey have been mobilized in various ways to construct the Canadian identity, I'd like to tease out the implications of the words comprising the organizing structure of professional ice hockey in Canada: the NHL, the National Hockey League.

N: NATIONAL

In the 1960s, The National Hockey League consisted of the Original Six: teams from Detroit, Boston, Chicago, New York, Toronto and Montreal. Notice that the *National* Hockey League could consist – without contradiction – of teams based both in Canada and in the US. Notice, too, the two Canadian-based teams: one in Ontario, the other in Quebec. "National" then, as constructed by this league pre-1967 expansion included two nations, and, effectively, framed Canada with the Ontario and Quebec borders. This is a geopolitical emblem of issues that continue to characterize Canada – those of centrism and western alienation. Furthering the elasticity of the "National," ice hockey was not then Canada's official national sport, lacrosse was. But ice hockey was and is both embraced as and constructs the public concept of nation because it airs on Canada's national broadcasting corporation, CBC, on the almost ritually titled *Hockey Night in Canada*. It came into our homes, first via radio, then television, on Saturday nights, and whether you liked it or not, tuned into it or not, you grew up knowing who the hell Howie Meeker was and wondering, if you didn't give a fuck about hockey, why. And if you were from Western or Eastern Canada, you had two choices of Canadian teams – the English one from Ontario and the French one from Quebec.

Notice, too, that the organization rests on the myth of Canada as founded by the French and the English alone. While, by 1972, there was a real, though small, First Nations, Metis and Inuit presence in the game, culturally through the controversially named Chicago Blackhawks as well as personally in the form of famously 'Indian' players – George "Chief" Armstrong, and Jim (also "Chief") Neilson, there was no constitutional, organizational native presence – which, in turn, no doubt, limited and continues to limit native involvement on ice and behind the bench. Why? Because First Nations, Metis and Inuit peoples don't own NHL teams. Though the first one-piece hockey sticks were carved by Mi'kmaq tribes in New Brunswick, and these sticks are the root of the game, it is the colonizers who hold on to its economic power and assimilating strategies such as privileging written rules and building official teams on the basis of prior-existing white institutions such as universities, military colleges and towns. In effect, to be included in the hockey nation, one had to live the white man's game.

What, exactly, does "National" mean, then, when one looks at the history of Canada?

As Rinaldo Walcott describes it:

> with its ethnic mix of English, French, Ukrainians, Italians, Jews, Germans, Poles, Portuguese and other Europeans as well as Japanese, Caribbean, Chinese, South Asian, continental African, black Canadian and Native peoples, we get a very complex picture of who or what the Canadian might be. All of these groups (except for the Natives) migrated at different points in time and have found themselves placed differently in narratives of the nation, in ways that complicate the fiction that the modern nation-state is constituted from a 'natural' sameness.[5]

Walcott argues that politically the Canadian nation struggles with making sense of communities founded across and upon difference. In answer to this challenge ice hockey declares its own nation. In the hockey nation (and within that such fan tribes as the Leafs Nation) First Nations, Metis, Inuit, European, Ukrainian, African, French-Canadian and American "differences" are assimilated under the community of those pledging allegiance to the game. Part of the hockey nation-building machinery involves what Pierre Bourdieu calls the "symbolic conquest of youth."[6] For instance, there is considerable pressure – on young boys primarily – to play hockey, and for families to support the practices and tournaments that take over family life. And of course, once one has played a sport, there is usually an interest in continuing to follow the game, whether through coaching or simply continuing to watch, fuelling membership in the hockey nation. We now also have European players being drafted here, leaving their homelands behind and becoming honorary Canadians. As well, the 'racial purity' notion infuses team-building. For years, it was assumed the Montreal Canadiens would have first dibs on Francophone players and more recently, the Quebec Nordiques franchise had their trades tied to the draft of Francophone players. An ideal Canada is produced in the craze of its national game.

Where the discourse of heritage in Canada proper, with its official multicultural policies, seems to suggest that "heritage" always means coming from elsewhere, heritage in the hockey nation seems to mean nostalgic repetition, as in November's Heritage Series 2003 – an outdoor game between Canadiens and Oilers old-timers, complete with the players wearing toques and -40°C weather in Edmonton. Again, I am not trying to be a killjoy here – there is and was something oddly inspiring about this spectacle visually, particularly the sight of forty thousand fans sitting for two hours in that cold.

However, taken in the twenty-first century, this celebration-by-recreation of hockey's – and by implication Canada's – heritage, reveals the way in which hockey, in revaluating itself, might be said to falsify the truth of the nation in favour of its ideal. The Heritage Classic, acknowledging the failure of Toronto to hold up the English-language side of the game, went back to hockey's original dynamic in pitting the best of the English-Canadian teams against the best of the French-Canadian. This is the division which is so accepted as to seem a necessary part of the game. But Canada is composed of more groups than those defined by speech. We are a nation of ethnicities as well as languages. Hockey uses this to its advantage, ignoring it under some circumstances, and acknowledging it in others. Where the face of hockey in the Heritage match was primarily white, with no effort (probably not even a thought) to include a population-based proportionate number of non-white (and possibly non-NHL) veterans of the heritage game, April 2004's *The Calgary Herald* offered us in its headline "The new face of hockey," Jarome Iginla, Captain of the Flames, dubbed during the Flames' winning streak that year as "Captain Canada." Ironically, perhaps, Captain Canada regularly honours Grant Fuhr, another player of African descent[7] and the only non-white in the Heritage Classic. On the national level, however, the country cannot treat race as if it is subordinate to purpose, or less real a political fact than language, as much as hockey's re-presentation of heritage and the future might pretend that it can.

Throughout the years and seasons, there are regular reconfigurations of the national. In 2004, with the Montreal Canadiens and Toronto Maple Leafs out of the playoffs, a big dilemma emerged in Ontario about whom to cheer for. *The National Post* printed a list of Canadian players on US-based teams, encouraging people to cheer for some of them – this against the alternative of cheering for Calgary, the only Canadian-based team in the playoffs. However, the latter idea won out. When The Flames won the Western Conference, *The Post* printed its front page banner in red, as opposed to blue, and declared Calgary "Team Canada." The article was titled "One Nation One Goal," evoking the Summit Series of 1972, with Calgary becoming The National. So this game can overcome western separatism, and the west can provisionally become the centre as "Team Canada" united once again to attempt to defeat a US-based team, the Tampa Bay Lightning, whose roster then included three American, seven European and thirteen Canadian players![8] Even Edmonton, the capital city of Alberta and rival city to Calgary, decided that year to put aside historical grudges and in *The Edmonton Journal*, labelled the Calgary Flames "Team Alberta." Calgary became The Provincial as well. Still, however – two nations. Asked who he was cheering for, Bloc Québécois leader Gilles Duceppe answered "Tampa Bay" because its stars – Vincent Lecavalier, Martin St. Louis and Brad Richards – represented as far as possible "the French team."

H: HOCKEY

According to Roland Barthes, professional sport operates by virtue of myth. Following Barthes' model, we can see that ice hockey is not necessarily anchored in any one national trait and so captures many, and it is this flexibility that allows hockey to signify the equally flexible nationalism. If we ask exactly what game is being played, hockey provides an abundance of seemingly contradictory answers, and that's because rather than confining experience, it adapts itself to the conditions of the experience in which it is said to be found. That's why we can hear hockey defined as the game played equally on frozen ponds, roads, in the gym or on a tabletop; as folk expression and commodified spectacle; as both diversion from political life and a unifying political force, or, most famously by poet Al Purdy as "this combination of ballet and murder."

Hockey has recently been signified in Freudian terms by another of the game's poets, Richard Harrison, author of *Hero of the Play*. At a conference in Hull commemorating the opening of the Rocket Richard exhibit, weeks after Todd Bertuzzi's neck-breaking attack on Steve Moore, Harrison, in conversation with Roy MacGregor, articulated that "Hockey is the National Id," a phrase which captivated MacGregor and served as the epigraph to his article in *The Globe and Mail* in April 2004 called "Cultural Power Play." To suggest that hockey is the national id is to suggest that hockey is our irrationality, our pleasure and impulse centre, detached from the intervention of the superego's conscience mechanism. To say that hockey is the national id is to say that hockey is sheer animal intensity that we can all experience or share. But what exactly are we sharing? Some would say it is not a terribly refined collective experience; after all, it's largely about screaming, beer and, more than occasionally, streaking and stripping (kind of like a Hip concert!).

While certainly hockey language lacks the substance, flexibility and variety of other languages, it performs a useful community-building function. It is an easy language to be literate in – for instance, think of how many situations for which "they need to create a scoring opportunity" can work its way into the conversation. It creates points of contact where there might not normally be any. A social lubricant, hockey talk can be guaranteed to evoke at least an opinion from just about anyone. Of course, it can also function as a substitute for substantial communication. The clichés, the small talk, the quips make it a less complicated language to utter … less risky, perhaps?

Hockey continues to signify a particular kind of masculinity-in-action, as typified by the words of my hockey-playing brothers – "it's the rush of endorphins that you feel because of the speed; it's the velocity; it's the physicality," – as well as a not-all-that-sublimated homoeroticism – all those fit male bodies, proudly displaying battle scars and lost teeth. However, it is also adding to its definition with the rapidly-expanding world of women's hockey, a game which embraces a different kind of toughness, one that holds on to the exertions of the body but lets go of the idea that strength is measured by injuries endured.

Yet no cultural creation moves as a unit. There are (as there must be) those who try to anchor the floating signifier that is hockey. Don Cherry fulfills the role of Raymond Williams' concept of "the residual" – those aspects of the present that preserve the past and appear as constant or universal values. The über-hockey dad, Don breaks off from his slot on "Coach's Corner," a five-minute segment during at least one intermission on *Hockey Night in Canada*, in an attempt to resurrect the differences that hockey is in the process of erasing as it expands its definition. So he declares his definition of hockey (and simultaneously, masculinity) – grinding, physical, Canadian, not the game that wussified Europeans play – and feeds us our definition of Canada: anti-immigration and anti-bilingual. A figure who reminds us of "the greatness" of our game as played, and of our nation as constituted in 1972, The Coach seemed to be on his way out in 2004, but due to his enormous popularity (he was even voted one of the ten Greatest Canadians in a national poll) the CBC, who had him on a seven-second delay after his particularly inflammatory remarks about Franco-Canadians, renewed his contract.

Ice hockey is the distillation of our terrain – the ice and cold of Canadian winters, which all of us share in varying degrees and lengths – into a game space. It is a marker of our cultural differentiation from every other part of the Commonwealth; unlike other colonies, we didn't take up the flat bat or the football, but crooked timber and a rubber disc.

In his book, *National Dreams: Myth, Memory and Canadian History*, Daniel Francis speculates that "because we are spread out so sparsely across such a huge piece of real estate, Canadians depend on this habit of 'consensual hallucination' more than any other people."[9] Hockey is visual. It engages the act of imagination and this in turn facilitates mental construction of the nation and national identity.

Francis's point goes some way in explaining the patriotic, nostalgic iterations that comprise the cultural field of hockey. American culture so infiltrates our national space, it seems imperative to us to claim supremacy in something we think we own.

Some suggest that the nostalgic iterations of ice hockey are an attempt to recapture something; and there is no lack of cultural material on ice hockey that demonstrates a hero-worshipping, sentimentalizing discourse. Still others suggest that the increasingly rich body of work about hockey is proportional with the nation's attempts to create a myth, one perhaps as celebrated in literature and rich in exploration as baseball is in the US. There is much evidence to say so.

For instance, David McNeil of Dalhousie University has researched and organized HIP: Hockey in Print, devoted to hockey texts and songs, and the list is extensive. What is striking is the amount of evidence of what Gary Genosko refers to as non-normative representations of ice hockey in popular culture.[10] Hockey was queered with the production of Brad Walton's opera, *The Loves of Wayne Gretzky* and its bad boy dramatized in *The Lindros Trial*. A film called *Chicks with Sticks* premiered in 2005. Of the many songs about hockey, not all are anthems of normative masculinity – Jane Siberry's "Hockey"; The Tragically Hip's "Fireworks" and Stompin' Tom Connors' "Ode to Hockey Moms," to name a few. Even if we examine so-called classic hockey literature like Roch Carrier's *The Hockey Sweater*, we recognize that the book is not so much about the sweater as it is about the connection between a mother and a son. The opening poems of Richard Harrison's *Hero of the Play* collection are about ice hockey in the Ivory Coast, and in A. M. Arruin's collection, *Crooked Timber: seven suburban fairie tales*, the story "Rumpelstiltzky" focuses on a veritable united nations of a hockey game with Russian, Transylvanian and Antarctic players, as well as Irish dwarves, girls and "boodists." Erotica has entered the arena with Dave Bidini's *The Five Hole Stories* collection and the play upon which it was based. A final delightful example, this of the multicultural manifestations of hockey, emerges in Srinivas Krishna's film, *Masala*. Focusing on the challenges of identity formation in South Asian diasporic communities, Krishna, a Toronto filmmaker, includes a scene in which Lord Krishna, the deity, outfitted with a Leafs' jersey, confronts a van of Canada Post workers in a back alley game of ball hockey.

L: LEAGUE

Hockey allows for leaguing, but, as much as it organizes games, leaguing also destabilizes the game. It is the critical term that talks of exclusion. Leaguing, after all, has to do with allegiances you do and do not form. With whom is one in league? In hockey, you are drafted onto a team. Ideally you are in league with your fellows, a class of contestants, mutually helping the team. But how does one become "in league with" from the outside? One of the ways is through ritual. During the Flames' run, the Calgary CBC radio show, *The Calgary Eyeopener,* held a contest asking for people to submit their sports rituals. What follows is the winning entry, submitted by Mr. Bukhari and copied to me by the CBC with his permission:

> Absolute Ritual for my Team
>
> Being new Canadian, still big traditional fan of Cricket and I am telling the story of ritual we used to follow during India Pakistan cricket matches in South Asia –
>
> Follow this always to make your team winner:
>
> Minimum three (max no limit) families should watch together the game on one TV set and potluck menu arranged by women with trad but delicious food items and three quart of food contains all kinds of dishers should sent first to orphan house. Harmony and enthusiasm among fans is very important during watching the game – if there is an argument OR fight between viewers it could create curse on favourite team:) that's right – I am witness…. Key point of ritual: if your team is loosing – among viewers whoever feels more heartbreaking should take off his shirt and go outside the house and yell in favour of his team and run at least 100 meter on the street. And if that person is female she should

go and start cooking something more yummy for all and some other male volunteer should go for her without shirt 100 meter running ... folks! I have tons of stories to tell how we won the game because of this :) Flames fans – I am not joking believe me it works :) watch hard – don't give it up... :)

So in this ritual, we have men doing the watching and running around shirtless while women are forced to beat a hasty retreat into the kitchen! It was interesting to note that the overriding characteristic of the females' rituals in this CBC contest had to do with avoiding watching or hiding during the game.

Then on May 19, 2004, in Calgary, we saw women baring their breasts in the postgame frenzy on the Red Mile. Commentators talked about the carnivalesque atmosphere where the body is freed up – where taboos are broken – and spoke of this as the reason for the women's entry into the arena. Others decried what they saw as a performance of old sexualized roles and lamented that young women's "way in" was again sexual as opposed to political and economic.

I had a different view. A new ritual began: instead of hiding in the house or hovering in the kitchen, women entered the streets, baring their backs or their fronts. Or both. And I wondered: is this how some women who aren't players themselves get in league with the hockey nation? Not just as puck bunnies or athletic supporters, hockey wives, sisters or mothers, but as participants in the celebration of bodily power, as totems of victory, as frontrunners in the parade? Parades are often linked with the idea of nation – Bastille Day, May Day, Independence Day, even the Calgary Stampede parade – and they function to display an idea, create a feeling about something, and to galvanize the spectators. And what is one of the things a spectator can do when galvanized? Join the parade.

But what began as random acts of spontaneity quickly became objects for speculation. The media hyped the issue. Men, women and children went out to gawk and record, and the infamous "Calgaryflameschicks" website got up to one million hits in a single day.[11]

League implies a class of contestants. The ones who are worthy, who are in a league of their own, are usually men. Some of the exceptions in hockey are Hayley Wickenheiser, who played for a time on a men's team in Finland, and Manon Rhéaume, who once played goal in the NHL. There are difficulties to getting "in league with" – elitism, sporting clubs and their colonizing structures, tradition – so what women have typically done is create a league of their own; it is usually not well-funded, doesn't get the time, support, money or coverage that men's leagues do, but it manages, nevertheless, to win.

But what is it that makes some of us want to be "in league with?" I think it's about hopefulness. It's about alliances. It's about mutuality and respect. It is The Tragically Hip, those hockey icons, flying to Salt Lake City to put on a concert for the Women's Olympic gold medal winners in 2002. It is thirty-five thousand fans in Calgary attending a rally in the heart of the city for the team that lost the Stanley Cup.

So ice hockey, I think, is something that can be appropriated, reused, revaluated and reconfigured. Two line passes, the return of the tag-up offside rule, the women's game, the enhancement of divisional rivalries, not just European players but European team captains, a salary cap, reduced goalie gear, a crackdown on obstruction, the Stanley Cup standing like a hero in Red Square and shootouts to end tie games ... hockey is always *becoming*, just as the nation is ... It provides us with exemplars of how the past forms of nation and present possibilities of nation come together and collide. In that sense, hockey can be understood not simply as a force in the creation of the Canadian national myth and identity, or simply as a mirror for the political and social forces with which it actually interacts, but as a means by which we get a glimpse of entities that form across nineteenth and twentieth century nations. Hockey gives Canada a role model for itself in a post-national world.

1   The Tragically Hip, "Fireworks," *Phantom Power* (New York: Universal, 1998).
2   In October 2003, I submitted a proposal about ice hockey and the imagined Canadian nation to an international postcolonial studies conference that I attend triennially. Held in Hyderabad, India, in August 2004, its theme was "Nation and Imagination," with one of the sub-themes being "Sport and the Nation." I did not "give a fuck" about

hockey in October 2003, and my proposed paper was attempting to explore those of us sidelined by this overarching national descriptor.

3   A recent CBC radio show reported this as the most shown and viewed clip in Canadian broadcasting history.
4   The leaf of the maple tree on which the Canadian flag is based is not even found in Alberta or British Columbia – it's a central Canadian tree, primarily, but that is another story ...
5   "Keep on Movin': Rap, Black Atlantic Identities and the Problem of Nation," 115.
6   "Sport and Social Class," 365.
7   Iginla's honouring of Grant Fuhr is an example of how the hockey archive can transform the hockey nation's present by expanding its past.
8   Many thanks to the Ontario-based members of the Hewson clan, the legitimate hockey fans, who contributed these and other important observations to this paper.
9   Page 10.
10 "Hockey and Culture," 231.
11 Dr. Mary Valentich, an expert in human sexuality, recently retired from the University of Calgary, proposed a study to explore the reasons for so many women's toplessness during the Flames' run. She felt it was important to ask the women themselves rather than accept the labels so many of us were so willing to place on them. The study earned the dubious distinction of being one of the "strangest stories in sport in 2005," according to www.badjock.com. Her findings, based on a sample of six women, were presented in May of 2006 in a keynote address at the Western Canadian conference of Sexual Health. Dr. Valentich discovered, from her in-depth discussions with her subjects, that "going topless was a complex phenomenon, with varying motivations expressed by women in the sample." (Greg Harris, "Red Mile research," *OnCampus Weekly* [University of Calgary], May 5, 2006).

Works Cited

Barthes, Roland. *Mythologies*. Compiled and translated by Annette Lavers. London: Random House, 2000.

Bourdieu, Pierre. "Sport and Social Class." In *Rethinking Popular Culture: Contemporary Perspectives in Cultural Studies*. Edited by Chandra Mukerji and Michael Schudson, 357–373. Berkeley: University of California Press, 1991.

Francis, Daniel. *National Dreams: Myth, Memory and Canadian History*. Vancouver: Arsenal Pulp Press, 1997.

Genosko, Gary. "Hockey and Culture" in *Landmarks: A Process Reader for Canadian Writers*. 2nd edition. Edited by Roberta Birks, Tom Eng and Julie Walchli. Toronto: Pearson, 2003.

McNeil, David, dir. Hockey in Print (HIP): A Bibliography of Writing on Hockey. http://www.hip.english.dal.ca/.

Walcott, Rinaldo. *Black Like Who? Writing Black Canada*. 2nd ed. Toronto: Insomniac Press, 2003. See esp. "Keep on Movin': Rap, Black Atlantic Identities and the Problem of Nation."

Contributors

Michael P. Buma holds a PhD in English from the University of Western Ontario. His dissertation examines the cultural work of Canadian hockey novels, focusing particularly on the ways in which the game has been mythologized as a marker of nationhood and masculinity. He currently teaches at Western and Redeemer University College.

Jamie Dopp is an Associate Professor of Canadian Literature at the University of Victoria. He has published a variety of articles on Canadian fiction, poetry, and culture, as well as one novel and two books of poems. In 2004, during a very rare cold spell in Victoria, he stayed up all night to build a backyard ice rink and managed to have three blissful days of outdoor hockey with his family.

William M. Foster is an assistant professor of management at the Augustana Campus of the University of Alberta. He received his PhD from the University of Alberta School of Business and the Faculty of Physical Education. His main hockey interest is being an avid fan of the Edmonton Oilers. He is also looking forward to the day when his daughter will join him on the ice.

Stephen Hardy, PhD, is Professor of Kinesiology and Affiliate Professor of History at the University of New Hampshire, where he also serves as Faculty Representative to the NCAA. His publications include *Sport Marketing* (3rd ed., 2007), *How Boston Played* (1982, 2005) and numerous articles, reviews and book chapters, several of which deal with early hockey in America. He played hockey for Bowdoin College in the late 1960s and co-captained the 1969–70 team with his twin brother, Erl. After coaching stints at Vermont Academy and Amherst College, he joined the Eastern College Athletic Conference in 1976, where he served as an assistant commissioner and hockey supervisor until 1979. During this time, he helped manage collegiate tournaments in venues such as the Boston Garden and Madison Square Garden, and worked closely with the NCAA Ice Hockey Committee and its affiliated championships. He is a founder of the Charles Holt Archives of American Hockey, located at UNH's Dimond Library. In 2003, he was selected by the Hockey East Association as one of twenty "special friends" to celebrate the league's twentieth anniversary. He and his wife Donna live in Durham, NH.

Richard Harrison is the award-winning author of six books of poetry, among them *Hero of the Play* (now in a 10th Anniversary Edition), the first book of poetry launched at the Hockey Hall of Fame, and the only one read at the Saddledome, home of the Calgary Flames. Richard was the University of Calgary's Markin-Flanagan writer-in-residence for 1994/95. In the spring of 2000 the Calgary Booster Club honoured Maurice Richard, Jean Beliveau, Bobby Hull and Gordie Howe at the club's Annual Sportsman of the Year dinner, the first and last time all four were honoured together. Richard wrote four poems specifically for the occasion and read them as part of the ceremony. Richard's other hockey writings – both poetry and prose – have been published widely in Canada and the United States. Currently he lives in Calgary with his wife and family, and is a professor of English and Creative Writing at Mount Royal University.

Anne Hartman is a PhD Candidate in Social Anthropology at York University. Her research interests include the anthropology of settler societies, Canadian nationalism, postcolonial theory, sexuality studies, the politics of affect, public space and play. She is currently writing her doctoral dissertation on women's shinny in Toronto parks, based on her ethnographic fieldwork during 2007 and 2008, which gives her the perfect excuse to lace up her skates at every opportunity. She continues to live, and play, in Toronto.

Kelly Hewson joined Mount Royal's English department in 1993 where she teaches postcolonial literatures, film studies and composition. Her hallway colleague is Richard Harrison whose thoughtful passion about ice hockey sparked her initial thinking about the sport. She is still astonished by how generative and engaging her foray into this arena is proving.

Andrew Holman is a professor of History and Canadian Studies at Bridgewater State College in Massachusetts. He is the author of several studies on hockey's history and meaning and, most recently, editor of *Canada's Game: Hockey and Identity*, published by McGill-Queen's University Press in 2009.

Craig G. Hyatt is an Associate Professor in the Department of Sport Management at Brock University, St. Catharines, Ontario. His research focuses on sport fans who fall outside of many of the existing sport fan models, such as fans who have lost their favourite team through franchise relocation, fans who switch loyalties from one team to another and fans who reject the obvious local option to cheer for a distant team instead. He has been published in such journals as the *Journal of Sport Management*, *European Sport Management Quarterly*, *Journal of Sport Behavior* and the *International Journal of Sport Management and Marketing*.

Mark R. Julien, PhD, is an Assistant Professor in the Faculty of Business at Brock University in St. Catharines, Ontario. His doctorate is from Carleton University, Ottawa. His research interests include: how Aboriginal leadership differs from non-Aboriginal leadership, how Aboriginal network groups are an effective retention strategy, what employers can do to help employees balance work and family and the impact of gender roles and gender socialization. He has published in such journals as: *Human Resource Professional*, *Leadership Quarterly* and *Advancing Women in Leadership*.

Brian Kennedy, PhD, is an associate professor in the English department at Pasadena City College, where he teaches contemporary British and Commonwealth literature (including Canadian literature) as well as writing classes.

He is the author of two recent works of creative nonfiction, *Growing Up Hockey* (Folklore Publishing, 2007) and *Living the Hockey Dream* (Folklore Publishing, 2009), as well as the co-editor of an anthology, *The People and Promise of California* (Pearson-Longman, 2008). He has also published academic articles on a variety of topics including WWI fiction, Virginia Woolf, Henry James and Mikhail Bakhtin.

In addition to his academic work, Dr. Kennedy covers NHL hockey for *Inside Hockey* and other media outlets.

E.W. (Ed) Mason is a Canadian Kiwi. Ed lectures in communication degrees at Unitec New Zealand in Auckland. He played recreational hockey in Ontario before immigrating to New Zealand in 1980. Ed is a Life Member of the New Zealand Ice Hockey Federation having handled the Federation's media for seventeen years and serving as Junior Vice President.

Sam McKegney is a scholar of Indigenous and Canadian literatures at Queen's University in Kingston, Ontario, Canada. His book, *Magic Weapons: Aboriginal Writers Remaking Community After Residential School*, examines the ways in which Indigenous survivors of residential school mobilize narrative in their struggles for personal and communal empowerment in the shadow of attempted cultural genocide. He has published on Indigenous literature, politics and activism in journals like *English Studies in Canada*, *The Canadian Journal of Native Studies*, *Studies in American Indian Literatures*, *Topia* and *West Coast Line*. Sam considers himself the worst in a long line of pretty good hockey players; his uncle Tony McKegney amassed three hundred twenty goals and three hundred nineteen assists over thirteen seasons in the NHL and his father played three games for the Chicago Blackhawks in the 1976–77 season – the year Sam was born.

Contributors

David McNeil is an Associate Professor in the Department of English at Dalhousie University, where he gets to teach, among other things, a class on "Sports Literature and Culture: Hockey." He has completed a biography (with companion DVD) of his father Gerry McNeil who played for the Montreal Canadiens (1950–54). He also maintains an online bibliography "Hockey in Print" (HIP) at www.hip.english.dal.ca.

John Soares teaches history at the University of Notre Dame in Indiana, USA. He is writing a book about international ice hockey and relations among Canada, the USSR, Czechoslovakia and the United States during the Cold War. Among his recent publications are articles about US foreign policy in *The Journal of Cold War Studies* and *Cold War History*; and articles about international hockey in the *Journal of Sport History* and the *Brown Journal of World Affairs*. The son of a former minor league player, college coach and NHL scout, he has played the game for years and is currently a cautious, stay-at-home defenceman for the Notre Dame faculty-staff team.

John Soares would like to acknowledge the support and encouragement he has received on this project from the organizers and participants of the 2007 conference on Canada & the League of Hockey Nations and from Jim Hershberg, Jeremi Suri, Fred Logevall, Leo Ribuffo and from the scholar who first encouraged him to pursue hockey and the Cold War as an academic project – his wife, Linda Przybyszewski.

INDEX

Air Canada Centre, 188
Amateur Hockey Association of Canada (AHAC), 23
Amateur Hockey Association of the United States (AHAUS), 99–100
American Hockey Coaches Association (AHCA), 31
Anaheim Ducks (formerly The Mighty), 47, 152, 163–65, 175, 183n2. *See also* Disney
Avalanche. *See* Colorado Avalanche

Baker, Hobey, 28, 63, 67n33
Balsillie, Jim, 38–39, 51n1
bandy, 23–24
Barbour, Ralph Henry, 55, 58–62, 66n17
Barilko, Bill, 81–83, 94n2, 188
baseball, 24, 56, 64, 173, 198
Bettman, Gary, 39, 51n1
Blackhawks. *See* Chicago Blackhawks
Blues. *See* St. Louis Blues

Calgary Flames, 187, 194–95, 199–200, 202n11
Canada: culture in, 20, 133–139, 187; hockey in, 22–27, 39, 84, 149, 1920; in literature, 10–15, 41–50, 54–64; in world hockey, 24, 98–99, 102–107. *See also* Team Canada, Summit Series, Canadian identity
Canada: Our Century, 84
Canada's game, 37, 47, 53, 115, 121
Canadian Amateur Hockey Association (CAHA), 98
Canadian Amateur Hockey League (CAHL), 25
Canadian Broadcasting Centre (CBC). *See under* CBC

Canadian identity: national patriotism of, 8–9, 37, 40, 77, 182, 196–97; imagined self-image of, 115–19, 121, 134–35
Canadiens. *See* Montreal Canadiens
Carrier, Roch, 198
CBC, 10, 90, 199, 202n3. *See also names of individual programs*
Cheechoo, Jonathan: as "sidekick," 113–15, 119–20; in youth, 116-17
Cherry, Don, 149, 188, 197
Chicago Blackhawks, 99, 192
Christian, Bill, 104
Christian, Roger, 104
Clarke, Bobby, 97, 190
Cleary, Bob, 103
Cleary, Bill, 28, 108n5
Cold War, 10, 97–98, 103, 107, 189
collective bargaining agreement (CBA), 171
Colorado Avalanche, 39. *See also* Quebec Nordiques
Coyotes. *See* Phoenix Coyotes
Cree, 115, 117, 119
cricket, 133, 145, 199
Crimson Sweater, The (Barbour), 60, 66n17

Death of Hockey, 38–39, 49
Detroit Red Wings, 87, 90
Disney, 47, 51n4, 163, 165. *See also* Anaheim Ducks
Divine Ryans, The (Johnston), 11, 90
Dryden, Dave, 147
Dryden, Ken, 10–11, 28
Ducks. *See* Anaheim Ducks

Edmonton Oilers: fans 175–80, 182, 183n2; in The Heritage Series, 194; Pronger trade from, 171; Stanley Cup loss, 172
Eposito, Phil, 190

Erewhon Cup, 146

fan: experience, 156, 160–67, 182, 199–200; reaction, 172–73, 175–81, 183; satisfaction, 157–59, 174
field hockey, 23
"Fifty Mission Cap," 82, 188
First Nations, 133, 192–93. *See also* Cree, Mi'kmaq, Native American, Native Canadian
Flames. *See* Calgary Flames
football, 19, 55, 64, 163, 172
Fuhr, Grant, 194, 202n7

game presentation, 158, 164–65, 167
Guarding His Goal (Barbour), 58–59
global sport, 21, 32n1
golf, 174–75
Gretzky, Janet, 182
Gretzky, Wayne, 85, 152
Guarding His Goal (Barbour), 58

Hart Trophy, 113
Henderson, Paul, 85, 90, 188–98, 202n3
Heritage Classic, The, 194
Hero of the Play (Harrison), 11, 70, 196, 198
Hockey Hall of Fame, 85, 90, 92
hockey literature: American, 53, 58, 61; as fiction, 11, 40, 51n3, 54–56, 198; as poetry, 11–12, 69–70, 196, 198. *See also names of individual titles*
Hockey Night in Canada, 136, 192, 197
Hockey Sweater, The (Carrier), 198
Horn of a Lamb (Sedlack): summary of: 41–46; as nostalgia, 48–50
Howe, Gordie, 69, 84–89, 93

Hull, Bobby, 70, 84, 191

Ice Blacks, 146, 149–50
International Hockey League (IHL), 25
International Ice Hockey Federation (IIHF): in Europe, 105, 107; governance of, 28, 31, 98, 153; in New Zealand, 147–47, 149–50
International Olympic Committee (IOC), 247, 97, 101

Jets. *See* Winnipeg Jets
Johnston, Wayne, 11, 90–91, 95n11

Kharlamov, Valery, 28, 190
Kilpatrick, James "Scotty", 81, 86–88, 93
Kings. *See* Los Angeles Kings

Landin, Steve, 41, 46, 49
Leafs. *See* Toronto Maple Leafs
League of Hockey Nations (LHN), 78
Lecavalier, René, 90, 95n10
Lemieux, Mario, 69
Lightning. *See* Tampa Bay Lightning
Ligue International de Hockey sur Glace (LIHG), 24
lockout, 30, 77, 171
Los Angeles Kings, 152, 163, 164

Madison Square Garden, 63, 158, 161, 205
Maple Leaf Gardens, 81–82
McNeil, Gerry: in *The Divine Ryans*, 90–91; in Kilpatrick photo, 85–89, 93; in Turofsky photo, 82–85, 93; portrait of, 92, 94
Merriwell, Frank, 55, 64n5
Mi'kmaq, 193

INDEX

Montreal Canadiens, 11, 69, 83, 162, 192, 194
Montreal game, the, 21, 23, 57
Murray, Ron, 164–65

Nashville Predators, 38, 51n1
National Collegiate Athletic Association (NCAA), 22, 25, 30–31
National Hockey Association (NHA), 25
National Hockey League (NHL). *See under* NHL
Native American, 20, 22. *See also* Cree, First Nations, Mi'kmaq, Native Canadian
Native Canadian, 115–19, 193. *See also* Cree, First Nations, Mi'kmaq, Native American
New York Rangers, 84, 162
New Zealand Ice Hockey Federation, 146–47, 150, 152–53
New Zealand Ice Skating Association, 146
New Zealand National Hockey League (NZNHL), 145, 147
NHL: expansion, 30, 39, 59, 191–92; corporate, 27–29, 147, 150, 160; governance, 22, 30–32, 76–77. *See also* lockout, *names of individual teams and players*
Nike Bauer, 28
Nordiques. *See* Quebec Nordiques

Oilers. *See under* Edmonton Oilers
Olympia, 81, 87–88
Olympics: early 24, 26; New Zealand in, 150, 152; during Cold War, 97, 101; Women's team, 136, 201. *See also* Team Canada
Ontario Hockey Association (OHA), 24, 116, 161

Orr, Bobby, 82, 188

People's History, A, 12, 133
Pearson, Lester B., 97, 190
Penguins. *See* Pittsburgh Penguins
Phoenix Coyotes, 38–39, 51n1. *See also* Winnipeg Jets
Pittsburgh Penguins, 38, 51n1
political economy
polo: 23; "ice," 57
pond hockey, 46, 139, 146, 196
Predators. *See* Nashville Predators
Pronger, Chris: trade request, 171–72, 175, 180, 182; fan anger at, 176–79
Pronger, Lauren, 179–82

Quebec Nordiques, 39, 194. *See also* Colorado Avalanche

Rangers. *See* New York Rangers
Reardon, Ken, 162
Red Wings. *See* Detroit Red Wings
Reebok, 28
Richard Riot (1955), 10, 84, 162
Richard, Maurice "Rocket," 84, 87, 90, 162, 196
ringette, 135–36
Rocket Richard Trophy, 113, 119
rugby, 24, 145, 148–50

San Jose Sharks, 113, 120
Sawchuk, Terry, 12, 88
Sedlack, Robert, 41
Sharks. *See* San Jose Sharks
shinny: at *Canada's Game?*, 7; as Canadian symbol, 135, 123–25; vs. organized hockey, 116, 130–31; as social commentary, 134–40; women's, 125, 127–130, 133, 137–38
Sinden, Harry, 8

Skate Glendale! (Barbour), 60–62
skiing, 106
soccer, 19, 21, 24, 26
Society for International Hockey Research (SIHR), 22
Sologubov, Nikolai, 104, 108n5
Soviet Union, 26–27, 35n17, 98–107. *See also* Cold War and Summit Series
Spirit of Manitoba, 44
St. Louis Blues, 152
Stanley Cup: Ducks' 165; Flames' loss, 187, 201; history of, 72, 74–75; Leafs', 81; Oilers', 171–72; like Superman, 72–73, 75–76
Stanley, Lord Frederick, 74
Stanley, Isobel, 133
Stewart, Bill, 99
Summit Series (1972): Cold War link, 10, 75, 98, 189; and the WHA, 29, 191

Tampa Bay Lightning, 187, 195
Tardiff, Patrice, 147, 152
Team Canada: in 1972 Summit Series, 8, 29, 75, 189–91; and Calgary, 182, 195
Thornton, Joe, 113–15, 118–20
Toronto Gay Hockey Association, 137
Toronto Maple Leafs, 82–84, 188, 192, 195
Tragically Hip, The, 82, 187–88, 198, 201
Trudeau, Pierre Elliott, 191
Turofsky, Nat, 81–84, 92, 94

United States: civil rights in, 86–87; in the Cold War, 102–103; cultural distinction from Canada, 37–38, 50, 187; hockey expansion to, 22, 30, 39, 41, 59, 76; in hockey literature, 41, 53–57; in world hockey, 24, 99, 105

violence: Canadian, 22, 27, 102, 149; fan, 161–62, 166; in sports, 7, 148–49, 151, 156, 163

Winnipeg Jets, 39, 41, 44, 47. *See also* Phoenix Coyotes
Winsor, Ralph, 58
women's hockey, 32, 136, 147, 149, 201
Women's Hockey Club of Toronto, 127, 137
World Championship, 8, 27, 98–107, 147, 149
World Hockey Assocation (WHA), 29, 73, 191
World War I, 25, 58, 63